KU-579-433

The Hamlyn Book
of Garden Flowers

The Hamlyn Book
of Garden Flowers

By Vladimír Mölzer

HAMLYN

LONDON · NEW YORK · SYDNEY · TORONTO

Authors of illustrations: F. Severa, J. Kaplická, V. Štolfa,
K. Švarc, J. Windsor
Line drawings by F. Severa

Translated by Olga Kuthanová
Designed and produced by Artia for
The Hamlyn Publishing Group Limited
London · New York · Sydney · Toronto
Astronaut House, Feltham, Middlesex, England

Copyright © 1979 Artia, Prague

All Rights Reserved.
No part of this publication may be reproduced
or transmitted
in any form or by any means,
electronic or mechanical, including
photocopy, recording, or any information storage
and retrieval system,
without permission in writing from
the copyright owner.

ISBN 0 600 34085 6

Printed in Czechoslovakia
3/13/02/51-01

CONTENTS

FOREWORD

Although the present day and age provides us with all the amenities and advantages that modern civilization has to offer there are negative aspects as well. Many people seek respite from the rapid pace of modern life, and the stresses and strains of their jobs by taking up gardening. Pursuing an active out-of-doors pastime is one of several ways in which man tries to offset the effects of his 'artificial environment', which is often at odds with the natural environment. The owner of a small plot who can create a garden to his taste should consider himself lucky. A garden gives us beauty, health and the joy of creative activity—three of the most precious values in life. However, only a garden that is well cared for provides all three. If the work entailed can be tackled by the gardener himself then it will be a pleasure, and for it to remain so the options open to him should be carefully considered.

Factors that must be taken into consideration when laying out a garden are time, the amount of work involved, the effort required and the costs. The experienced gardener knows that all these are required to establish and keep a beautiful garden and therefore he plans it so that it will not take up all his free time and, become a 'second job', but will still be a place which will serve his needs and give him pleasure.

Plants are continually growing and require constant care, which entails work and money. Structural elements such as pathways, walls, patios, furniture and fences also require care and upkeep. Tools become worn and need to be replaced and supplemented. It is easier and cheaper to carry out maintenance regularly, a little at a time. A garden that has been neglected for a long period necessitates a great deal of labour and expense to put back into shape.

WHAT SHOULD BE EXPECTED OF A MODERN GARDEN?

First it should be beautiful. Plants and other elements should form a harmonious whole that creates a restful atmosphere. Plants should be laid out in attractive combinations, according to form and colour, that are pleasing to the eye. They should also be in harmony with the structural elements, such as the house, so that the whole blends with the surroundings. That is why plants that grow together in the wild, should be combined similarly in the garden. For instance, dahlias, gladioli or annuals should not be planted next to pine trees; it is far better to use catchfly, *Lychnis viscaria* (campion), heathers, and similar plants. When creating a beautiful garden much can be learned by observing any of the many lovely parks around us, seeing how the various elements are grouped and arranged.

Secondly, it should be a place where one can rest and relax. This purpose can be fulfilled by a bench under an attractive shrub, a deck chair on a lawn, an alcove, a pergola or a patio with garden furniture. The choice depends on the layout of the garden; here, too, it is necessary that whatever is chosen should blend with the surroundings.

Thirdly, it should be an outdoor room, an extension of the living quarters, an added dimension providing a unique atmosphere with its combinations of scents and colours, its play of light and shade; a place where flowers, ornamental trees and shrubs and other natural elements reflect the passage of time, changing with the hours of daylight as well as with the seasons.

In such a garden not only is it possible to rest and relax but also to eat, study, and sleep. It is an ideal setting for solitary thought. It is in this need for privacy that the garden and park differ. Both parks and gardens are refreshing with their expanses of green, pleasing to the eye with their beauty of arrangement and soothing in that they afford a place to relax, but a park can never provide the privacy and intimacy of the garden.

The value of the garden as an outdoor room is enhanced by linking it with the living quarters. Each window opening into the garden should frame a picture that changes, in the morning, at noon and in the evening, and with the seasons. There is more to an attractive home than just tastefully furnished rooms; the view from the window is equally important. The outdoor area should be planned so that the part most often seen from the inside is the most attractive. The garden should link up with the living quarters not only scenically but also practically; at least one door should open into the garden. A garden that is used and lived in by the family should be furnished, not with discarded seats and tables but with furniture specially designed for the purpose and made from a material that blends with the surroundings. The pieces may be put on the patio or out on the lawn, which, of course, must be kept trim and tidy and cut at least once a week in the growing season. Such a lawn fulfills an aesthetic function and it is almost impossible to imagine a garden without one.

A live-in garden should be used not only during the daytime, but, weather permitting, also in the evening and at night. This, of course, requires some form of lighting and heat. Illumination in the garden creates a special magic and makes it seem even more intimate than in bright daylight. The light source may be permanently positioned —unobtrusively in a flower bed or tree-top—or movable; or else it may be purely decorative. The heat source should be unobtrusive too and should harmonise with the setting, for example a permanent bonfire area, an earthenware bowl for burning charcoal, or an outdoor fireplace.

If such a garden is to serve its purpose it must be attuned to the needs of the people concerned, to their way of life, and is thus generally unique. There can be no general rule on how to plan it, but when doing so it is necessary to keep in mind the obvious needs—room to sit in sun or shade, a working area, a place for children to play, lawn space, flower beds, trees and shrubs—and to keep these in proper balance.

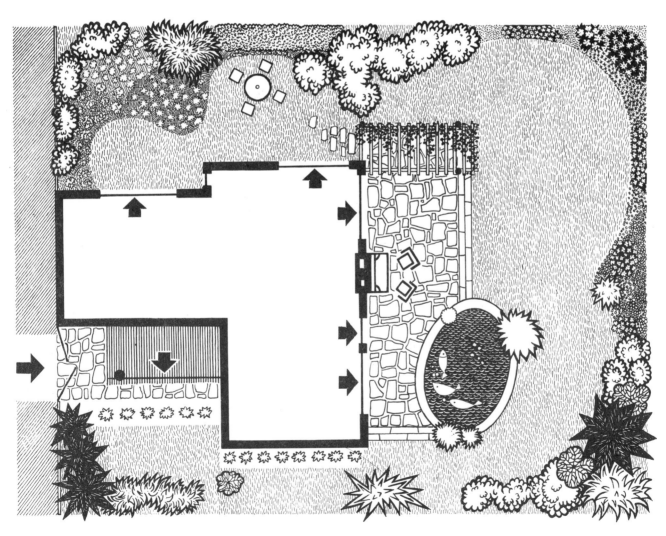

A garden designed for the whole household should be an extension of the living quarters.

STARTING A GARDEN

Learning how to set out and arrange plants in a garden is far more difficult than learning how to grow them. Every arrangement bears the stamp of the gardener's personality—it is influenced by his talent, experience and taste.

A beautiful garden is a work of art which must take into account not only the aesthetic aspect but also the laws of nature and the specific, practical needs of the owner.

To create such a work of art is a difficult task even for the expert. If he has no experience in this field the owner of the garden can have it designed by a landscape architect who knows the laws of aesthetics and of plant cultivation.

Even the owner, however, can gradually create such a work of art over a period of time. But he must learn the basic rules of garden aesthetics, of the attractive arrangement of space, and must give serious thought to preparing a plan of the finished product as well as the successive stages of its execution.

The garden should not only be attractive but should also serve practical needs; neither the one nor the other aspect should be overestimated. When designing a garden it is necessary to observe certain rules and principles which will assure a pleasingly—attractive result.

WHAT ARE THE AESTHETIC PRINCIPLES OF GARDEN DESIGN?

The layout should be logical, in other words everything in the garden should create a natural and not a forced and contrived effect. The rock garden is best placed on a slope, not level ground; plants that thrive in dry locations should not be planted beside a pool; if a table is of wood then the seats should not be of stone; plastic materials should not be painted to resemble wood; a lovely view should not be concealed by plants while an unsightly spot is left unmasked. Good common sense should be the guiding principle throughout.

The various elements should be suitable and appropriate, that is the size, shape, colour and positioning of every item should conform to its purpose and be in harmony with the environment and nothing should appear forced. A garden is the place for a lilac bush, not a poplar tree, and garden furniture should be simple and, where possible, of natural materials. The scheme of planting green elements in a garden is dif-

ferent from their layout in a park, a formal ornamental flower bed has its place in a city park but not in a garden.

In a garden everything should be in proportion, and there should be a harmony of dimensions. Shapes should be clear and definite. For example, both circles and ovals are suitable shapes for a flower bed, but an oval that is almost a circle is not correct proportionally. The same is true of rectangles with little difference in length between the long and short sides. The most important element should be located in the most important spot and should also be large. Without careful planning of the elements, so that some are emphasised while others are played down, the resulting garden will lack character and beauty no matter how many lovely plants and fittings it contains.

Every garden needs a dominating feature, a central motif that sets the tone and gives it a certain character. In a larger garden there may be several such focal points, depending on the layout, but one should dominate the rest. The dominant feature is usually a summerhouse, swimming pool, or pergola, or may be attractive groups of conifers, a solitary tree, a shrub with brightly-coloured foliage, a flower bowl or a handsome piece of sculpture. Even the overall dominant feature must be in harmony with the setting and have intrinsic aesthetic value. The eye should not be drawn away from it by distracting features. It would be wrong, for instance, to put a brightly-coloured flower bed next to a piece of modern sculpture. The dominant feature should always be well lit—with artificial light in the evening if so desired. The dominant feature may also be a particularly attractive element in the immediate surroundings, for instance a group of handsome trees, a nearby church spire or the shimmering surface of a pond. In this case the garden layout should be planned so as to draw attention to the feature outside its boundaries.

Harmony and contrast are both important in a garden. To achieve a general effect that is restful but not monotonous, contrasting, brightening elements should be included. Care, however, must be taken not to go to extremes so that the outcome proves irritating instead of giving pleasure. Harmony and contrast are used in mutual combination. Harmony is achieved by using elements of like character (for instance trees of similar form but varying height) and placing them randomly in an attractive arrangement, in a group or line or in a regularly repeated rhythm. Contrast is achieved by placing next to each other two elements that are markedly different in form or colour, for instance dark conifers next to a light-coloured house, white garden furniture against a background of green, or a bright flower bed set in the lawn.

All these rules should be applied with an eye to a number of other factors, foremost of which is optical aspect. Every object, though it has certain specific dimensions, may appear otherwise to the beholder, that is it may seem larger or smaller than it actually is, depending on the point from which it is viewed. This fact can be put to good use in designing the garden. Everyone knows building two parallel lines converge in a perspective view. By suitable planting—by planting a regularly expanding row instead of a straight row—such an optical illusion may be limited or even reversed. A light object against a dark background seems larger than a dark object against a light back-

Every well-placed focal point gives the garden character.

11

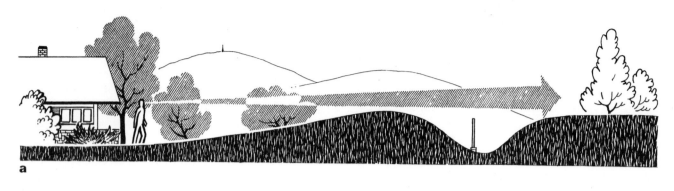

a

b

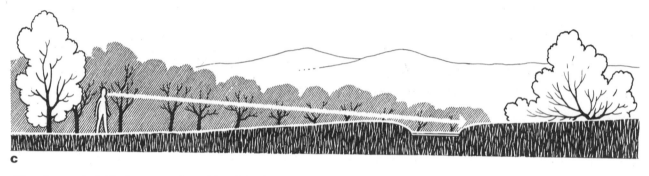

c

Attractive optical illusions may be achieved by landscaping: a — a fence concealed by being placed at the bottom of a shallow ditch; b — suitable location of a fence at the foot of a slope; c — concealment of a path creates the impression of an unbroken expanse of lawn.

ground. An interrupted line seems longer than a continuous line. A large tree set in a large expanse of turf appears to be smaller. A circle viewed in frontal perspective looks like an oval, a square like a rectangle. Fewer trees and shrubs and more grass make the garden seem larger. We know by using these principles a garden can be made to appear larger, longer or shorter.

This effect can be further promoted by incorporating views. In large parks unexpected views and vistas are a tribute to the art of the landscape architect, but the same can be achieved in the private garden, not by copying from parks, of course, but by suitably arranging the planting of trees and shrubs and the placing of seats. The landscaping of parks is of two basic kinds. One is the natural landscaping of English parks, the other the formal landscaping of the French. The first is better for large areas,

the second for small landscaping schemes. The trend of recent years is towards the natural landscaping scheme, partly because it requires less maintenance, and this aspect is also important in the private garden. In general, it is best to choose the natural scheme incorporating the odd view and vista and the element of surprise, but there is no reason not to choose a formal plan with clearly defined views. Taste is the determining factor. A formal garden requires regular care and upkeep whereas a natural one can succeed under sporadic care. However, the amount of work and time entailed is about the same for both schemes. In a large garden one section may be formally landscaped and the rest naturally landscaped.

In a natural scheme viewing positions of interesting features inside or outside the garden should be arranged in a natural, unaffected manner whereas in the formal garden they are arranged according to a precise scheme in line with the main axis. They should not be positioned in the direction of prevailing winds, and should be equipped with seats. An undulating surface offers more opportunities for exploiting such views than level ground. If the viewed building is to be edged with trees and shrubs they should be low and broad if surrounding a tall, narrow building and columnar or conical if the building is wide. Colour contrast is also important.

When planning pleasant and surprising views of nearby and more distant objects keep in mind that the trees and shrubs you plant will grow and spread and in time may form a dense mass that affords no views whatsoever. They must be shaped by trimming or else replaced by other woody plants.

When designing any garden one must take into account the effects of light and shade. The constrast between the two, especially on a sunny day, can create wonderful effects. Light, of course, is a necessity and we must try to make the garden as sunny as possible. Plants need light to flourish. Shaded positions are pleasant to sit in summer and shade is also used to highlight views. Always, however, the garden should have more sunny areas than shaded ones if possible. Light and shade in the garden are important not only from the grower's viewpoint but also as an aesthetic element.

A garden without the play of light and shade lacks character. The best effects are achieved by light coming from the side; least suitable is direct light in the same direction as the view which provides a sunlit picture but one with little contrast. Equipped with this information one can choose a suitable combination of trees and shrubs for various views. Shade creates the illusion of greater privacy and striking effects can be achieved when such a shaded spot affords a view of a sunlit, brightly coloured part of the garden. Generally, views of sunlit objects from shaded positions are more striking. For that reason, all dominant elements should be well lit. The magic play of light and shade should be remembered when planning pathways and locating sites to sit and rest, which are the points from which the garden will be viewed most frequently.

Contrast of colour goes hand in hand with contrast of light and shade. Colour is extremely important, besides brightening the garden and heightening its effect, certain combinations can evoke pleasant moods. Knowledge of the rules of aesthetics in the use of colour is important not only in daily life but also in the realm of art, including garden landscaping.

The circle in the drawing shows the primary colours. Warm colours are stimulating, joyous, warming, definite; cold colours evoke feelings of shade and coolness. Sub-

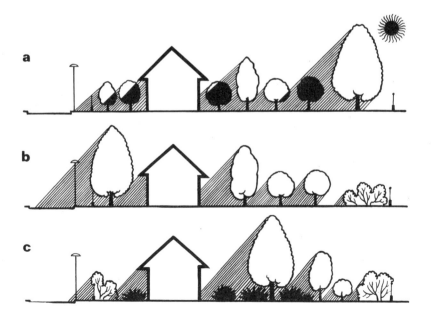

When planting trees it is necessary to keep in mind the shade they will cast when fully-grown: a — not a good layout; b — better arrangement with lower elements on the southern side; c — utilization of shaded areas by planting out shade-loving shrubs and flowers.

13

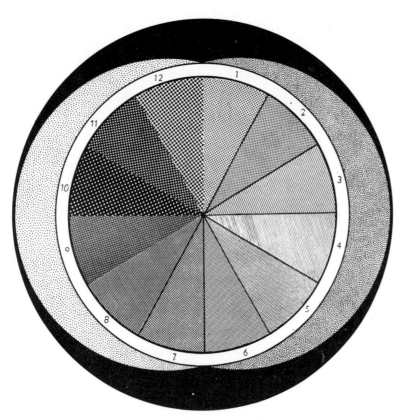

Colours arranged according to the dial of a clock: 1 — red, 2 — orange-red, 3 — orange, 4 — yellow, 5 — greenish-yellow, 6 — yellowish-green, 7 — green, 8 — blue-green, 9 — greenish-blue, 10 — blue, 11 — blue-violet, 12 — violet. Those in the top half (10—3) are stimulating colours, those in the bottom half (4—9) calming hues, those at the left (6—12) cold colours and those at the right (1—6) warm ones.

dued colours evoke feelings of peace and harmony; stimulating colours evoke feelings of excitement. Natural colours (grey, white, black) do not evoke any particular feelings or impressions in themselves but soften transitions between contrasting colours. These aspects of colour are naturally taken into account when planning the garden but so are the various possible combinations of colours, because these, too, have different effects. The two colours that are directly opposite each other in the circle are complementary, while those adjacent to each other harmonise. Intensity of colour is also important. Deeper shades are brighter, more striking; paler shades are softer, more subdued. These facts must be kept in mind particularly when planting flowering plants such as annuals, bulbs and alpines.

Combinations of colours and their varying degrees of intensity do not always produce the same effects; much depends on the setting, the environment. This also has its own colour and thus evokes various impressions and feelings. The sky, for example, is the lightest feature of all. Water and grassy areas are also light. Deciduous shrubs and trees are darker, and darkest are conifers, the yew being the darkest of all. The surrounding environment also influences the

combination of colours in the garden. Meadows, expanses of water and roads are light elements; hills, hillocks and trees create a darker effect.

The influence of colour on the overall effect of the garden is immense and would be even greater if green did not predominate, for green softens contrasts and in itself has a calming, restful effect. Pale shades of green are the most pleasant and that is why the garden, and nature in general, is loveliest in spring.

Monotony should be avoided, which could be the case if it included only grassy areas and conifers, or else only grassy areas and flowers without any trees or shrubs. Nor should a feeling of chaos be created, which could occur by indiscriminate collection and unplanned planting resulting in a garden without any form or character. Variety is important in a garden. This is achieved by the number and quality of plants and supplementary objects, by their arrangement and also by movement, for example flowing water. Number and quality are determined by the selected assortment of plant species and varieties. Some plants remain the same troughout the year (older conifers), others change during the course of the year or only during the growing season

14

(deciduous trees and shrubs), and many live only part of the year. It is thus possible to have beauty the whole year round or only during certain seasons. In the garden of a summer cottage which is inhabited only during the summer months, plants that are loveliest in summer either for their beauty of shape, flowers or foliage are grown. To be interesting for as long as possible should be the aim of town gardens which are enjoyed the whole year, as they are attached to the permanent residence. This can be achieved only by selecting the widest possible assortment of plants. In a cottage garden just shrub roses could be grown, but in the town garden the selection should include plants ranging from early-flowering bulbs to deciduous trees and shrubs that have such beautifully coloured foliage in autumn, as well as conifers and evergreens, particularly important in winter.

When the whole garden can be viewed at a glance immediately on entering it the effect may be lovely but is still lacking in variety. There should be a number of views, each more striking than the preceding one. It is best to plan the layout so that plants form smaller units with a new and different vista opening up every few steps. Planting schemes should not be repeated, they should alternate or each should be quite different. One arrangement may be symmetrical and another asymmetrical, or the various sections may differ in substance—a perennial border, a rosarium, a heath garden, a pool with aquatic plants. In planning the various

sections it is necessary to keep in mind the overall layout of the garden. The whole may be unified by a continuous expanse of turf which flows through and holds together all or most of the various sections, by paths with the same surface, or by the use of the same type of earthenware containers, decorative objects and furniture throughout. The greatest thought and consideration should be devoted to that section of the garden that is used the most—the area around the house or cottage, the patio.

Movement of any kind adds variety to the garden. It may be the movement of water—a stream, waterfall or cascade, or trees with leaves that flutter in the wind such as aspen or birch—but the best and most common is that provided by songbirds which can be attracted to the garden by putting out feeding trays and nest boxes.

It is obvious that there are many aesthetic aspects to be considered when planning a garden. However, these principles are the same in all fields of art and life: in architecture, fashion design and painting. They are applied all the time in daily life, some with greater, others with less success, and are relevant to the planning of a new garden or improving an existing one.

The best teacher of aesthetics is nature. Individual elements of beauty as well as groupings in the countryside can be incorporated in the garden, though in stylized form and adapted to the size of the garden. The results are striking and distinctive—a concentrated essence of nature's beauty.

Two different schemes of arrangement of a garden: at left — a chaotic arrangement which is better avoided; at right — a well-balanced arrangement.

WHAT PLANTS TO CHOOSE

In order to have a perfect garden, it is crucial to know which plants to use, which are the most suitable for a given purpose and the most striking. It is an art to select from the hundreds and thousands of species and varieties, ranging from the smallest to the largest, from those that flower a long time every season to those that only flower a few days in a single year. Each is lovely in its own right and if properly used will help make the garden a place of beauty. When choosing plants, however, we must also keep in mind economical factors. Some plants require practically no care whatsoever whereas others need constant attention. The most economical in the long term are those that are the most rewarding. It is difficult to think in terms of economy when the subject is the beauty of the garden but it must be taken into consideration. The choice, then, is influenced by the gardener's personal taste, his finances, the amount of time at his disposal and his ability to do work requiring hard labour or expertise. It is best, therefore, to choose plants which will give the most effective result for the time, effort and money spent.

CAN GARDEN PLANTS BE JUDGED BY THEIR EFFECTIVENESS?

There are many opinions on this subject and the following is just one.

Conifers are the most rewarding. They are fairly expensive initially but in ensuing years they require very little maintenance and they usually dominate the garden. Planted aesthetically conifers give excellent value.

Next to be considered is the lawn, a green, matt-textured carpet. It is costly to establish, must be mown, watered and fertilized regularly, bald patches must be sown with new seed, and occasionally the whole lawn must be renewed. However, a well kept lawn is a beautiful sight and no garden is complete without one. It can be used as a place to sit and rest, sunbathe, play games and it improves the atmosphere. A well-tended lawn is always a good investment.

Roses entail more work and are time-consuming (pruning in spring, feeding, watering, weeding, pruning after flowering, protection against pests and diseases) but they bloom from early June (sometimes even sooner) until the frost and few flowering plants can match them for their wide range of shapes, colours and scents. They are lovely both in the garden and as cut flowers in the home. It is no accident that the rose is considered the queen of flowers. Because of their striking effect during the growing season they are the most widely cultivated plants in the world, gracing public areas, private gardens and homes. The pleasure derived from roses far outweighs the cost, work and time they require.

Members of the heath family are also interesting: rhododendrons, deciduous azaleas (mollis azaleas), heathers (calluna), heaths (erica), and others. Besides the initial purchasing cost, they require special preparation of the soil, but afterwards only occasional feeding and watering, although rhododendrons require removal of dead flowers.

The cost and work are not too great when the final result is considered. The blooms of rhododendrons and azaleas are extremely beautiful although they have a short life. Heaths are the first to flower in late winter or early spring and heathers are in flower late into summer and autumn. Growing heath plants is rewarding as their foliage is a decorative feature even in winter.

Next to be considered are bulbs. The principal ones—tulips and narcissi—must be lifted occasionally, otherwise they spread freely. This is also the case with lilies. In summer the bulbs can be lifted, stored, sorted, and then planted out again. The results, however, are worth the effort for they are among the first plants to flower after the long, dreary winter, contributing a bright display of colour. The garden would be a bleak place without them in spring.

After bulbs come corms and tubers—chiefly gladioli and dahlias. They are not as rewarding as bulbs because they must be lifted every year before winter, dried, over-

Two main groups of roses: a — hybrid teas (chiefly for cutting); b — floribundas (mainly for edging and bedding in parks)

Growth cycle of a garden tulip: from left to right — October, December, March, April, May, June

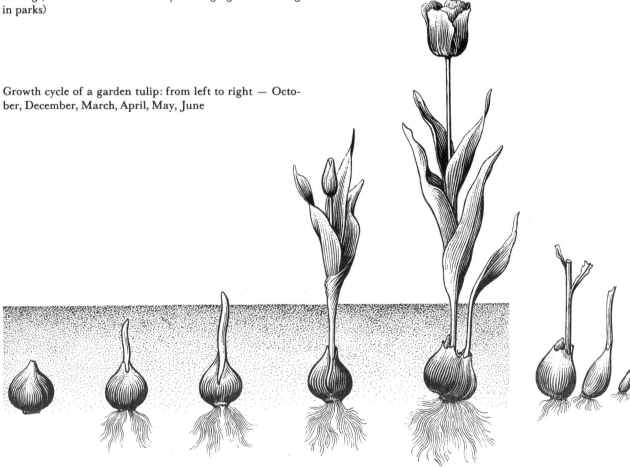

wintered and planted out again in spring. The beauty and bright colours of the many gladiolus and dahlia varieties, however, make them great favourites. As cut flowers gladioli are almost as popular as roses. Although corms and tubers entail more work a garden is incomplete without them.

Evergreen shrubs require a certain financial outlay (purchase of young plants), good care and pruning, but their evergreen foliage is an asset to the garden in winter. Many also have lovely flowers and decorative fruits (brightly coloured berries) in the autumn.

The deciduous shrubs, besides normal care, need pruning and the fallen leaves in the autumn have to be swept up. Many also tend to spread freely. They require less work than roses and are not so rewarding as the flowering period is comparatively short. Often, however, they are prized not only for their decorative aspects but because they serve other purposes as well—to mask unsightly spots, as hedges, and to conceal walls.

Perennials are classed as one group although they differ in beauty of form and use. The choice should be based on the time and length of the flowering period, the number of years the plants will last in the border, how freely they spread, and the uses they are to serve. Considering the time taken up by sowing, planting, hoeing, watering, feeding, care after flowering, and weeding, careful thought should be given to choice. It is important to select a few species and varieties of the best quality for a rewarding outcome. Rock garden plants form a special group.

Biennials bloom when bulbs have finished and before the annuals start flowering. As they only flower for one year, considering the amount of work required, they are not so rewarding as plants such as bulbs.

Annuals, although they flower only once, include a great many magnificent flowers that no garden should be without, and ready-grown seedlings can be purchased, or seeds can be grown in a greenhouse, frames and boxes. They are popular and widely grown for their variety, wide range of size, shape and colour, and, perhaps, also for the very fact that they are of short duration and allow for changes and thus greater interest in the garden.

Comparisons based solely on economic factors give a distorted picture, other values must also be taken into account. Individual species within the above groups vary in effectiveness. For instance, roses are placed high on the list and annuals at the bottom, but one of the best annuals—the sweet pea (*Lathyrus odoratus*)—is far more satisfying in the garden than a climbing rose that is susceptible to disease.

PLANTING POSITIONS IN THE GARDEN

Knowing what plants to choose for the garden is one thing, knowing where to put them, both from the viewpoint of cultivation and aesthetics, is another. Every plant should be placed where it will thrive and where it will be most effective for the rest of its life. Plants are not static; they grow and change. Their ultimate size and shape must be taken into account, so that views are not blocked and unwanted shade is not cast. It is absolutely necessary for the gardener to arm himself with adequate information and plan his layout with care and forethought, as mistakes will last for years.

The garden is divided into several layers on the horizontal plane: the carpet, bottom layer, middle layer and top layer.

The carpet is composed of the grassy areas which are an essential part of every garden. It creates a restful atmosphere and it holds together all the other plant layers in the garden. It is the first of the decorative elements to make an impact in the garden; other layers, particularly woody plants, come into their own much later. When planning the layout decide first on the grassy areas, which should be in the most important part of the garden (such as around the house and if possible in full sun). The lawn, of course, must be of good quality, and well

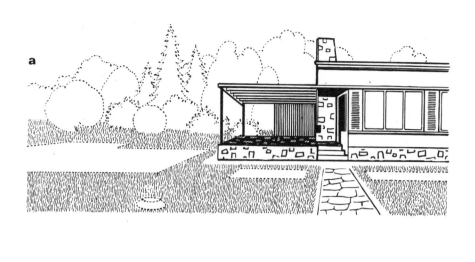

a

b

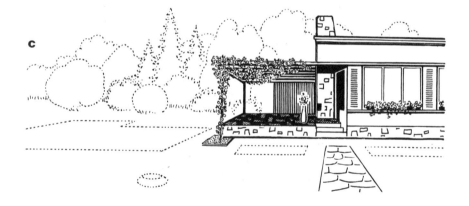

c

d

Horizontal division of a garden:
a — carpet, b — bottom layer,
c — middle layer, d — upper
layer

19

and regularly cared for. An attractive carpet of grass demands much work in comparison with that required by other plants in the garden. However, with an efficient, light lawnmower the task of cutting the lawn becomes pleasant physical exercise instead of heavy drudgery. The quality of the lawn is often indicative of the quality of the mower.

The bottom layer is composed mostly of flowers which brighten the garden with their colour and variety, adding beauty and interest to the principal elements. These are mostly rock garden plants, carpeting plants, edging plants, low ornamental grasses, bulbs and water and bog plants. They are the last items to be considered in the planning and planting of the garden, firstly because their space requirements are not very great and secondly because they are not permanent fixtures. The bottom layer is also a necessity in the garden but one should take into account that it requires a lot of maintenance. It is composed of a great many species, some of which are perennial, others annual, some are too invasive, some are easy to grow, others have special requirements and require special care. When choosing plants for this layer the principles of aesthetics (variety, colour and harmony) should be observed, but mistakes can be put right fairly easily.

The middle layer is usually composed of some of the loveliest and most rewarding flowers, ones which not only add beauty to the garden but can also be used for cutting. These are mainly roses, perennials and annuals for cutting, tulips, gladioli, dahlias, climbing plants—in short, the most widely grown and most popular flowers. When planning the garden this layer comes third in order of importance, after the green carpet and upper layer. They should be planted in well defined beds in a sunny, eye-catching spot where they can be easily cared for. Being the most numerous type of plant in the garden they require a lot of work and some must be planted out or moved every year. They include countless species and varieties and it is important to blend the aesthetic with the practical aspects, such as when planting flowers for cutting it must be kept in mind that the effect of the whole must remain attractive even when some have been removed for floral decoration.

The top layer is composed of ornamental

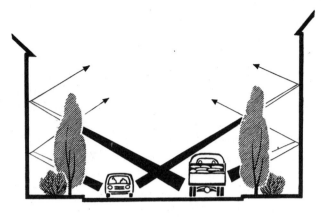

Hedges with dense foliage play an important role in deadening sound and keeping out dust. Thick foliage can be achieved by trimming shrubs suitable for the purpose or else by growing shrubs of various heights.

shrubs and trees. It is the main structural element of the garden. The placing of trees and shrubs is the first and most important step in deciding the layout for they determine the basic character of the garden. It is very difficult to move full-grown shrubs or trees so it is important to know their growth rate and final size and plan the scheme accordingly. It is also necessary to know which are best planted as solitary specimens and which to plant in groups. The composition of the upper layer is more uniform than the middle and bottom layers but the range of choice is still wide. Once planted this layer requires the least maintenance.

The division of plants into the layers just described makes it possible to combine them so that the whole as well as the details are lovely and give pleasure. However, everybody has different taste, so a universal plan is impossible to conceive. In the wild one finds different types of scenery, each in its own way as beautiful as the next. Much can be learnt from nature.

Natural materials should be used. Boundaries and space divisions should appear natural, not contrived, as even in nature sharp lines of demarcation are not found. It is inadvisable to improve the garden with various exotic plants where it is not certain that the end result will compensate for the work entailed and there is a danger that the whole effect might appear forced. A garden should reflect the character of its owner.

A garden is more than just living plants. It is also the proper use of stone, wood, and water, all harmoniously arranged.

Making the boundary. A defined boundary is usually a necessity. Without such a boundary even the best of gardens looks unfinished. Hedges, wooden fences, wire fences, iron railings or brick walls may be used. The choice should always be made with an eye to the locality even though it is also a matter of personal taste, available material, and cost.

Hedges have many advantages. They muffle sounds, keep out dust and exhaust fumes, act as windbreaks, provide privacy, create a pleasant, secluded spot for the family, afford nesting places for songbirds, and in an urban area the large quantities of oxygen evolved are an added advantage. The one drawback of hedges is the need for constant upkeep. The hedge can either be clipped or unclipped, depending on the type of garden, cottage or house and on the locality. A clipped and carefully shaped hedge would be inappropriate for a woodland cottage, but it is very attractive in a residential neighbourhood.

A wooden fence is usually cheapest if made of poles, especially if these can be purchased locally; it does not require much work but is not particularly attractive. A picket fence with supporting columns of roughcast brick or concrete is better. Plank gates are best for these types of fences. A wire fence is the most common type chosen nowadays and the initial cost is not very high. The supports are either concrete piers or else iron uprights embedded in concrete. Brick walls are expensive and if they are high can shade the garden needlessly. Low fencing of openwork or ornamentally arranged bricks round certain areas inside the garden enhances the aesthetic effect of the whole.

Paths and paving. Another important item in the garden are pathways. A path that cannot be used at all times of the year is not worth having. It must be sufficiently firm so that it is convenient to walk on and to carry out various gardening chores. Every

Two ways of concealing an unattractive wire fence with greenery. The one shown below — a multi-level arrangement of mixed shrubs — is the better method.

21

path should take you where you want to go.

Paths are usually surfaced with sand, or bricks, precast paving, or stone paving. Concrete is generally unattractive, and asphalt does not fit in a modern garden even though both are sometimes used. Sand has the disadvantage that it may be carried into the house. The width should be such that it is possible for two people to walk comfortably abreast on the path and thus the main path should be 1.20 to 1.50 m (4 to 5 ft) wide. Only in very small gardens where every centimetre of space counts is the main pathway about one metre wide. Other pathways connecting various parts of the garden should be about 60 cm (2 ft) wide and slightly curved; paths following a straight line or with too many curves appear forced and arbitrary. A width of 40 cm (16 in) is sufficient for paths between flowerbeds.

All paths should be inclined both lengthwise and crosswise so that water will run off. It is a good idea to lead the water off at the lowest point into the sewage system or else into a sump so that it does not form puddles.

If a path crosses the lawn it should be set about 1 to 2 cm ($^1/_2$ to 1 in) lower than the lawn surface. Sanded paths do not need to be edged. Paths bordered on either side by areas where plants grow and soil is tilled should be edged either with curbstones, stones or suitable plants such as madwort (alyssum) and candytuft (iberis).

For casual use, stepping stones carefully placed in grass may be used instead of a formal path (e.g. leading to a secluded alcove, bird-bath, rock garden). These may be of precast paving slabs or flat stones either regularly or irregularly shaped. They should be about 4 to 6 cm ($1^1/_2$ to $2^1/_2$ in) thick and should measure 40 by 60 cm (16 by 24 in). They should be level and again set slightly below the level of the turf so that mower blades can pass unharmed over the top.

Patios and places to sit can also be paved. It is important to remember that the paving must be laid so that water will run off, in other words it must slope from the centre to the edges and, in the case of a patio away from the house.

Every material requires its own type of finish, anything else appears incongruous and alien. Trying to colour a concrete surface to make it look like natural stone or bricks is rarely successful. If concrete must be used in the garden the effect may be softened by a suitably placed dry wall of natural, flat stones or else a decorative wall of patterned bricks, which can also serve as edging for a bonfire area or an outdoor fireplace.

Steps. Steps in the garden should be comfortable to use. The average length of a man's stride—64 cm (25 in)—is the measure that is used as the basis for determining the height and breadth of the steps. In general, steps should be broad and shallow, that is if the rise is 12 cm (5 in) then the width should be 40 cm (16 in). The width of the steps can be determined by subtracting twice the height from the length of a man's stride.

Where possible there should be an odd number of steps and never more than five in one stretch. It is better to break them up into sections so that in addition to their practical aspect the steps will also add beauty to the garden. A greater number of steps in a stretch is used only in a garden located on a steep slope. Steps may be made of various materials—logs, bricks, stones or precast slabs—and the choice depends on the material with which the paths are surfaced.

Coping with slopes. Sloping ground always poses difficulties, even though it can be turned to advantage. Terracing is the usual landscaping scheme selected for gardens on slopes. If the terraces are higher than 50 cm (20 in) it is necessary to build retaining walls of stone or concrete as a safeguard against heavy rain. Terraces less than 50 cm (20 in) high are spaced according to the steepness of the slope and decorated with beds of flowers or they can be turfed. Such grassy terraces are attractive but the grass must be kept neat and tidy and requires regular mowing. Various chemical agents may be used to retard the growth of grass on terraces but they sometimes spoil the appearance of the turf. Carpeting plants may also be used to cover the slope, such as stonecrops with trailing stems, sedum, periwinkles, vinca for shaded areas, or the vigorous snow-in-summer (cerastium) for sunny situations. All however, need care, mainly weeding, and must not be allowed to invade the flowerbeds.

The best, but fairly expensive method of strengthening a slope or equalizing differ-

Stones for the rock garden, pathway and steps should be uniform, of one and the same kind.

ences in height on sloping ground is to build walls planted with flowers. If the wall is to be higher than 60 to 70 cm (24 to 28 in) and if the stones are to be joined by mortar a mason should be employed. Dry walls, however, in which the stones are not joined by cement, are far more common. Foundations are not necessary if the wall is less than 60 cm (2 ft) high. Nevertheless, it is better to build the wall on a foundation [about 20 to 30 cm (8 to 12 in) deep] to preclude any possibility of shifting due to frost or excessive water in spring.

The wall should be inclined backwards so that the top layer of stones is about 10 to 20 cm (4 to 8 in) closer to the slope than the bottom layer. A dry wall should be planted with suitable rock plants.

Rock gardens. A correctly constructed and well planted rockery is a decorative asset throughout the year. A rock garden looks best if located on a rise or on a slope. Rocks found in the surrounding countryside and always of the same kind, with a weathered surface if possible, are best. The basis of a rock garden is large stones placed so they look as natural as possible, with medium-size and small stones in between. It is recommended to plan the layout of the rockery beforehand and then proceed according to the plan. In a larger rock garden stone paths and steps make it easier to reach the various parts of the rockery. The stones should be arranged in irregular formations to create large and smaller spaces to accom-

modate the various plants. Plants should be selected with an eye to providing harmonising colour for as long as possible.

Most rock garden plants look best if planted in large groups. Spreading junipers and dwarf pine make effective backgrounds in front of the rockery. The level space can be planted with groups of bulbs or ornamental grass. The beauty of every rock garden is enhanced by including a small pool round which interesting marsh plants may be grown.

Odd stones add interest to the level spaces in the garden. They may be single rocks in grass or may form an attractive nook with a bird-bath; they can also be placed at the edge of a paved surface. Stones for this purpose should be large, at least 40 to 50 cm (16 to 20 in) high, have an attractive form and a weathered surface and can be surrounded by prostrate shrubs, ornamental grasses, and cushion plants.

Furniture and ornaments. Garden furniture should blend with the general character of the garden and all should be of the same kind, whether it is a permanent fixture or movable, whether it is of wood, wicker or metal. Old discarded furniture no longer needed in the house should not be used.

Attractive decorative objects of wood or stone, including statues, add interest to the modern garden. These objects should be placed in an open space, such as on the lawn, at the edge of a pool, on a paved patio, or beside steps. Shallow garden urns are best planted with bright flowers such as petunias, nasturtiums, combined with other trailing plants. Tall, narrow urns are used as a decoration by themselves, without any plants.

A bird table may be an attractive addition. The best material for such a table is wood combined with wicker or else an interesting branch or log adapted for the purpose. Logs and branches of unusual shape are an interesting decoration in the garden but must be selected with care. Like statuary they need to be put in a suitable place and need to be surrounded by space. Even the most beautiful decorative object loses its attraction if it is placed incorrectly.

Screens. Pergolas, archways and screens are enhanced by climbing plants which can be heavy so the structure must be solidly built. Treated wood is most suitable.

Pergolas and archways cannot be placed as solitary, isolated structures in the garden. Usually they extend from some building and end at a specific point the gardener wishes to emphasise. They lead somewhere. Archways can decorate an entrance, may lead from the house to the garage, or from the ornamental to the kitchen garden.

Screens covered with climbing plants may be used to block off sections of the garden, for instance a spot where children can play, or else conceal dustbins or a compost heap. They can be used as protection against wind, and placed round a bench. It is important to choose climbing plants carefully. For example, the Russian vine, *Polygonum baldschuanicum* (polygonum) is suitable for a large garden, parthenocissus for a smaller garden, ivy (hedera) for shady places, and *Clematis alpina* for sunny spots.

The role of water. Water is a necessity in every garden. Sometimes pools are built purely for practical reasons (as a reserve supply for purposes of watering, as a paddling pool), and sometimes only as a decorative element (an ornamental basin, birdbath) but it is possible to combine the practical with the pleasant, usefulness and beauty.

A pool enhances the beauty of a garden. The sky and garden are mirrored in its surface thus doubling the effect. Water is a living thing, it is in constant motion, the slightest movement ripples the surface. A pool makes it possible to have a wider assortment of ornamental plants by including aquatic and marsh plants. Furthermore, pools are visited by birds that come there to drink.

A pool should always be placed where it produces the greatest effect. The spot should be chosen with care for a basin is a permanent expensive fixture. Its shape, size and depth should be well thought out in advance.

Bird-baths are also decorative. They may be of widely varied design as well as material. However, they must form a shallow bowl with shallow edge no deeper than 3 to 4 cm (1 to 1¹/₂ in) so that the birds will not drown. The water must be changed regularly. Bird-baths should be put in an open spot where the birds will feel safe and where they can be observed.

A brook running through a garden is a great asset. It can be widened at one point to form a pool and the soil on either side held in place by edging of water-loving plants. Water used in this way is perhaps the loveliest of all.

Other garden facilities. The modern garden needs a bonfire area, outdoor fireplace or at least a barbecue pit. The bonfire site should be located in a spot free of draughts and distant from any buildings. A very attractive effect is obtained if the area is edged with flat paving stones which help keep the place tidy and prevent the possibility of fire spreading to the surrounding grass. When building the raised edge, cement a short iron tube in place on either side through which spits can then be inserted. An outdoor fireplace, also located in a draught-free spot, generally on a paved terrace sheltered by climbing plants, is very useful. It is also possible to purchase portable grills.

Lighting in the garden is used primarily on patios and in other places designed for use in the evening. Various lighting fixtures concealed in the vegetation can also illuminate one or more attractive spots. Electric cables should be placed underground and deep enough so that they are not damaged by garden tools.

A garden should also cater for childrens' taste. A sandpit placed in a warm and sunny spot free of draughts is always popular. The size depends on the number of children. The bottom should be paved with bricks laid flat and far enough apart to allow for drainage after a rainfall so that the sand will dry quickly. Bricks can also be used to pave the area around the sandbox. Planed edging boards should be nailed on top of the wooden framework for the children to sit on and to use as a 'workbench'. In a large garden one section can be set apart for children to play games, linked to the area where the sandpit is.

In every garden there should also be a place for dustbins and compost heaps. It is thus best to select a corner of the garden, a low, shaded spot, separated from the rest of the garden by a pergola covered with climbing plants or by suitably placed flowering shrubs.

ANIMAL LIFE
IN THE GARDEN

The garden is a haven for many forms of animal life. Garden soil contains many microscopic as well as larger organisms that feed on plant remnants and organic waste, transforming it into humus and thus enriching the soil. The small tunnels that earthworms burrow aerate the soil. The soil they consume in the lower layers passes through their digestive tract together with the plant remnants they eat and is then deposited either on or below the surface, thereby cultivating the soil and at the same time enriching it with humus. About one gram of soil passes through the earthworm's digestive tract in twenty-four hours. In one year earthworms on an area of one square metre will bring to the surface some five to six kg (12 lb) of humus. Experiments have shown that crops grown on soil worked by earthworms give far greater yields.

Soil, however, is also inhabited by undesirable creatures, such as the larvae of harmful insects which should be destroyed. Ants are also unwelcome in the garden.

The mole can be disastrous in the garden, particularly if it chooses a smooth, clipped lawn for its activities. There are many ways of getting rid of moles, but none are very effective. Moles avoid fertilized soil. Rather than killing them it is best to try to drive them away as far as possible from the garden.

The hedgehog is a welcome helper as it captures various beetles and small mammals and causes minimum damage to plants. It can easily be tamed.

Even frogs, including toads, are beneficial. They eat large numbers of slugs and various insects and should therefore be protected. Snails and slugs, on the other hand, will eat whatever vegetable matter they come upon in the garden and even though the gardener wages constant war on them they always reappear.

Bees are extremely important as pollinators. To produce 1 kg (2 lb 4 oz) of honey, bees must visit at least 40,000 flowers. A garden is fortunate if there is a bee-hive nearby and the work of bee-keepers should be supported.

Wasps are serious pests. They pierce ripening fruit and spread rot (*Monilia fructigena*), and they sting. The best way to get rid of them is to put some beer or sweet syrup in several wide-necked bottles and hang them on trees. Attracted by the sweet fragrance the wasps climb into the bottles and are unable to get out.

Part of the living environment in the garden are various species of birds. Most are welcome visitors because they help control insects, being the best means of keeping these in check, and their song brightens the

Location of a beehive in the garden — away from the section designed for the use of the household.

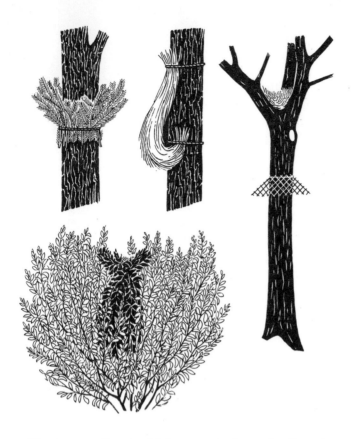

Simple ways of getting birds to nest in the garden. Round the tree trunk at the right is a wire ring to keep cats at bay.

atmosphere. Only the blackbird, starling, pigeon, and sparrow will frequently eat part of the garden's harvest leaving insects unnoticed. In severe winters birds often die of hunger and we should try to save them by regularly putting out food at this time and enticing them to the garden even during the growing season. Remember, however, that it is better not to feed them at all rather than to do so irregularly. Birds become accustomed to having food put out for them and wait patiently by the feeding trays even if these are empty. In some cases the birds may become so weak that they finally die. It is also important to know what kind of food to put out. Water should never be put in feeders in winter. Neither should birds be given food remnants from the table that are salty, spicy or of leavened dough. Tits, finches and

chaffinches like sunflower seeds. Best for buntings, linnets and bramblings is a mixture of grain-seeds and poppy-seeds and various dried berries such as rowan berries. Remnants of bread and rolls should be left to harden and then grated. Excellent for all species of tits are bits of raw suet as well as pork fat. These may be attached so they hang freely from the roof of the feeder because troublesome blackbirds and sparrows will not perch on swaying food whereas tits find it to their liking. Feeders should always be protected from rain, snow and wind as well as cats. There should also be a loose shrub or tree branch nearby.

Help should also be given by providing them with nesting opportunities. Natural nesting sites are becoming continually scarcer not only in the wild but also in gardens as thickets give way to carefully tended shrubs. A good substitute for natural thickets are various man-made nesting sites of pine, spruce or fir twigs on the trunk or at the base of a tree. The tops of gooseberry bushes grown as standards are particularly good places for nesting because the thorns provide reliable protection against cats. It is also possible to tie the shoots of ornamental shrubs about 1 m (3 ft) above the ground to form a kind of 'basket' suitable for nesting. The tie may be removed and the shoots allowed to spring apart again after the young birds have fledged and left the nest.

Some birds are in the habit of nesting in tree cavities and the scarcity of old, hollow trees should be made up for somehow. Tits, in particular, prefer nesting in cavities. For these birds we can put out various types of nest boxes, generally made of wood, putting them up in a tree or else building them directly into a wall. They should be placed about 3 m (10 ft) above the ground or at least at eye level. For tits the entrance hole should measure about 32 mm ($^1/_4$ in) in diameter; a larger hole would enable other, less welcome birds to usurp the abode. If nest boxes are used they must be cleaned regularly, at least once a year—anytime between September and November.

PICTORIAL SECTION

On the preceding pages we discussed the principles that should be observed when establishing a new garden. The following pictorial section is intended primarily for those who already have a garden and wish only to adapt it to their taste. It deals with the subject in greater detail, with the various groups of plants arranged not according to the botanical system of classification but according to gardening practice and practical uses. Discussed in this section will be the requirements of the various plants, the best place to put them in the garden, their possible combinations with other plants, and the particulars of their cultivation and use.

Putting theory into practice, however, applying what one has learned and bringing it to life will depend on the individual gardener's talent, industry, imagination and taste.

ORNAMENTAL TREES AND SHRUBS

Ornamental trees and shrubs make up a large group of garden plants that can be used in a great many ways. In general they are easy to grow and yet they are elements that determine the character of the garden. They also improve the environment by reducing the amount of dust in the atmosphere, oxygenating the air, and muffling the noise of passing traffic.

Included in this group are coniferous trees and shrubs, deciduous trees, as well as deciduous and evergreen shrubs, plus other plants such as heath plants, climbers and roses. Some woody plants, particularly trees, eventually attain a large size and these are not usually used in the small garden. Shrubs afford a wide selection from which to choose.

What points should we consider when selecting trees and shrubs for our garden?

1. The size and shape. Some shrubs are prostrate, while others may be tall and narrow. They may be spherical or pyramidal and they may have arching or climbing shoots. Some grow rapidly, reaching their full height in three to four years and then remain the same height for years; others grow continually, sometimes for as long as forty years or more. Type species are becoming increasingly rare in gardens. Grown in their place are various cultivars of varying form, usually smaller, lower. In the case of woody plants these forms are generally described by Latin names—columnar forms by the term 'Columnaris' or 'Fastigiata', pyramidal forms by the term 'Pyramidalis' or 'Monumentalis', pendent, drooping forms by the term 'Pendula' or 'Inversa', spherical or umbrella-like forms by the terms 'Globosa', 'Compacta', forms with twisted branches by the terms 'Monstrosa' or 'Tortuosa', low, dwarf forms by the terms 'Nana', 'Compacta', 'Nidiformis', 'Tabulaeformis', 'Prostrata'.

Colours differing from that of the type species are designated in the same manner: red forms by the term 'Rubra', 'Purpurea', 'Atropurpurea', yellow forms by the term 'Aurea' or 'Lutea', silvery or bluish forms (in the case of conifers) by the term 'Argentea', 'Glauca', 'Violacea', three-coloured forms by the term 'Tricolor'.

2. The site or location. Some trees and shrubs are very adaptable and will grow in almost any place they are put whereas others will not thrive unless in ideal conditions. Many trees and shrubs originally grew under conditions quite different from those in our gardens and it is particularly important that these be provided with the type of soil, light and climate they require.

3. Expediency (suitability to the end in view). In the garden this always goes hand in hand with the aesthetic effect created by the planting. Some trees and shrubs are best as specimens, others are good for hedges, others as edging or bedding plants, others are best in the rockery and some conceal unsightly spots. Some lighten the environment, others produce a dignified effect,

some create a feeling of warmth, others of coolness, some are of precise, geometrical shape, others are of loose, twiggy habit.

Conifers generally do best in moist soil and a clear, moist atmosphere. In parks and gardens they are important and striking elements mainly because they are green in winter. In summer they appear cool, but in winter, when they are practically the only bright spot out-of-doors they evoke a feeling of warmth. Conifers covered with snow or hoar frost are attractive and most effective are those with branches close to the ground.

Evergreen broad-leaved trees and shrubs are very popular in the garden. For these the most important factor is a suitable site, for they are either plants of warmer and damper climates or else of arctic and high-mountain regions. A shaded location is best. They need an adequately moist soil throughout the year, even in winter, because the evergreen leaves transpire during the cold winter months. A site exposed to winds is also unsuitable, for wind dries out the soil and leaves. The only pruning evergreens require is to improve their shape.

Evergreen shrubs are so striking that they are planted out either as specimens or separate, individual groups. If planted in combination with other woody plants they should not be placed with deciduous ones but rather with conifers. They are often planted beside buildings, even on the northern side, and some are good as hedges.

Deciduous shrubs are the most popular group of woody plants in the garden. Of the many genera, species and cultivars the flowering shrubs are the favourites. Many decidous shrubs spread rapidly and may become invasive after several years if allowed to grow freely. Therefore, they must be pruned and thinned occasionally. For a shrub to grow well and flower it must be planted in good soil, the ground must be kept weeded and loose by hoeing, and it must be watered and fertilized.

Pruning ornamental deciduous shrubs is basically the same as pruning fruit-bearing shrubs. The oldest shoots should be cut off at ground level and young immature shoots should also be removed; only strong young shoots should be left and the shrub trimmed so that it is attractive, shapely and tidy. Some species must be pruned every year, others need hardly any pruning at all, some are trimmed in winter, others after the flowers have faded. In all cases, however, the faded flowers should be removed.

Heath plants. These plants have quite different uses and requirements. Most are evergreens but some are deciduous or semi-evergreen. For the successful cultivation of all heath plants a woodland environment is necessary, that is a light, moist, acid soil and partial shade. A special section should be set apart in the garden for heath plants, suitably supplemented with conifers, ferns, and a pool. Most heath plants grown and propagated in nurseries are hardy and will tolerate even the atmospheric pollution of large cities. They all require soil rich in humus and frequent application of lime-free water. Only acid fertilizers should be applied (sulphates and superphosphate).

Climbing woody plants create a marvellous effect in the garden. They are grown not only for ornament but for practical purposes as well—to conceal unattractive walls, fences and unsightly spots, to keep out dust from the road, to separate one section of the garden from another. As a rule, however, their purpose is ornamental—adding colour to fences, summerhouses, archways, pergolas, brick or concrete walls, gateways, pillars and dead trees. One must know how to manage climbing plants. They need not cover the whole object but may be used only to frame or to highlight, particularly if it has an architectural beauty of its own.

Climbing woody plants are divided into the following groups according to the way in which they are attached to the support: twining plants (these are the majority), plants with tendrils, plants with sucker-tipped rootlets, and plants without organs that enable them to climb. Climbers with sucker-tipped rootlets will climb up and retain a firm hold on a rough surface without any support, plants without organs that enable them to climb must be tied to a support, the remainder will climb up wires or wood strips placed upright for twining plants and crosswise for others. Some climbers are rapid growers and tend to become invasive. When choosing climbers, therefore, it is necessary to be guided not only by the purpose they are to serve but also by their specific requirements and whether these can be fulfilled. This, of course, applies to all ornamental trees and shrubs.

The plant groups are arranged on the basis of their permanent importance in the garden with an eye to the work required for their care. Within the separate groups the species are arranged on each double page either on the basis of common characteristics or common uses.

CONIFERS

Conifers head the list of ornamental trees and shrubs and the following is a basic selection.

Chamaecyparis. These are trees with a dense, conical crown and are native to North America and Japan. The type species are large trees growing to a height of 20 to 50 m (65 to 160 ft) in their native land; only small forms of the species are used in gardens. They have the great advantage of being quite tolerant of the atmospheric pollution of large cities.

The Sawara cypress—*Chamaecyparis pisifera*—is native to Japan. In Europe the type species grows to a height of 20 m (65 ft); only cultivated varieties, which are broader and of looser habit than other cypresses and require a light, nourishing and sufficiently moist soil, are grown in gardens. *C. pisifera* 'Filifera Aurea' is a golden-leaved form of the cultivar *C. pisifera* 'Filifera'. It is a broadly conical tree growing to a height of 5 m (16 ft) with long branches and slender, string-like, drooping twigs.

Chamaecyparis pisifera 'Squarrosa Dumosa' is a dwarf form of the cultivar *C. pisifera* 'Squarrosa'. It is a slow grower, reaching a height of 3 m (10 ft) and

is asymmetrical with an irregular outline. The leaves are needle-like, silvery, and blue-green in colour. Young trees are very beautiful but after a few years they shed the bottom branches. This is a good tree for shaded locations. It must be sheltered from dry and freezing winds for otherwise the needles on the windward side turn rusty-brown and fall.

The Lawson cypress—*Chamaecyparis lawsoniana*—is a native of California and Oregon, where it grows to a height of 50 m (160 ft). Specimens grown in Europe, however, are much smaller, no more than 20 m (65 ft) high. It has a narrow, conical, densely branched crown with blue-green needles. The terminal shoots are usually pendulous. The twigs spread out horizontally but not in a precise and regular pattern; they give off a strong scent when rubbed between the fingers. This species and its many forms is the least hardy of all the cypresses. In severe winters or unsuitable situations it is damaged or even killed by frost. The hardiest forms have a greyish tinge; yellow-leaved forms have a low resistance to frost and are therefore cultivated less frequently. They succeed best in lower altitudes and sheltered situations. The illustrated *C. lawsoniana* 'Ellwoodii' (see p. 34) is ovate-conical in outline, up to 4 m (13 ft) high and 2 m (6 ft) wide, bluish, and comparatively hardy.

The Hinoki cypress—*Chamaecyparis obtusa*—is a native of Japan, where it grows to a height of 40 m (135 ft). In Europe its growth rate is very slow and it attains a maximum height of 10 m (33 ft). The type species is little known in Europe. Usually cultivated are the dwarf forms which are excellent for ornamental miniature Japanese gardens. They may be grown in a sheltered spot and also in the rock garden. The most commonly cultivated form is *C. obtusa* 'Nana Gracilis', which is broadly conical and grows to a maximum height of 2 m (6 ft). The twigs, arranged in a fan-like pattern, are beautiful and dainty. This form requires a site sheltered against frost, wind and sun scorch and a more nourishing soil that tends to be on the moist side.

Thuja. Arbor-vitae are trees with a dense conical crown and flat twigs and are native to North America and eastern Asia. Of the six species found in the parks and gardens of Europe the one most commonly grown is the American arbor-vitae or white cedar *(Thuja occidentalis)* of North America, which grows to a height of 20 m (65 ft). It is very hardy, the hardiest of all conifers not indigenous to Europe, and has no special requirements. It tolerates dry conditions as well as atmospheric pollution but does best in a warm and moist soil. In extremely dry conditions it thins out prematurely and dries up; in shade the growth is less dense. Of the many cultivated forms— slender, conical as well as spherical—the most rewarding is *T. occidentalis* 'Elwangeriana Aurea Rheingold', which grows to a height of 3 to 4 m (10 to 13 ft), is strikingly broadly conical in outline and has lovely golden twigs which keep their colour until winter. The twigs are slender, dainty and full. In winter the branches spread and droop under the weight of snow rendering them unsuitable as hedges. Other arbor-vitae and yews, however, are excellent for clipped hedges and screens.

Chamaecyparis pisifera 'Filifera Aurea'

Chamaecyparis obtusa 'Nana Gracilis'

Chamaecyparis pisifera 'Squarrosa Dumosa'

Thuja occidentalis 'Elwangeriana Aurea'

33

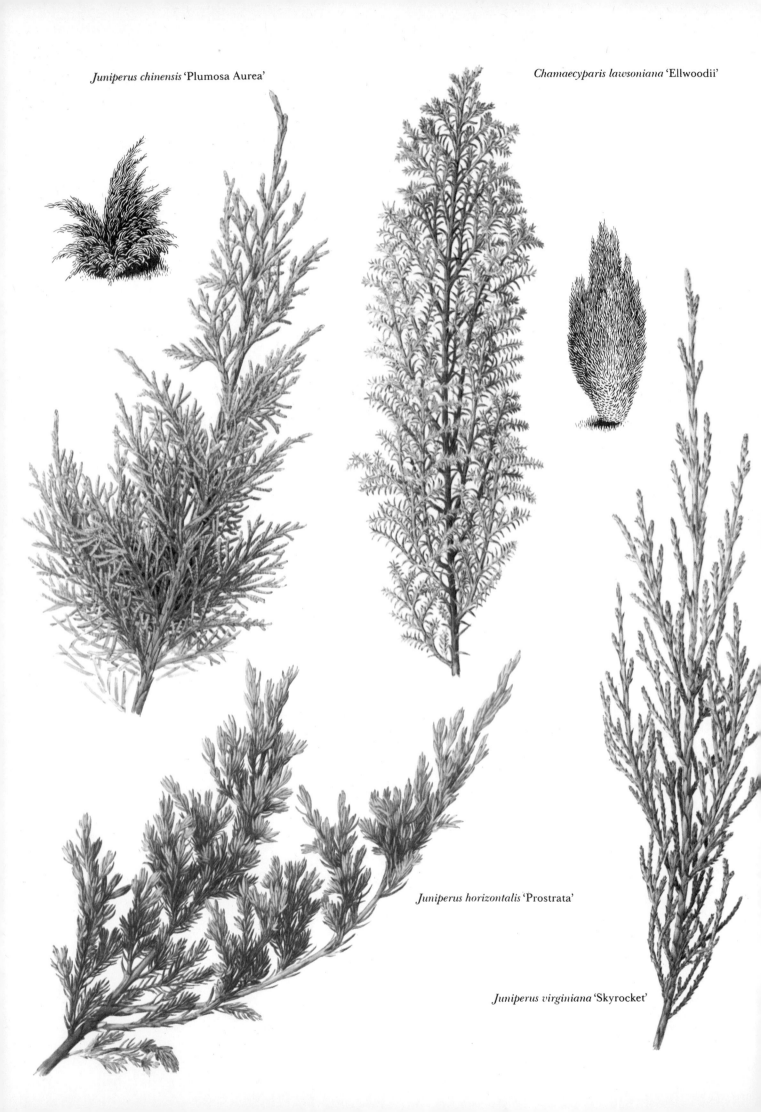

Juniperus chinensis 'Plumosa Aurea'

Chamaecyparis lawsoniana 'Ellwoodii'

Juniperus horizontalis 'Prostrata'

Juniperus virginiana 'Skyrocket'

Juniperus. These are trees and shrubs of diverse habit found throughout practically the entire northern hemisphere. Many of the 60 species grow wild in the mountains and hill country of central and western Europe. The juniper is the most widely and commonly used conifer in Europe's parks and gardens. There are many species, cultivars and forms, all with no particular requirements. They like ample light but will grow even in poorer soils, are hardy and tolerate atmospheric pollution.

The following are six cultivated varieties recommended for the garden:

Juniperus chinensis 'Plumosa Aurea' is a lovely cultivar of the species *J. chinensis*. It is hardy and will grow even in alkaline soil but requires a sunny position. Of spreading habit, it reaches a height of 2 to 3 m (6 to 10 ft) and has yellow twigs. It is a slow growing juniper for planting as a solitary specimen in grass or a larger rock garden.

Juniperus chinensis 'Pfitzeriana' is the most widely cultivated form. It is very dense, has a broad and irregularly spreading habit, and grows to a height of 2 m (6 ft). The branches are long and stout, slanting upwards or horizontally, pendulous at the tip and slightly greyish. This variety has no special requirements, but the branches tend to break under the weight of heavy snow and it is sometimes attacked by insect pests such as *Linneaspis junipericola*.

Juniperus horizontalis is an American species of prostrate or creeping shrubs with long branches and numerous short, blue-green twigs. It is hardy with no special requirements and invaluable in the rock garden and on top of dry walls. It is also good as a ground cover on slopes as a substitute for grass. The illustrated *J. horizontalis* 'Prostrata' is one of the several cultivated varieties.

Juniperus virginiana is a native of North America. It resembles the Chinese junipers and the type species is a slender tree 10 m (33 ft) high. Though hardy it does not tolerate atmospheric pollution. It requires a more nourishing and moister soil than other junipers for good growth, even though it stands up fairly well to temporary drought. It is a typical plant for use as a specimen tree, for it does poorly and tends to dry up when planted in groups. There are several cultivated varieties, the most noteworthy being *J. virginiana* 'Skyrocket', which grows to a height of 3 m (10 ft) and is the slenderest conifer grown in European gardens.

The Common juniper—*J. communis*—is a native of Europe. It is a tall, slender tree with sharp, prickle-pointed needles which will grow almost anywhere. However, it is one of the few conifers which will not tolerate the atmospheric pollution of industrial regions. It also occurs as a low, prostrate shrub, the lowest form *J. communis* 'Repanda', being no more than 50 cm (20 in) high but with a spread of 1.5 m (5 ft).

Juniperus squamata is native to Asia. The form generally cultivated in Europe is *J. squamata* 'Meyeri', which is a spreading, forked shrub of loose habit up to 3 m (10 ft) high with short, stout twigs. The needles are set close together and have a silvery tinge. It is attractive and hardy and tolerates atmospheric pollution but at lower altitudes is attacked by pests.

Juniperus squamata 'Meyeri'

Juniperus communis 'Repanda'

36

Picea. Spruces are trees with a conical crown terminating in a point, which distinguishes them from the firs (abies). Some 40 species are distributed throughout the temperate and cold regions of the northern hemisphere, but only the garden varieties are cultivated. Even though native to Europe spruces have fairly exacting requirements. They grow best in moist soil and a moist, clear atmosphere, even though some species are hardier. If conditions are unfavourable the bottom branches die.

The Colorado or blue spruce — *Picea pungens* — is a North American species commonly grown in Europe. It is noted for its regular shape. Seedlings and cultivated varieties vary in colour from dull green to whitish-grey and bluish-grey. This spruce is a hardy tree with few requirements. It tolerates both dry conditions and atmospheric pollution. It is used as a solitary specimen; when planted in groups it soon loses the bottom branches. The illustrated *P. pungens* 'Glauca Globosa', a low, dwarf form of fairly spreading habit, is one of the several cultivated varieties.

The common or Norway spruce — *Picea abies* — grows in mountainous regions. This means that it has no particular light or heat requirements but needs both a moist soil and atmosphere. In warm and dry conditions in the lowlands it dries up and is prone to disease, also it does not tolerate atmospheric pollution. Cultivated varieties grown in gardens are dwarf and of unusual shapes, such as cushion-like, spherical, broadly conical, drooping, asymmetrical. The one shown in the illustration is *Picea abies* 'Dumosa'.

Picea pungens 'Glauca Globosa'

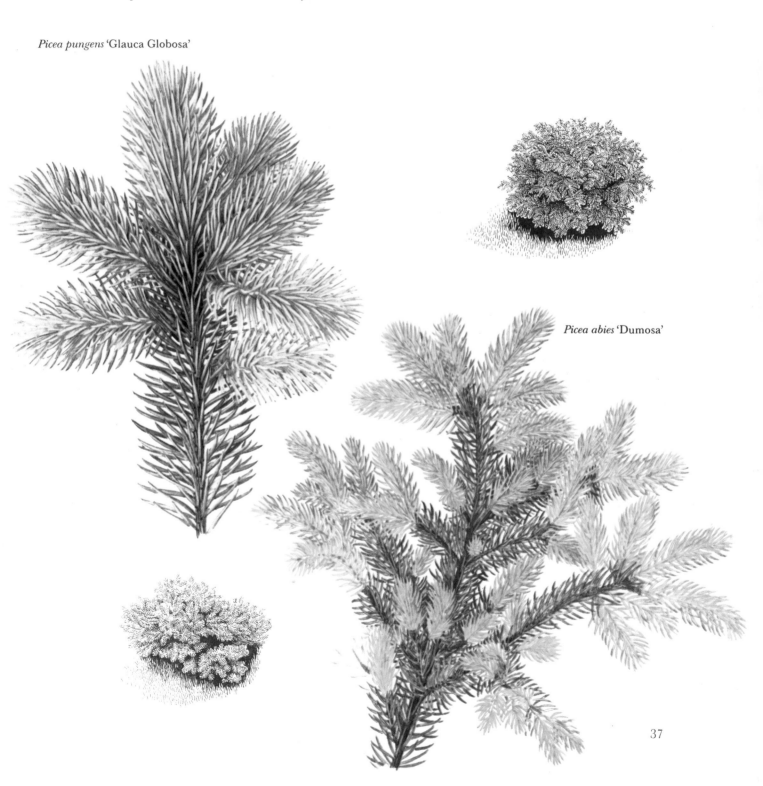

Picea abies 'Dumosa'

Picea glauca is native to the western part of North America. Only the cultivated variety *P. glauca* 'Conica' (syn. *P. glauca albertiana conica*) is generally grown in Europe where it is one of the most popular of conifers, highly prized for its symmetrical shape, dense conical crown and slow rate of growth. Mature specimens are not higher than 2 m (6 ft). It is a hardy tree requiring a moderately moist soil and is fairly tolerant of atmospheric pollution. It is usually planted as a specimen subject where the beauty of its symmetry is shown to best advantage. It is the most valuable of all spruces for the garden.

Picea glauca 'Conica'

Pinus. Pines are trees that differ from other conifers in the arrangement and placing of the crown, which marks a sort of transitional stage to the broad-leaved trees. There are some 115 species distributed throughout the temperate regions of the northern hemisphere only a few of which are grown in parks and gardens, mostly the low and dwarf species or their cultivated varieties. Whereas the spruce is a tree of the mountains the pine is a tree of the lowlands, except for dwarf mountain pine and certain exotic species. All pines need ample light. Given this as well as ample space they will retain their lower branches for a long time, otherwise these are soon shed. Most species have no special requirements and will grow even in poor, sandy and stony soil. They are tolerant of drought.

The Swiss mountain pine — *Pinus mugo* 'Mughus' (syn. *P. montana*) — differs somewhat from the typical pines in that it has a dwarf form which grows in mountains and peat bogs throughout most of Europe. This is a slow-growing, prostrate shrub of great importance on slopes as it prevents soil erosion by holding the earth together with its roots. It is extremely variable. The form generally grown in parks and gardens is *P. mugo pumilio* which has no special requirements and will grow in both dry and wet soil. It measures up to 1 m (3 ft) in height and 4 m (13 ft) across. At lower altitudes the shrub forms are generally of looser habit; denser, branching shrubs may be obtained by removing the terminal shoots. In the garden it should be planted in a suitable spot — in the rock garden, on slopes to hold the soil, or with birch and heaths. It is also good for freely-growing hedges.

Scots pine — *Pinus sylvestris* — is a tall erect tree with loose spreading branches and beautifully coloured bark, rather thick and fissured. On shallow, rocky foundations the trunk is crooked. This pine has no special requirements and is very adaptable but does poorly in heavy soil and peat bogs. The smaller cultivars are usually grown in parks and gardens, one of the most popular and most widely grown is *P. sylvestris* 'Watereri', also known as *P. sylvestris* 'Pumila'. It has a slow growth rate, a dense, conical to ovate crown up to 3 m (10 ft) high, and a greyer hue than the usual pine.

The Weymouth or eastern white pine — *Pinus strobus* — is native to North America. It is a tall, handsome tree with slender needles. Grown in gardens is the dwarf form *P. strobus* 'Nana' which grows to a height of about 5 m (16 ft) in Europe. It is very hardy and tolerates even shade when young. Its requirements are similar to those of spruce; it needs deep soil as well as atmospheric moisture. It is planted as a solitary subject so that it will retain its lower branches a long time.

Pinus mugo

Pinus sylvestris 'Watereri'

Pinus strobus 'Nana'

39

if conditioned to light from youth. In shaded locations they tolerate dry and poor soils and they are also tolerant of atmospheric pollution. They are planted either in groups or as specimens.

The common or English yew — *Taxus baccata* — is native to Europe but is rarely found in the wild. It is a tree with a conical crown that grows very slowly to a height of 10 to 12 m (33 to 40 ft). Often it produces several shoots at ground level and develops into a large shrub of broadly spreading habit. This yew has yielded many cultivated varieties that are very valuable for parks and gardens, such as *T. baccata* 'Fastigiata Aurea' — a yellow-leaved form of dense, columnar, often asymmetrical habit with upright branches which grows to a height of 3 to 5 m (10 to 16 ft). Though prized by gardeners it is less resistant and is damaged by frost in severe winters, however, it puts out new shoots again in spring.

An excellent yew for the garden is *T. media* 'Hicksii', one of the group of upright yews of which it is the hardiest. It grows to a height of 3 to 4 m (10 to 13 ft) but the branches of older specimens tend to spread. The needles are a glossy dark green. This yew

Tsuga canadensis

Taxus baccata 'Fastigiata Aurea'

Taxus. Yews are trees and shrubs for shady locations. All parts are poisonous. There are 8 species distributed throughout the northern hemisphere, all very much alike. Yews are the darkest of the conifers, ideal for hedges, screens and contouring because they stand up well to pruning and regenerate even from stumps. They do best in partial shade, a moist atmosphere and deep nourishing soil. However, they are very adaptable and will grow in a light situation

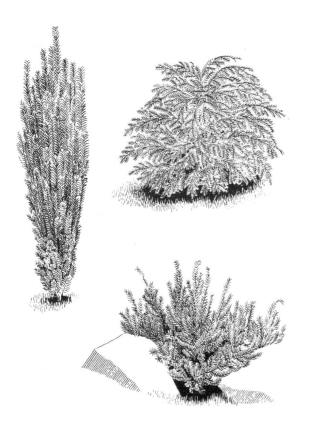

is a hybrid between *T. baccata* 'Fastigiata' and *T. cuspidata* and is becoming increasingly common in parks and gardens.

The Japanese yew—*T. cuspidata*—differs from the common yew mainly by its lower crown and more spreading habit. It is also less demanding and does better in open situations exposed to winds. Most widely grown is *T. cuspidata* 'Nana'—a very dense form rarely exceeding one metre in height and 2 to 3 m (6 to 10 ft) in width.

Tsuga. The hemlock is a tree rarely seen in Europe. However, there are 14 species in North America and eastern Asia of which only the Eastern or Canadian hemlock *(Tsuga canadensis)* is grown in parks and gardens. A native of the colder regions of North America, it is a handsome, beautifully branched tree growing to a height of 15 m (50 ft). It is suitable for both higher and lower altitudes but for vigorous growth requires atmospheric moisture and rich, deep, moist soil. It tolerates slight shade. Of the several cultivars the one most widely grown in the garden is *T. canadensis* 'Nana' which is low, semi-spherical and of dense habit.

Taxus media 'Hicksii'   *Taxus cuspidata* 'Nana'

41

Mahonia aquifolium

Ilex aquifolium

BROAD-LEAVED
TREES AND SHRUBS

Of the large selection of broad-leaved trees and shrubs available the first on the list that follows are the most widely grown evergreen species.

Mahonia aquifolium. The Oregon grape is native to North America. This is a shrub up to 1 m (3 ft) high with glossy, sharply toothed leaves. It is hardy and has no special requirements but grows best in partial shade and moist, rich soil. It is used as underplanting in loose groupings of trees, amidst early-

flowering shrubs, for freely-growing hedges and in the rock garden. Rich yellow pendulous flowers open in early spring.

Ilex aquifolium. Holly is native to the Mediterranean region where it reaches a height of 15 m (50 ft); in the temperate zone, however, it is usually seen as a small tree or large bush. It is a beautiful tree with dark green, glossy, serrated leaves. Bright red berries are produced in the autumn and winter. The variety *I.a.* 'Bacciflava' has yellow berries. Hollies can be used as hedges.

Rhododendron hybridum. This is a wonderful shrub for the garden. Cross-breeding of the botanical

Rhododendron hybridum

Rhododendron japonicum

species has produced hardy cultivated varieties differing in the size of the shrub, size of the blooms and colour. It requires a woodland environment, in other words partial shade and moist, acid, fertile soil. The garden soil where it is planted should be a mixture of peat, forest litter and sand.

Rhododendron japonicum. This is better known by the synonym *Azalea mollis;* it is a semi-evergreen shrub growing to a height of about 1 m (3 ft) and bearing pastel-coloured flowers in early spring (mid-May). It requires the same woodland conditions as *R. hybridum* but is less demanding. It is usually planted in groups.

43

Buxus sempervirens

Berberis julianae

Prunus laurocerasus

44

Berberis julianae. This evergreen shrub belongs to a large genus which comprises mostly deciduous species. *B. julianae*, a native of China, grows to a height of about 1.5 m (5 ft), is of sturdy habit and has beautiful foliage. Like all berberries it is a thorny shrub. In May till June it bears yellow to orange blossoms and in the autumn it is lovely with its bluish berries and reddish leaves. It requires well drained soil that is not unduly moist, and partial shade. It is planted in groups, as a hedge or as a solitary subject in the rock garden.

Buxus sempervirens. The common box is native to the Mediterranean region, where it grows to a height of 8 m (26 ft). In the temperate regions of Europe, under the best possible conditions, its maximum height is 3 m (10 ft). All parts of the plant are poisonous. It is a thick shrub of symmetrical habit with light, leathery leaves. The flowers are inconspicuous and borne in clusters in the leaf axils. Box has no particular requirements; it tolerates dry conditions, sun scorch as well as shade and atmospheric pollution. It does best in partial shade and rich soil. Several cultivated varieties exist, some with white or yellow variegated leaves. Its appearance is hard and stiff and it should therefore be placed together with similar trees and shrubs, such as cypresses and yews. It is good as an underplanting for taller trees. It stands up well to pruning and is thus excellent for clipped hedges and topiary.

Prunus laurocerasus. This shrub is native to southeastern Europe and Asia Minor, where it forms large shrubs; in the temperate regions of Europe, however, it reaches a height of no more than 2 m (6 ft). It has beautiful foliage and during the flowering period is covered with thick clusters of white flowers which in autumn give way to black fruits. The plant is poisonous. It is one of the most valuable of the evergreen shrubs. Requirements include partial shade, well-drained and nourishing soil containing lime and adequate moisture. It stands up fairly well to dry conditions and atmospheric pollution and has a comparatively rapid rate of growth. There are several cultivated varieties differing primarily in the size of the plant and leaves. Large-leaved cultivars are not as hardy. It may be used in many ways—planted in groups or as a solitary subject, also for decorating buildings and conservatories.

Calluna vulgaris. Scottish heather is widespread throughout Europe and Asia Minor. It is a small, twiggy shrub which flowers from July till September and forms large spreading masses. It likes sun, poor, sandy, acid soil and drier situations and does not tolerate lime or rich soil. Old specimens are not attractive for they have too many woody shoots and tend to be prostrate and therefore should be cut back in spring. There are many cultivated varieties of heather—white, pink, mauve and red, single and double, as well as dwarf forms.

Calluna vulgaris

DECIDUOUS TREES AND SHRUBS

These form a far more numerous group than the evergreens.

Viburnum rhytidophyllum. The leatherleaf viburnum is a large-leaved evergreen species of a genus which includes many deciduous shrubs. Native to China, evergreen viburnums are more valuable but in most cases less hardy. The leatherleaf viburnum is a shrub 2 to 3 m (6 to 10 ft) high which produces creamy white flowers in May. The oval fruits are red at first, later turning black. It requires partial shade but tolerates dry conditions growing best on chalk. The growth rate is quite rapid. To produce fruit it is necessary to plant two or more together.

Viburnum lantana

Viburnum rhytidophyllum

Viburnum lantana. Viburnum is one of the most widely grown ornamental shrubs in the garden. In the northern hemisphere there exist many species, both deciduous and evergreen. Native to Europe is one of the most widely distributed species, the wayfaring tree, *V. lantana,* which grows to a height of over 3 m (10 ft). The whitish flowers appear in May and June. The fruits are red at first, later turning black. It requires a deep, rich soil, preferring soil with lime, and prefers a sunny situation although it tolerates partial shade and fairly dry conditions. It can be used in a great many ways but only in larger gardens as it is a large shrub.

Ligustrum vulgare

Symphoricarpos albus

Ligustrum vulgare. Privet grows throughout the whole of Europe in woodlands in warmer areas. It is a dense shrub about 3 m (10 ft) high with no special requirements. It tolerates dry conditions as well as atmospheric pollution and thrives in sun as well as partial shade. Quick growing it is a most valuable shrub for clipped hedges. The cultivated varieties that do not shed their leaves till spring (*L. vulgare* 'Atrovirens', *L. vulgare* 'Lodense'—dwarf) are best. The plant is poisonous, especially the berries. When grown in groups it requires frequent thinning so that it does not become twiggy.

Symphoricarpos albus. The snowberry is native to North America, is a shrub about 1.5 m (5 ft) high which produces root suckers freely and forms spreading masses. The small flowers are borne in succession from June until August and the berries are white. It will grow practically anywhere, even in poor soil and shade, and tolerates a polluted atmosphere. It is important as food for bees but tends to spread too freely. The root suckers must be cut back regularly and old branches removed every five years.

Laburnum anagyroides. Golden rain is a native of southern Europe and Asia Minor. It is a slender, small tree growing to a height of 6 m (20 ft) which is gorgeous in May with its chains of golden flowers, some as long as 20 cm (8 in). The leaves, flowers and seeds are very poisonous. It prefers warmer situations, and sun or at most light shade. It does best in medium-heavy, well-drained soil containing lime and is moderately tolerant of dry conditions and atmospheric pollution. Only young shrubs must be pruned. It is striking as a solitary subject but is also effective planted in groups, particularly with lilac (syringa) and forsythia.

Laburnum anagyroides

Cornus mas

Cornus mas. The cornelian cherry is native to Europe, where it grows in groves and on shrub-covered hillsides in warmer regions. It is a spreading shrub or small tree that reaches a height of 3 to 7 m (10 to 23 ft). It is particularly attractive in March and April, when it is covered with yellow flowers, which appear before the leaves, and then again in autumn with its fruits. It has no special requirements, thriving in sun as well as partial shade and tolerating soil with lime, drought and atmospheric pollution. Planted in groups of several shrubs, it holds the soil on banks and hillsides and is also used for hedges. There are several cultivated varieties; particularly attractive is *C.m.* 'Variegata' with white-edged leaves.

Buddleia davidii. The butterfly bush also known as Tibetan or summer lilac, is a native of western China. In Europe it reaches a maximum height of 2 m (6 ft) because it must be pruned every year. The flexible annual shoots bear beautiful long clusters of fragrant, mauve flowers at the tips in July and August and form a shrub of regularly spreading habit. It requires a sunny site, and rich, well-drained soil. It is planted as a solitary subject or in small groups with perennials and ornamental grasses, which it resembles by its habit of growth.

Hibiscus syriacus 'Rubin'

Buddleia davidii

Hibiscus syriacus. Rose of Sharon is native to China and India. It is a slender, upright shrub, 2 to 3 m (6 to 10 ft) high, with lovely large, papery flowers. The leaves and flowers appear late, from August till October. These may be single or double, monocoloured or bicoloured, and various hues of pink, mauve, purple, white, blue and red. This shrub requires a warm, sunny situation and rich, well-drained soil. It stands up well to pruning but should be trimmed only to keep it tidy. In normal European winters it may be damaged and in severe winters even killed by frost. It should therefore be planted only in warmer locations, in a sheltered spot and not in great numbers. It is splendid as a solitary subject or in groups consisting of variously coloured cultivars. Illustrated is the popular and commonly grown variety *H.s.* 'Rubin'.

49

Philadelphus coronarius. Mock orange is native to southern Europe. It grows to a height of 3 m (10 ft) and is noted for the penetrating, sweet scent of its creamy-white flowers resembling that of orange blossom which appear in June or July. It is long-lived and suitable for dry conditions. Numerous hybrids have been produced in recent years, some small (up to 1.5 m [5 ft]), others taller, with single, semi-double as well as double blooms. These cultivars are hardy but require good garden soil, a sunny site or one that is only lightly shaded and are tolerant of atmospheric pollution. Small cultivars are also good for freely-growing hedges and borders.

Syringa vulgaris. Lilac, a native of south eastern Europe, is the second most widely grown ornamental shrub. It is a large shrub or small tree growing to a height of 4 to 5 m (13 to 16 ft) and flowering profusely in May. It has no special requirements but produces less flowers when grown in shady conditions. It tolerates atmospheric pollution. Cultivated varieties require good soil and an occasional application of feed. Lilac (both on its own roots and grafted) puts out numerous root suckers and these must be continually removed. Only cultivated varieties, with large, richly scented, single and double blooms in a wide range of colours (shades of mauve, pink and white) are generally grown in gardens nowadays.

Philadelphus coronarius

Syringa vulgaris

Forsythia suspensa. Forsythia or golden bell, native to China, is a shrub with long, arching branches growing to a height of about 3 m (10 ft). If the branches touch the ground they will take root. The yellow flowers appear in early spring. Forsythia requires a sunny spot (in shaded locations it flowers poorly) and rich, well-drained soil. It does not do well in unduly dry or wet conditions, but tolerates atmospheric pollution. It is best planted on banks, by the waterside and above terraces from which the drooping branches make a lovely display. It can also be tied to a support like a climbing plant. There are several cultivated varieties as well as a dwarf form suitable for the rock garden.

Forsythia suspensa

Paeonia suffruticosa

Paeonia suffruticosa. The tree peony is native to north-western China. It grows to a height of about 1.5 m (5 ft) and is noted for its huge blossoms (10 to 30 cm [4 to 12 in] in diameter) either single or double and in a number of different colours, appearing in May till June. It requires a warm, sheltered site and sun or better light shade. The soil should be rich, well-drained and continually moist. The roots should be protected against spring frosts. The tree peony is generally planted as a solitary subject in turf as well as in smaller groups so that it shows to advantage when in bloom.

51

Kerria japonica. The Japanese rose is native to China. It is a dense shrub growing to a height of about 1.5 m (5 ft). The golden-yellow flowers, appearing in May and June, cover the whole shrub and make a spectacular sight. The variety *K.j.* 'Pleniflora' is more vigorous and has double flowers. It does best in a sunny position though it tolerates partial shade, requires a good, well-drained garden soil and is moderately tolerant of dry conditions. It should be thinned after flowering and when cut back it puts forth a great number of shoots. Kerrias may be planted as solitary subjects, in groups, in borders, in mixed informal hedges and with perennials.

Kerria japonica

Cytisus scoparius

Cytisus scoparius. Scotch broom (syn. *Sarothamnus scoparius*) is a member of the large genus of brooms. This twiggy shrub growing to a height of 1 to 1.5 m (3 to 5 ft) is native to Europe. It flowers in May and June; in winter the branches are green and covered with black pods. It grows everywhere but is found mainly on sandy and dry, acid soil, forming large spreading masses on banks. If it is to be transplanted it should be moved only with the root ball. It is ideal for hillsides and railway embankments but is not particularly suitable for the garden.

Ribes alpinum. Mountain currant grows throughout all of Europe. It is a dense shrub reaching a height of about 1.5 m (5 ft), which comes into leaf early in spring. The inconspicuous flowers appear in April and the berries remain on the shrub a long time. This currant has no special requirements, tolerating drought, sun as well as deep shade and atmospheric pollution. It is often grown in parks and gardens, being suitable for planting in groups, as an underplanting to tall trees, for covering banks, and also for clipped as well as freely-growing hedges. *R. alpinum* 'Pumilum' is a very attractive, low (about 1 m [3 ft] cultivar.

Chaenomeles speciosa. Japanese quince or japonica (syn. *C. lagenaria*) is native to eastern Asia. It is an upright, thorny shrub up to 2 m (6 ft) high. The flowers, which appear in April and May, resemble large apple blossoms (in shades of red, orange and white), and the fruits are yellow quinces. It is a relatively undemanding shrub which tolerates drought and requires ample sunshine. Because the flowers are borne on the side shoots the shrubs should not be pruned but only thinned. They may be planted as solitary subjects, in groups by themselves, as well as in freely-growing hedges. The related species *C. japonica* reaches a height of only 1 m (3 ft) and is ideal for the rock garden.

Ribes alpinum 'Pumilum'

Chaenomeles speciosa

53

Hippophae rhamnoides

Daphne mezereum

Hippophae rhamnoides. Sea buckthorn grows from south-western Europe to the Himalayas. It is a thin, slightly thorny shrub or tree up to 6 m (20 ft) high and 3 m (10 ft) wide. The insignificant flowers appear in April. In the autumn the male plants are covered with fruits rich in Vitamin C. This is a sun-loving species that requires a light, sandy, dry, lime-rich soil. It tolerates salty soils and atmospheric pollution but is sometimes damaged by frost in severe winters. Lovely with its silvery colouring and orange berries it is not particularly good for seaside gardens.

Daphne mezereum. Mezereon, native to Europe, is a small shrub growing to a height of about 1 m (3 ft). The sweet-smelling flowers appear before the leaves from February to March, sometimes even as early as December. The attractive fruits, which ripen in summer, are poisonous. Mezereon requires partial shade and light soil with humus. It should be moved with the root ball. This is a very valuable shrub for the rock garden and is effective grown with low ever-green shrubs.

Cotoneaster horizontalis. Rock cotoneaster is one of the best prostrate species of the large genus cotoneaster. It is native to China. It reaches a height of 1 m (3 ft) and width of at least 2 m (6 ft) and bears small flowers in May; the most ornamental part, however, is the fruit. This shrub has no particular requirements but does well in a sunny situation and a well-drained soil. It tolerates atmospheric pollution and is invaluable for the rock garden, and on top of dry walls.

Hydrangea arborescens. Snowhill hydrangea, native to North America, is a dense, broad shrub growing to a height of 1 to 1.5 m (3 to 5 ft). The flowers appear from June to August. Grown in gardens is the cultivated variety *H. arborescens* 'Grandiflora' which bears white heads of flowers up to 20 cm (8 in) across and has a long flowering period. It does best in a sheltered site in partial shade and moist, acid, nourishing soil, and tolerates atmospheric pollution. The roots should be provided with a protective cover for the winter. It is planted alone or in groups to form a wide border.

Hydrangea arborescens 'Grandiflora'

Cotoneaster horizontalis

flowers, *L.t.* 'Rosea' with large pale-pink flowers, and *L.t.* 'Louis Leroy', a thick, slow-growing shrub of almost perfectly spherical habit, one 1 m (3 ft) high and very good for hedges.

Fly honeysuckle—*L. xylosteum*—is native to the temperate regions of Europe, where it grows chiefly on banks and in the woodlands of warmer, dry areas. It is a thick, spreading shrub growing to a height of 2 to 3 m (6 to 10 ft). The flowers are yellowish-white, the berries dark red. These honeysuckles, and practically all those grown in Europe, are invaluable shrubs for parks and larger gardens and may be used in a great many ways. They are particularly good as

Euonymus europaeus

Lonicera tatarica

Lonicera. Honeysuckle is a large genus of shrubs, trees and climbers, distributed throughout the northern hemisphere. Deciduous shrub species are hardy, have no special requirements and tolerate dry and sandy soil, sun as well as partial shade, and atmospheric pollution. One of the most commonly grown shrubs in Europe's parks and gardens is the Tatarian honeysuckle—*Lonicera tatarica*—which is native to central Asia. It is a dense shrub of upright habit growing to a height of about 3 m (10 ft). The leaves appear early in spring, the white or pink flowers in May and the red berries ripen in July. Attractive cultivated varieties include *L.t.* 'Grandiflora' with larger white flowers, *L.t.* 'Punicea' with rosy-carmine an underplanting or a temporary stop gap for odd spaces.

Euonymus europaeus. Euonymus is a very large genus distributed throughout Europe, Asia and North America. The most commonly grown in parks and gardens is the spindle tree, *E. europaeus,* widespread throughout all Europe in lowlands and hilly country, on the edges of forests, on hillsides and alongside brooks. It is a shrub growing to a height of 2 to 4 m (6 to 13 ft). The flowers are insignificant, small and greenish, the leaves turn purplish in the autumn. The pretty scarlet fruits are four-valved capsules. This shrub does best in partial shade and

Lonicera xylosteum

Rhamnus frangula

in moist soil, but it will grow well under any conditions. It is often attacked by aphids and the ermine moth, *Hyponomeuta cognatella.*

Rhamnus. Buckthorn is a large genus distributed throughout the northern hemisphere. The two species generally cultivated are the common buckthorn, *Rhamnus catharticus,* which grows in dry regions, and the illustrated alder buckthorn, *R. frangula,* which grows in damp and swampy sites. It is a shrub of upright habit growing to a height of 6 m (20 ft). The flowers appear from May until August. The fruits are red at first, later turning black. It requires moist soil and the vicinity of water and is suitable only for parks and large gardens.

57

Deutzia scabra

Rhus typhina

Rhus typhina. Staghorn sumach is an interesting shrub native to North America. It is widely grown in Europe and sometimes becomes naturalized. It reaches a height of 3 to 5 m (10 to 16 ft) and is a very fast grower. The shoots are stout and rusty-brown with velvet-like hairs. The greenish flowers, borne in dense, conical panicles, appear from June to July, followed in the autumn by dark red, hairy fruit. It does best in a sunny position and light, well-drained soil, tolerating dry as well as damp conditions, light shade, atmospheric pollution, and is rigorously hardy. It may be planted as a solitary subject or in groups with other shrubs. It suckers freely and is a good shrub for large gardens, particularly on banks, but in the small garden this feature is a disadvantage.

Deutzia scabra. Deutzia is a popular shrub of European gardens. It is native to eastern Asia—China and Japan. One of the most widely grown species is the rough deutzia, *D. scabra,* which reaches a height of 2 to 3 m (6 to 10 ft). The flowers appear in June and July. For good growth it requires a light, well-drained and sufficiently nourishing soil. It does poorly in unduly dry as well as unduly wet conditions. It is generally planted in groups by itself or together with other trees and shrubs and is also good for freely-growing hedges. Cultivated varieties include *D.s.* 'Candissima' with white, fully double flowers, *D.s.* 'Plena' with pink, double flowers, and *D.s.* 'Watereri' with single, bicoloured flowers.

Spiraea. This is a large genus of low to medium-high shrubs widely grown in gardens and distributed throughout the temperate regions of the northern hemisphere. One of the most popular, is *Spiraea ×*

vanhouttei, which is 1.5 to 2 m (5 to 6 ft) high with arching branches covered profusely with clusters of white blossoms in May, the foliage turning orange to red in the autumn. Preferring sun it will tolerate moderate shade but poor flowering results. It has no special requirements but succeeds best in rich soil. It tolerates atmospheric pollution. Its uses are many and it is one of the best shrubs for freely growing hedges and borders.

The willow spiraea, *S. salicifolia,* bridewort, is a native European shrub of upright habit growing to a height of 1 to 2 m (3 to 6 ft). The pink flowers appear in summer, from June to August. It requires atmospheric moisture and fertile soil, but tolerates atmospheric pollution. It puts out a great number of suckers and its growth needs to be kept in check. It is particularly good for freely growing hedges.

Spiraea salicifolia

Spiraea × vanhouttei

Corylus avellana. The hazel grows throughout all of Europe. It is a dense shrub of spreading habit reaching a height of 5 m (16 ft). Although producing edible nuts it is usually cultivated for the beauty of its catkins in the spring. It is not particularly demanding in its requirements, tolerating both sun and shade as well as atmospheric pollution, but needs a moist, rich soil. It is generally used to conceal unattractive spots, on banks, and also as a freely growing hedge. There are several attractive cultivated varieties— *C. avellana* 'Aurea' with yellow leaves, particularly when they first appear, *C.a.* 'Fuscorubra' with brownish-red flowers, *C.a.* 'Pendula' with pendent twigs, and *C.a.* 'Contorta' with crooked twigs.

Sorbus aucuparia

Corylus avellana

Sorbus aucuparia. Mountain ash or rowan is the best known member of this huge family which includes some 80 species and numerous hybrids growing in the moderate regions of the northern hemisphere. *S. aucuparia* grows throughout all of Europe and western Asia. It is a small tree with open crown reaching a height of 6 to 10 m (20 to 33 ft). Its most decorative features are the red berries which remain on the tree until late winter and the reddish to golden-yellow foliage. It does best in acid, loamy soil, at higher elevations and in peat-bogs. Although a light-loving species, it tolerates shade and is resistant to frost and industrial fumes. In large gardens it is attractive as a specimen tree but it is generally planted in avenues. Several cultivated varieties are grown, the best known being *S. aucuparia* 'Edulis' (syn. *S. aucuparia moravica*) with edible fruit that is used by the food industry.

Salix alba. The white willow is the most widespread European willow. It reaches a height of 25 m (80 ft) and is usually planted as solitary subject in damp places. Often grown in gardens is the weeping willow—*S.a.* 'Tristis'. Of the many other tree and shrub willows, the most favourite is the goat willow—*S. caprea*—whose branches with their catkins are used as decoration at Easter time. It grows to a height of 12 m (40 ft) and is noted for its ease of cultivation. It likes sunny sites but is also tolerant of semi-shade, and it does best in moist soil. It is planted as a solitary subject or in groups of three. It serves as a spring source of food for bees.

Salix alba

Magnolia stellata

Magnolia. These are native to North America and eastern Asia, where some 30 species grow in the wild. Most commonly grown as an ornamental in the garden is *Magnolia soulangiana,* a shrub or tree growing to a height of 8 m (26 ft) with beautiful pinky-white, tulip-shaped blossoms appearing in May. Requirements include a sunny position, sheltered, if possible, from the early morning sun, and a rich, acid soil. Also beautiful is *M. stellata,* a shrub with saucer-like, white blossoms borne in April. It grows to a height of only 3 m (10 ft). Magnolias are not pruned but allowed to grow freely.

Tamarix tetrandra

Weigela florida

Acer palmatum 'Atropurpureum'

Tamarix. Tamarisk is a striking, feathery shrub with long, graceful broom-like, arching branches. The genus includes some 75 species growing in the warmer regions from western Europe through the Mediterranean region to eastern Asia. Species grown in Europe reach a height of 3 to 5 m (10 to 16 ft). The twigs are interesting and resemble those of heather. Two different types exist—those that flower in spring, mainly *Tamarix tetrandra* (light pink flowers) and *T. parviflora* (deep pink flowers), and those that flower in summer (from June to September), chiefly *T. pentandra* (rose-pink flowers, the most valuable of this group) and *T. gallica* (pink flowers). The former flower on shoots of the previous year and the latter flower on the current year's growth. Tamarisks need a well-drained soil. They stand up well to drought and sun scorch, and tolerate atmospheric pollution and poorer, salty soil. They differ in appearance from other trees and shrubs and are generally planted as solitary subjects; best companions are evergreens such as junipers and pines.

Weigela florida. Pink weigela is one of the most valuable flowering shrubs for the garden. Native to northern China and Korea it grows to a height of 2 to 3 m (6 to 10 ft) and bears a profusion of tubular flowers in May and June, single blooms appearing even later. It requires a rich, well-drained soil that is not heavy and neither moist nor unduly dry. It likes sun and tolerates light shade. In general only the beautiful hybrids of the type species—designated as *W. hybrida*—are cultivated nowadays. These include the white cultivars 'Candida' and 'Dame Blanche', the pink 'Avantgarde', 'Floreal', 'Rosabella' and 'Styriaca', and the red 'Bristol Ruby', 'Eva Rathke' and 'Fiesta'. They may be used in a great many ways as solitary subjects and in groups.

Acer palmatum. Japanese maple is one of the many shrub-like maples that are of great value in the modern garden. It is native to Japan, where it grows to a height of 8 m (26 ft). In Europe, however, it is much shorter. It is prized mostly for its beautifully shaped and coloured foliage. Of the several cultivated varieties the one most commonly grown is the red-leaved *A. palmatum* 'Atropurpureum', a lovely shrub but demanding in its requirements. It does not tolerate sun scorch, or conditions that are too dry or too moist. It does best in dry soil and situations sheltered from cold winds. It is particulary tender in youth and if it survives the first four years then it will tolerate less expert handling. Planted as a solitary subject or in groups in front of a suitable backdrop, Japanese maples are very effective in a larger rock garden, beside a dry wall or pool, near a paved path or beside the house entrance.

Carpinus betulus. The hornbeam, native to Europe and the Caucasus, is a tree growing to a height of 20 to 25 m (65 to 80 ft) but in gardens it is used primarily as a hedge as it retains old leaves until spring like beech and stands up well to pruning. It can be kept quite low, about 1 m (3 ft) and can form a dense hedge. It is comparatively undemanding in its requirements. It does best in moist, loamy soil, is resistant to frost and tolerates industrial fumes. It has a wide range of uses in the garden. Besides hedges it is also used to hold the soil on banks and in smaller gardens as a single specimen, chiefly the cultivated varieties *C. betulus* 'Columnaris', *C. b.* 'Fastigiata' and *C. b.* 'Pendula'. It has attractive hop-like fruit.

Carpinus betulus

Sambucus racemosa. The red-berried elder is a shrub native to Europe that grows to a height of 2 to 4 m (6 to 13 ft). The creamy-white flowers appear in April and May, and the red berries that follow make this shrub a bright ornament of Europe's woodlands, together with the mountain ash. It tolerates dry soil, as well as moist conditions, and sun as well as shade. It is particularly good for higher altitudes. It does not spread as freely as the related European elder, *Sambucus nigra*. In gardens it is mostly used to conceal unsightly spots.

In conclusion to this section on ornamental trees and shrubs several of the best known climbers are mentioned.

Clematis. Plants of the genus clematis cultivated in the garden are both type species and large-flowered hybrids. Traveller's joy—*Clematis vitalba*—

shown in the illustration, is a rapid grower reaching a height of 10 m (33 ft) and bearing small white flowers from July to September. In the illustration their size is compared with the blossoms of a large-flowered hybrid. It has no special requirements and often becomes naturalized in gardens, spreading freely and turning into an undesirable weed. It is generally used to cover wire fences or roughly plastered walls on which it keeps a firm grip. Other type species grown in the garden include slender *C. alpina*, 2.5 m (8 ft) high with violet-blue flowers, dense growing *C. tangutica*, 4.5 m (15 ft) high producing yellow flowers in autumn, vigorous *C. montana* reaching 8 m (26 ft) in height with white flowers in May and graceful *C. viticella* reaching 3.5 m (11 ft) in height bearing violet flowers from June to September. All have small flowers.

Sambucus racemosa

Clematis vitalba. Bottom right—a large-flowered hybrid.

The large-flowered clematis hybrids, *C. hybrida,* are far more spectacular, perhaps ranking amongst the most beautiful flowers in the garden. They are, however, more demanding, requiring a sunny location, rich, well-drained soil, yearly pruning and the application of fertilizer. The base of the plants, or rather the surface of the soil covering the roots, should be shaded; for that reason it is good to plant annuals at the foot of the plant. Clematis hybrids reach a height of 2 to 2.5 m (6 to 8 ft) and flower profusely. Grown in the garden are following cultivated varieties: 'The President' (Patens group) — deep violet flowers June to September, 'Ville de Lyon' (Viticella group) — deep red flowers July to October, and 'Nelly Moser' — pink flowers in May and June and then again in early autumn. They should be planted in eye-catching spots.

Hedera helix. Ivy is a European species that grows to a height of 20 m (65 ft). It is one of the few evergreen climbers and the only self-clinging one. The variety *H.h.* 'Cristata' has pale green rounded leaves with crinkly edges and those of *H.h.* 'Glacier' variegated leaves. Only older plants bear the inconspicuous flowers, in late summer and autumn and only then if provided with sufficient light. The berries ripen the following spring. Ivy has no special requirements but does best in moist soil and partial shade, though it also does well in full shade and established specimens tolerate even dry conditions and atmospheric pollution. It is excellent for covering the corners of buildings, walls and rocks and for climbing up old tree trunks. Ivy may be used to form a green carpet in place of grass in deep shade, particularly under dense trees.

Clematis 'Durandii'

Hedera helix

Lonicera caprifolium

Parthenocissus tricuspidata

Lonicera. Perfoliate honeysuckle, *Lonicera caprifolium,* is one of the many species of the genus lonicera that are native to Europe. It is the most widely grown of the climbing honeysuckles. It reaches a moderate height (up to 6 m [20 ft]) and begins flowering in late May. The creamy-white flowers have a lovely, penetrating fragrance, particularly in the early evening. It tolerates sun as well as partial shade but not dry conditions. It should be thinned occasionally and sometimes also cut back. Honeysuckle is excellent for covering gateways, summerhouses, ornamental iron-work and wire fences.

Parthenocissus. This is a climber of many uses. There are two basic species; *Parthenocissus quinquefolia,* Virginia creeper, grows to a height of 8 m (26 ft) and is native to North America. It is hardy and has no special requirements. When young it must be tied in to a support and excess wood must be cut out. The other is *P. tricuspidata,* Boston ivy, of eastern Asia, also reaching a height of 8 m (26 ft). It climbs without a support and spreads evenly, therefore being used to cover straight walls. The leaves make a bright attractive display in the autumn with their wide range of colours.

Campsis radicans. The trumpet creeper is a gorgeous climbing plant when in flower. It is native to North America and it may reach a height of 8 m (26 ft), but must be tied in to a support at first. The brilliant orange and red flowers appear from August to September. It prefers a sunny, sheltered spot and good, well-drained soil. It may be pruned every year in spring—dry and undesirable wood is cut out and stout shoots are cut back by one third or more. Pruning does not deter flowering. This creeper is used to cover tall pillars, ironwork and pergolas.

Wisteria. This is splendid climber with hanging clusters of flowers up to 50 cm (20 in) long. It reaches a height of 8 to 10 m (33 ft) and flowers from May to June. Requirements include a warm, sunny and sheltered site and well-drained soil with sufficient lime. It does not need pruning and is beautiful trained over house fronts, balconies, attractive walls, pillars, summerhouses, archways. Two species are cultivated in the garden: *Wisteria floribunda* from Japan 4 m (13 ft) tall, and *W. sinensis* 18 to 30 m (60 to 100 ft) from China. Both have chains of mauve, pea-like flowers but there are cultivated varieties with white or pink flowers.

Campsis radicans

Wisteria sinensis

67

ROSES

The rose is called the queen of flowers, not only for its elegance, the wealth and beauty of its blooms, the great variety of type, shape and colour, but also because it is so popular. No other flower in the world is grown and sold in such vast numbers.

Continuous breeding, particularly cross-breeding, gave rise to growing numbers of varieties and it thus became necessary to divide and group them according to a systematic classification. The botanical classification of roses, however, is quite complicated and therefore in practice use is made of the so-called 'garden' classification which divides roses into the following groups.

Large-flowered roses. These are basically hybrid tea roses and large-flowered floribundas. They have a shapely bud and usually a single bloom or at most three blooms on one stem and are grown chiefly for cutting.

Multi-flowered roses. These include polyanthas, hybrid polyanthas and floribundas with smaller blooms, also miniature roses and the modern group known as garnettes. They bear clusters of flowers on one stem and are generally grown in beds, in parks and as specimens in smaller gardens.

Climbing roses. These must be provided with a support. Some have blooms like the large-flowered roses, others like the multi-flowered roses, some varieties are remontant (repeat flowering), others bloom only once a year.

Shrub roses. These are mostly large shrubs close, by origin, to the botanical species. They include species and varieties with single blooms; more recently developed varieties have blooms of the type borne by large-flowered roses. The species roses are also included in this group.

The garden classification of roses also indicates the purpose for which the plant can be used. Roses of the various groups should not be planted together; this may be done only in the case of climbing and shrub roses because they have similar characteristics. Large-flowered and multi-flowered roses should not be put in the same bed. Standard roses may be planted with multi-flowered roses in the same bed but never with large-flowered roses. Large-flowered roses are good for cutting and also for a striking colour display with at least three rows planted in one bed. Beds of these roses should have different varieties planted next to each other.

Multi-flowered roses are used for uniform, everblooming beds. A large number of the same variety planted in a single bed produces a striking effect. These roses are not used for cutting. The modern garnettes can be used for this purpose but it is necessary to pinch off the lateral buds so that they bear single blooms. Dwarfer, multi-flowerd roses can be used also for edging the main path; here, too, only a single variety should be used and the roses planted close together to form a continuous border. The lowest-growing forms, particularly the miniature roses, are attractive in the rock garden, especially if planted in groups of two or three.

Climbing roses are planted beside houses, entranceways and fences. They may also cover pergolas erected in the garden for this purpose. Wherever they are put they make a striking display when in bloom. In the case of pergolas it is recommended to plant several roses of the same variety together to heighten the colour effect. When a climbing rose is budded on to a standard the result is a so-called weeping standard which has again become popular in recent years.

Shrub roses grow into large bushes and are thus good for larger gardens, to fill a corner of the garden and to make a hedge. They are wonderful in country gardens where they blend well with the surroundings. In autumn and winter they are attractive with their bright-coloured hips. Also outstanding are certain species roses. These are generally planted as specimens, together with conifers and other inconspicuously-flowering woody plants with decorative foliage.

The more roses are bred and hybridized for greater beauty and elegance of form the more demanding are their cultivation requirements. Roses in the garden need ample light, warmth, moisture and nourishment. They do poorly in exposed, windy positions and are intolerant of bright, daylong sunlight. Full sun is required mainly by shrub roses; large-flowered varieties do better in situations that are lightly shaded at least part of the time during the heat of midday. Roses do not thrive in full shade. They do well in a loamy, neutral soil that is not too dry.

Roses may be planted out from mid-October until the first frost or in spring after the ground has thawed—in March and April. Roses planted in autumn generally do better the first few years. Before planting the roots should be trimmed as little as possible, and all damaged and dead wood pruned out down to healthy wood. The plant should be placed so that the junction of the rootstock and scion is about 2 to 3 cm (about 1 in) below ground level after the soil has settled, and when all is finished it should be watered thoroughly. When planting standards a stake of the same height as the top of the rose should first be driven into the ground.

Roses are pruned in spring. The rules of pruning are the same as for all woody plants. If a shoot is hard-pruned the plant will grow a strong new shoot. If a shoot is trimmed lightly new growth will be less. Because we want large-flowered roses to have long stems these are hard-pruned in spring, that is, cut back to two or three buds from the base. Multi-flowered roses, which we want to keep lower, are pruned lightly in spring. Because they do not need to grow new wood, they flower earlier. After a number of years all rose bushes will have old wood that makes them look unsightly and they should therefore be pruned harder from time to time, that is, the old wood should be removed, cut out, at most, however, only one-third of the bush.

In the case of climbing roses most important for healthy growth are the young shoots which are trimmed only to the extent of removing weak tips and ones damaged by frost. Otherwise the plant is merely thinned; that is, old shoots are cut back to the ground. Shrub roses are also only thinned and the tips of the shoots trimmed. In the case of species roses only dry and diseased wood is removed, otherwise they are allowed to grow freely. All leaves and wood that have been removed should be burned to reduce the spread of pests and diseases.

During the growing period the soil should be kept open by hoeing, the ground should be kept weeded, and feed and water should be applied. It is recommended to cover the bed with a mulch of peat.

Large-flowered roses are grown for cutting. To keep the plant strong and healthy, however, only about one third of the long-stemmed blooms should be cut, the remainder should be left on the plant and removed after they have faded. In the case of multi-flowered roses the whole flower cluster is removed by cutting it off above the first leaf below the cluster after all the individual blooms have faded. The faded flowers of climbing and shrub roses are cut off in the same manner except for those varieties that have decorative hips. Suckers—shoots arising from the roots—should be removed immediately by pulling them off at the root. These are easily recognized by the leaves which are small and light-coloured.

MINIATURE ROSES

These are rapidly gaining widespread popularity in recent years. They are used mainly in the rock garden and also as potted houseplants.

Some 40 varieties are propagated in Europe, ones with blooms that are miniature replicas of the large-flowered as well as of the multi-flowered roses. The best plants are those that are budded on *Rosa multiflora* rootstock; however, as budding on to the thin necks of the rootstock is difficult and laborious they are usually not grafted but grown on their own roots, even though they are not as hardy and bear somewhat fewer flowers. In general they are very rewarding plants.

Practically all miniature roses are derived from the type species *R. chinensis minima*, introduced into Europe from China in the year 1815 and very popular in the 1830's, though interest in it waned during the next twenty years.

Rosa chinensis minima, also known as *R. roulettii*, is a botanical species, a wild rose forming a 20 to 25 cm (8 to 10 in) high bush with leaves measuring about 2 cm ($^3/_4$ in) and rose-pink flowers also about 2 cm ($^3/_4$ in) across. It is comparatively demanding, requiring a soil that is moderately moist all the time and the removal of faded flowers. The leaves are susceptible to black spot.

'Baby Masquerade' was developed by Tantau in 1956 as a cross between 'Tom Thumb' and 'Masquerade'. In some countries and some nurseries it is listed under the synonym 'Baby Carnival'. It attains

Coralin

Baby Masquerade

Rosa chinensis minima

Pour Toi

a height of 30 cm (1 ft) and bears a profusion of yellow flowers, turning red as they age, measuring up to 2.5 cm (1 in) across, from June until the autumn. It is distinguished by good growth and has deep green foliage. It is used also as edging for striking beds and as a cover planting for romantic parts of the garden. It is exceptionally good as a pot plant and if properly cared for, will flower until Christmas.

'Coralin', developed by P. Dot of Spain in 1955, is a cross between 'Mephisto' and 'Perla de Alcanada'. It grows to a height of about 25 cm (10 in) and bears a profusion of red flowers, up to 4 cm (1$\frac{1}{2}$ in) across, until late autumn. These are individual blooms borne on separate stems and are therefore also good for cutting. This is a vigorous, healthy variety which, given good soil, will produce a main shoot up to 45

to 50 cm (1 ft 6 in to 1 ft 8 in) high; to keep growth low this shoot must be pinched in time to promote branching. This is also an excellent pot plant for the home.

'Pour Toi', developed by P. Dot in 1946, is a cross between 'Eduardo Toda' and 'Pompon de Paris', though some authorities list *R. roulettii* as one parent plant. In Britain it is known as 'For You'. It is only 20 cm (8 in) high and the cream flowers, usually borne singly on separate stems, are 2 to 3 cm ($\frac{3}{4}$ to 1 in) large. Though not of vigorous growth it bears many blooms. It is propagated with comparative ease from cuttings placed in a mixture of equal parts of sand and peat. Pour Toi is a very effective and ornamental plant for the rock garden; it does not grow very well in pots.

Rosmarin

The Fairy

Degenhardt

'Rosmarin', developed by W. Kordes in 1965, is a cross between 'Tom Thumb' and 'Dacapo'. It is a good grower and hardy, reaching a height of only 20 cm (8 in). The slightly fragrant pale pink blooms are also small, about 2 cm ($^3/_4$ in), and must be removed when they have faded to promote the growth of further blooms. It will then flower until late autumn. It is loveliest in a pot where it forms an attractive bush of regular habit. It is also good as edging beside stone walls where its red centres form a pleasing contrast against the natural hues of the stone.

'Degenhardt', developed by G. de Ruiter in 1959, is a cross between 'Robin Hood' and an unknown polyantha seedling. Up to 30 cm (1 ft) high, with flowers 3 to 3.5 cm (1 to 2 in) across, it has been rapidly gaining popularity in recent years for its lengthy and continuous flowering and because it is hardy as well as resistant to disease. It is propagated with comparative ease by means of cuttings. It is used chiefly in the rock garden though it is also good as a potted plant and as decoration in the cemetery.

'The Fairy', developed by J. A. Bentall in 1932, is a sport from 'Lady Godiva' and is one of the most valuable miniature roses for the rock garden. In some countries it is better known as 'Sweet Pink'. The shoots are up to 40 cm (1 ft 4 in) long, the individual blooms up to 4 cm (1 ^{1}/$_2$ in) across. The colour of the blooms changes, being paler in spring and darker in the autumn; the buds are also darker than the fully open flowers. This rose is noted for its healthy growth and continuous flowering until late autumn. It is particularly good for the rock garden, but not very attractive as a potted plant.

'Yellow Doll', developed by R. S. Moore in 1962, is a cross between 'Golden Glow' and 'Zee'. It is one of the best of the miniature yellow roses. It is only 25 cm (10 in) high and the fragrant flowers, generally borne singly, are only 2.5 cm (1 in) across with only the slightest fragrance. This rose is distinguished by healthy growth and by having the flowers more prominent than the leaves. It is grown in the rock garden and in pots.

Yellow Doll

The following four, most widely grown varieties belong to the garnette group of multi-flowered roses. It is a group that has gained wide popularity in the past twenty years when its advantages became known, chiefly the large profusion of blooms that when cut last far longer in the vase than other roses. They are used mainly for forcing in the glasshouse where they are pinched to a single bud. In the garden they form a cluster of flowers and are not nearly as valuable as for forcing. They are known as *roses for every day,* because most of the buds are slender and shapely though about half the size of the usual large-flowered rose. Care and maintenance are the same as for other multi-flowered roses.

This group was developed by further breeding of the original variety 'Garnette', developed by M. Tantau in 1947 as a cross between 'Rosenelfe' × 'Eva', and 'Heros'. These roses are noted for their healthy growth, reaching a height of 40 to 45 cm (1 ft 4 in — 1 ft 6 in), and repeated flowering. The foliage is a glossy dark green that blends well with the dark crimson blooms. The latter are about 5 cm (2 in) across. In full sun the edges of the blooms turn violet and they are less attractive.

'Zorina', developed by E. S. Boerner in 1963 as a cross between the seedling 'Pinocchio' and 'Spartan', is a healthy plant of compact habit growing to a height of about 50 cm (1 ft 8 in). The buds are

Zorina

Junior Miss

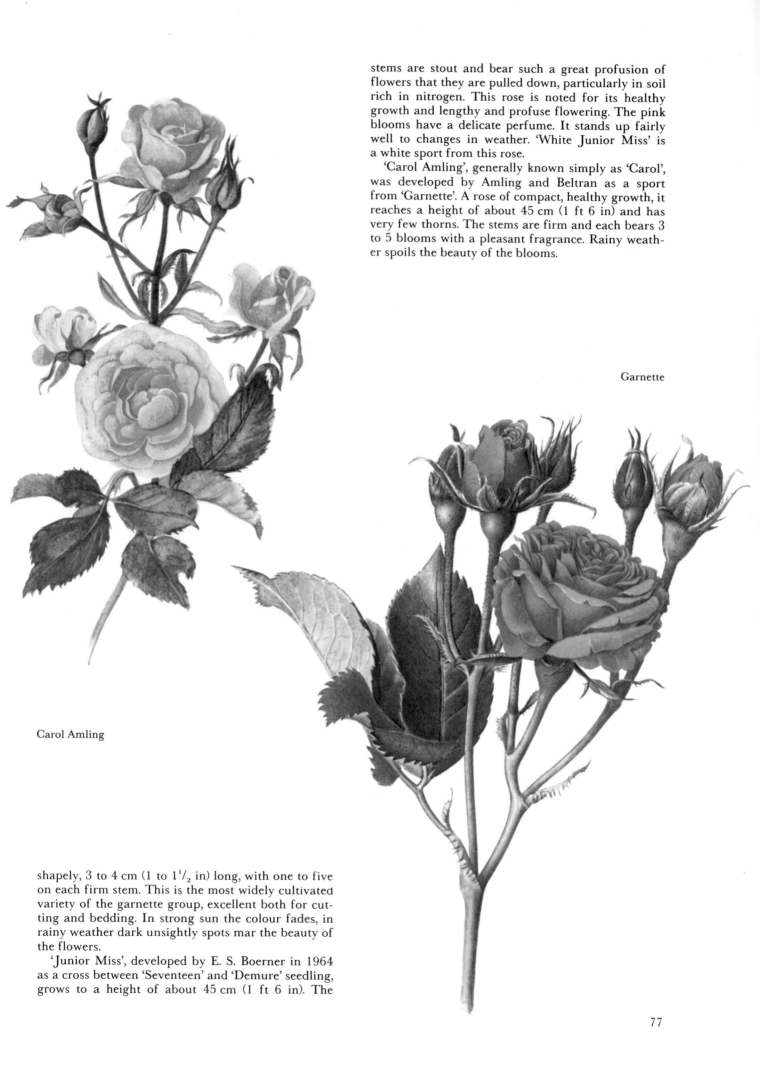

stems are stout and bear such a great profusion of flowers that they are pulled down, particularly in soil rich in nitrogen. This rose is noted for its healthy growth and lengthy and profuse flowering. The pink blooms have a delicate perfume. It stands up fairly well to changes in weather. 'White Junior Miss' is a white sport from this rose.

'Carol Amling', generally known simply as 'Carol', was developed by Amling and Beltran as a sport from 'Garnette'. A rose of compact, healthy growth, it reaches a height of about 45 cm (1 ft 6 in) and has very few thorns. The stems are firm and each bears 3 to 5 blooms with a pleasant fragrance. Rainy weather spoils the beauty of the blooms.

Garnette

Carol Amling

shapely, 3 to 4 cm (1 to 1½ in) long, with one to five on each firm stem. This is the most widely cultivated variety of the garnette group, excellent both for cutting and bedding. In strong sun the colour fades, in rainy weather dark unsightly spots mar the beauty of the flowers.

'Junior Miss', developed by E. S. Boerner in 1964 as a cross between 'Seventeen' and 'Demure' seedling, grows to a height of about 45 cm (1 ft 6 in). The

Paprika

Orange Sensation

MULTI-FLOWERED ROSES

In recent years breeders have devoted much attention to the garnette group and have come up with new varieties such as 'Prominent' and 'Sonia', which retain the advantages of garnettes (profuse flowering and long life as a cut flower) but have larger blooms, as large as those of the large-flowered roses. This group may be expected to yield beautiful new forms.

The following multi-flowered roses are suited chiefly for larger beds with individual varieties or at least roses of the same colour to a section. Red roses are most valuable as yellow and especially white varieties soon lose their beauty, either due to rain or to fading from the sun.

'Orange Sensation', developed by de Ruiter in 1961, is a cross between 'Amor' and 'Fashion'. It is about 50 cm (1 ft 8 in) high and distinguished by healthy growth. The dark green foliage makes an attractive background for the glowing flowers. The vermilion blooms are semi-double. They are produced continuously in rapid succession and for a long time.

'Paprika', developed by Tantau in 1958 as a cross

78

Concerto

Lilli Marleen

between 'Märchenland' and 'Red Favourite', is about 60 cm (2 ft) high with pale green foliage complementing the light red of the blooms. It is prone to black spot which disfigures the leaves and therefore needs to be protected. It flowers recurrently fairly well and when in full bloom brightens the whole garden.

'Lilli Marleen', developed by Kordes in 1959 by crossing ('Our Princess' × 'Rudolph Timm') and 'Ama', is one of the best red roses for group plantings. The plants, up to 50 cm (1 ft 8 in) high, form a beautiful growth of uniform height and thickness. The foliage withstands bad weather, the petals are shed easily after they have faded and the scarlet blooms appear in rapid succession. This rose is loveliest in a cut lawn against deciduous shrubs.

'Concerto', developed by Meilland in 1953 as a cross between 'Alain' and 'Floradora', grows to a height of about 60 cm (2 ft) and forms a rather thin bush. The blooms are rather small, about 5 to 6 cm (2 to 2¼ in) across, and placed at different levels. They face bad weather well and are produced freely and continuously. A group of these roses in the garden creates an illusion of greater space, and if planted in a row bordering the lawn they look like a natural, freely growing planting.

'Nordia', developed by P. T. Poulsen in 1967 by crossing ('Rosenmärchen' × 'Rosenmärchen') and 'Elsinore', is a bush about 70 cm (2 ft 4 in) high marked by vigorous, healthy growth until late autumn. The foliage is glossy dark green and resistant to disease. The scarlet blooms, one to five on a long stem, are produced freely and continuously. It is a valuable variety of the existing assortment, good not only for bedding but also for cutting, in which case the lateral buds are pinched, leaving only a single bloom on the stem. It is also frequently grown for forcing.

'Europeana', developed by de Ruiter in 1964 as a cross between 'Ruth Leuwerik' and 'Rosemary Rose', is one of the most valuable of the red, multiflowered roses. It forms a 60 to 90 cm (2—3 ft) high

Europeana

Nordia

ations and in bad weather the stems flatten and bend, giving to the whole shrub an untidy appearance. 'Scania' is best as edging for sections of lawn or for bedding in a sheltered part of the garden.

'Orange Triumph' is an older, tried and tested variety developed by Kordes in 1937 as a cross between 'Eva' and 'Solarium'. A vigorous grower, it forms a bush up to 60 cm (2 ft) high and is weather-resistant. In damper years the foliage is prone to black spot. The flowers are rather small, persistent and borne in profusion. They should be removed after they have faded. Bushes should be planted closer together so that they will fill out the space of the bed. This rose is also good as a border for beds and pathways. A climbing form called 'Climbing Orange Triumph' has been developed.

Orange Triumph

Scania

bush of regular habit with shapely, healthy, glossy dark green foliage. The blooms are fairly large and deliciously scented and are produced repeatedly. 'Europeana' is best for bedding. A group of these roses is attractive but the dark foliage and dark blooms create a somewhat depressing effect and thus in the landscaping scheme it should be combined with light green turf, light green grasses or light green foliaged deciduous shrubs.

'Scania', likewise developed by de Ruiter in 1965 by crossing 'Coccorica' with an unknown seedling, forms a thin bush of regular habit growing to a height of some 50 to 60 cm (1 ft 8 in — 2 ft). The leaves are large and dull green, the deep red blooms velvety and very attractive. In exposed, windy situ-

Multi-flowered roses of colours other than red are used rather less often in parks and gardens. However, they include some beautiful varieties.

'Zambra', developed by F. Meilland in 1961 by crossing ('Goldilocks' × 'Fashion' A) and ('Goldilocks' × 'Fashion' B), is a slow-growing plant reaching a height of some 40 cm (1 ft 4 in). The foliage is a pale, dull green. The shapely blooms have a heavy fragrance. Their colour changes from deep orange to a paler hue during growth. 'Zambra' is good chiefly for small beds where its beauty shows to best advantage. It is not as striking in larger groups.

'Elizabeth of Glamis', often better known as 'Irish Beauty', was developed by McGredy in 1963 as a cross between 'Spartan' and 'Highlight'. It is a healthy bush of compact habit growing to a height of 50 cm (1 ft 8 in). The foliage is glossy pale green. The buds, one to seven on a stem, are pointed and 3 to 4 cm (1¼ to 1½ in) long. The blooms are large and have a delicate golden tinge. This rose flowers profusely and has good powers of regeneration. It is used for group planting, individual flowers also for cutting.

'Rudolph Timm' was developed by Kordes in 1951 by crossing ('Johannes Böttner' × 'Magnifica') and ('Baby Château' × 'Else Poulsen'). A rose of modera-

Elizabeth of Glamis

Zambra

82

tely vigorous growth, it reaches a height of 40 to 50 cm (1 ft 4 in to 1 ft 8 in). The foliage is glossy pale green. The blooms are unusual in that they resemble petunias. The buds open rapidly and the opened blooms are long-lived, but their petals are spoiled by lengthy periods of rainy weather. They have a pleasant perfume. This rose is suited chiefly for large beds, such a bed looking its best from a distance of several tens of metres.

'Prominent' is the hit of the seventies. Developed by Kordes in 1971 as a cross between 'Königin der Rosen' and 'Zorina', it forms a bush 70 cm (2 ft 4 in) high and with its habit of growth, medium-large

Prominent

Rudolph Timm

blooms and profuse flowering, could be classed among the garnettes. This splendid rose represents a transition between the multi-flowered and large-flowered groups of roses. Besides having shapely and beautifully coloured blooms it is also hardy, flowers continuously and has a pleasant fragrance. The bright red blooms are borne on long stems and pinching also makes it an ideal rose for cutting. It is striking in beds of mixed roses, preferably with large-flowered varieties.

83

Iceberg

Jan Spek

'Iceberg', in some countries better known as 'Schneewittchen', was developed by Kordes in 1956 as a cross between 'Robin Hood' and 'Virgo'. It is a vigorous rose of spreading habit, up to 1 m (3 ft) high, with rich foliage. The blooms resemble water lilies and do not change colour. They are slightly fragrant. This rose is comparatively resistant to mildew and black spot and is the best of the white multi-flowered varieties. It is suited for planting in small beds by itself or in mixed beds with other multi-flowered roses whose bright colours it offsets.

'Jan Spek', developed by S. McGredy in 1966 as a cross between 'Clare Grammerstorf' and 'Doctor Faust', is a vigorous plant of spreading, bushy habit, about 50 cm (1 ft 8 in) high, with bright green foliage. The yellow blooms last long on the shrub and are slightly fragrant. New flowers are produced more rapidly if the faded ones are removed. This is a very good rose as a border in beds of darker plants.

'Rimosa', developed by Meilland in 1958 as a cross between 'Goldilocks' and 'Perla de Montserrat', is a dense shrub only 40 cm (1 ft 4 in) high with a great

so-called *dance* group. It is the healthiest of them all and therefore the most widely grown. It reaches a height of about 45 cm (1 ft 6 in) and flowers continuously. 'Rumba' is best planted by itself in beds, where it makes a brightly coloured display, and also for edging.

Rumba

Rimosa

profusion of small flowers. The blooms are deep yellow at first, later changing to a pale lemon colour. 'Rimosa' is not prone to black spot. The blooms fall easily when faded and thus do not spoil the appearance of the bush. In hot sunny weather they soon fade. This rose is excellent for low beds, especially in partly shaded locations.

'Rumba', developed by Poulsen in 1958 by crossing 'Masquerade' and 'Poulsen's Bedder' × 'Floradora', is a very popular variety because of its bright display of yellow. With 'Samba' and 'Charleston' it forms the

85

LARGE-FLOWERED ROSES

The most fragrant rose of the present assortment of large-flowered varieties intended primarily for cutting and floral arrangements is 'Duftwolke', or 'Fragrant Cloud', developed by Tantau in 1963 by crossing an unknown seedling with 'Prima Ballerina'. It is a medium-high bush of compact, upright habit with stiff, glossy, dark green foliage. The red buds, 1 to 4 on a stem, open slowly. Flowering is particularly good in the autumn. This rose is disease-resistant and one that belongs to the basic garden assortment.

'Queen of Bermuda' was developed by Bowie in 1956 by crossing 'Independence' × 'Orange Triumph' and 'Bettina'. An erect, healthy and vigorous rose, it grows to a height of 1.2 m (4 ft) and is remontant. There are one to three long-stalked buds to a stem. This is one of the best varieties for cutting as the blooms last a long time when cut. It is often used for forcing. It, too, is one of the varieties belonging to the basic garden assortment.

The 'Queen Elizabeth rose', also called simply

Fragrant Cloud

Queen of Bermuda

The Queen Elizabeth Rose

Milena

'Queen Elizabeth', was developed by Dr. W. E. Lammerts in 1954 as a cross between 'Charlotte Armstrong' and 'Floradora'. It is a tall plant, up to 1.5 m (5 ft) high, with deep red shoots, flowering freely and continuously until autumn. One to seven pink blooms are borne on a stem and have a slight fragrance. This rose is not susceptible to black spot. It shows to best advantage when planted in groups of three to five in a small garden. 'Scarlet Queen Elizabeth Rose' is a magnificent scarlet mutation of this variety.

'Milena' was developed in 1964 by L. Večeřa of Czechoslovakia as an induced mutation from 'The Queen Elizabeth rose'. (An induced mutation is obtained by the irradiation of seeds or grafts from a given variety with gamma rays which causes changes in the shape and colour of the blooms. This is one of the modern methods of rose breeding.) 'Milena' is a strong and tall-growing variety reaching a height of 1.2 m (4 ft). It flowers freely until the frost. The long, firm, reddish stems bear 3 to 7 blooms. It is fairly resistant to all diseases and is suited for planting as a specimen or in small groups of 3 to 5 against a darker background.

Bettina

King's Ransom

'King's Ransom', developed by D. Morey in 1961 as a cross between 'Golden Masterpiece' and 'Lydia', is a bush of slightly spreading habit growing to a height of 60 to 70 cm (2 ft to 2 ft 4 in). The foliage is a beatiful, glossy green. There is generally one yellow bloom to a stem; during the second flowering, however, there may be as many as five to a stem. It is used for mixed rose beds and is striking planted with large-flowered red varieties.

'Bettina', developed by Meilland in 1953 by crossing 'Peace' and ('Mme Joseph Perrand' × 'Demain'), is a popular variety growing to a height of 60 cm (2 ft) and flowering recurrently. The bud is shapely, slender, and has a faint, delicate perfume; there is

Peace

Sutter's Gold

usually only one to a stem. The bush is prone to black spot; it is also less resistant to frost and should therefore be provided with a protective cover for the winter. This is an excellent rose for cutting.

'Peace', also known as 'Gloria dei', 'Mme. A. Meilland' (in France), and 'Gioia' (in Italy), was developed by Meilland in 1945 by crossing 'Joanna Hill' × ('Charles P. Kilham' × *Rosa foetida bicolor* seedling), and ('Charles P. Kilham' × 'Margaret McGredy'). It is a healthy, weather-resistant, vigorous plant up to 1.2 m (4 ft) high. The stems are long and firm with 1 to 5 yellow flowers with pink edges to a stem. The blooms have a slight fragrance and are produced until late autumn. This rose is an out-

standing and very popular variety excellent for cutting, as a solitary subject and in groups. It belongs to the basic garden assortment and continues to be a bestseller to this day.

'Sutter's Gold', developed by H. C. Swim in 1950 as a cross between 'Charlotte Armstrong' and 'Signora', is an upright bush of rather tall, loose growth reaching a height of 80 cm (2 ft 8 in). The stems are rather spindly, usually carrying just one shapely flower which has a strong, pleasant fragrance. It flowers freely until late autumn and is moderately resistant to frost and diseases. It is best suited for cutting.

'Vienna Charm' ('syn. 'Charming Vienna', 'Charme de Vienne', 'Wiener Charme'), developed by Kordes in 1963 as a cross between 'Chantré' and 'Golden Sun', is a vigorous plant up to 70 cm (2 ft 4 in) high with long, strong shoots and lovely large leaves. There is usually one magnificent orange bloom to a stem during the first flowering; during the second flowering there may be several blooms to a stem but these are not as lovely as the first. This rose is susceptible to black spot and mildew and also has a low resistance to frost. It is a widely cultivated variety because of the unusual colour of the blooms, which are lovely and fairly long-lived in the vase.

'Piccadilly', developed by McGredy in 1960 as a cross between 'McGredy's Yellow' and 'Karl Herbst', is a bush of spreading habit growing to a height of 60 to 70 cm (2 ft to 2 ft 4 in). The foliage is glossy dark green. The firm stems bear one to five scarlet blooms edged with yellow that make a lovely contrast with the foliage. Flowering is early and profuse. This rose is moderately resistant to mildew but has little resistance to black spot. It is most attractive in the garden when planted in groups of three to five or with similar bicoloured varieties.

'Mitsouko', developed by Delbard in 1970, is a very popular variety of recent years. Of moderately

Vienna Charm

Piccadilly

Mitsouko

vigorous growth, it reaches a height of about 70 cm (2 ft 4 in). The foliage is dark green and disease-resistant and there are very few thorns on the stems. It flowers profusely and continuously. The blooms, usually one to a stem during the first flowering and sometimes several during the second flowering, are shapely and have a delicate fragrance. This rose is best suited for cutting but may also be used for planting in beds with other roses where its glowing blooms are set off against the dark foliage.

'Brasilia', developed by McGredy in 1968 as a cross between 'Kordes Perfecta' and 'Piccadilly', is a bush of moderately vigorous growth, reaching a height of 70 to 80 cm (2 ft 4 in to 2 ft 8 in), with thick, healthy foliage. The somewhat weak stems are terminated by single blooms which have a slight fragrance. The bud is shapely, opening into a glowing red star before fading. This is an interesting variety, good for cutting and for planting in beds with other roses.

Brasilia

'Super Star', known in the USA as 'Tropicana', was developed by Tantau in 1960 by crossing (seedling × 'Peace') and (seedling × 'Alpine Glow'). A vigorous, upright plant, it grows to a height of 90 cm (2 ft). The vermilion colour of the blooms, completely new among roses, created a sensation. There is sometimes only one flower to a stem but usually there are several, borne on 30 to 40 cm (1 ft to 1 ft 4 in) long side shoots, forming whole trusses. They have a strong fragrance and are more weather-resistant than many roses. This is an excellent freely-flowering variety but in recent years has become susceptible to mildew. Nevertheless, it is a rose that belongs to the basic garden assortment. It is used for bedding with other roses and for cutting.

'Duke of Windsor' was developed by Tantau in

Super Star

Duke of Windsor

1969. It is a cross between 'Spartan' and 'Montezuma', probably intended by the breeder to replace the ageing 'Super Star'. It is a healthy plant of moderately vigorous growth, reaching a height of about 80 cm (2 ft 8 in) and bearing a profusion of vermilion-orange flowers, one or more to a stem. The foliage is dark green, the blooms are weather resistant and very fragrant. This rose is good for group planting and is also outstanding as a solitary subject.

'Granada', known also as 'Donatella', was developed by Lindquist in 1966 as a cross between 'Tiffany' and 'Cavalcade'. It is a vigorous plant up to 1 m (3 ft) high with glossy dark green foliage. The firm stems usually bear only a single bloom during the first flowering; side shoots do not appear until the second flowering. This rose has a pleasant scent.

Both the bush and the blooms are disease and weather resistant. It is a very decorative variety for group planting as well as for cutting.

'Tapestry', developed by Fisher in 1958 as a cross between 'Peace' and 'Mission Belle', is a low bush, only 50 cm (1 ft 8 in) high, of regular habit, with attractive, dense foliage that is an excellent foil for the interesting colour combination of the blooms. There are one to three to a stem and they have a pleasantly spicy fragrance. The first blooms are large and striking, later blooms are increasingly smaller. This rose should be protected against black spot. It is used mainly with other large-flowered roses.

Tapestry

Granada

93

'Kordes Perfecta', better known simply as 'Pertecta', was developed by Kordes in 1957 as a cross between 'Spek's Yellow' and 'Karl Herbst'. This is a vigorous, freely flowering plant of upright habit, growing to a height of 90 cm (3 ft). The young budding shoots are red, the thorns reddish, and the foliage also has a slight reddish tinge. The strong, firm stems bear three to five pink blooms tinged with red, that are very large when open and have a pleasant fragrance. This is a lovely, remontant, but rather tender rose, affected chiefly by damp weather which causes the flowers to fade and become tattered. It is suitable for planting in protected places in the garden.

'Pink Peace', developed by Meilland in 1959, is an outstanding offspring of the famous 'Peace' produced by crossing ('Peace' × 'Monique') and ('Peace' × 'Mrs. John Laing'). This is a vigorous, upright plant up to 1.1 m (3 ft 6 in) high with large, dark green leaves. The long flower stem usually bears only a single deep pink bud; during the second flowering there may be another, secondary shoot. This rose flowers until late autumn and has a pleas-

Kordes Perfecta

Pink Peace

ant fragrance. It is fairly resistant to black spot and mildew, tending to be damaged more by bad weather, chiefly rain. It is excellent for cutting.

'Royal Highness', developed by Swim and Weeks in 1962 as a cross between 'Virgo' and 'Peace', is a slender, healthy plant with attractive dark green foliage. The first pale pink blooms are loveliest and borne singly, later blooms are smaller and borne three to five to a stem; they are very fragrant. This is a hardy, remontant variety good for cutting — it is most attractive in a bunch with salmon-pink and

Royal Highness

Prima Ballerina

blue varieties. In the garden it may be planted in a bed in partial shade where it flowers as well as in full sun.

'Prima Ballerina', developed by Tantau in 1957 as a cross between an unnamed seedling and 'Peace', is a strong, upright plant up to 90 cm (3 ft) high. The shapely buds are borne on strong stems, the first ones singly, later ones as many as seven to a stem. The deep pink blooms open slowly and do not change colour; they have a very strong fragrance. This is a healthy and freely-flowering variety, which looks best if used in groups of three to five. It is also good for cutting, being fairly long-lived in the vase.

95

'Blue Moon', also known as 'Mainzer Fastnacht', was developed by Tantau in 1967 and belongs to the group of *blue* roses. It is of moderately spreading habit and grows to a height of about 70 cm (2 ft 4 in). The strong stems bear single, large, shapely, lilac blooms with one or two secondary shoots below. They have a wonderful fragrance and are worth growing for this alone. The plant is fairly resistant to disease but rain causes unattractive spotting of the petals. It is used for cutting, and is an unusual variety in gardens.

'Pascali', developed by L. Lens in 1963 as a cross between 'Queen Elizabeth' and 'White Butterfly', is an upright bush 1.1 m (3 ft 6 in) high with dense, dark green foliage which is an excellent foil for the

Pascali

Blue Moon

blooms. They are fragrant and borne one to seven to a stem. This is a healthy variety, one of the most weather resistant of the white roses, and freely flowering. The first blooms are creamy-white, autumn ones are greenish. It is good in beds with other roses and for cutting.

'Chrysler Imperial', developed by Lammerts in 1952 as a cross between 'Charlotte Armstrong' and 'Mirandy', is a compact bush of upright habit reaching a height of about 90 cm (3 ft). The leaves are dark green with markedly pale veining and the stems are covered with large red thorns. The flower stems bear one or two deep red blooms that have a pleasant perfume. This rose flowers well into autumn, the later blooms being just as lovely as those borne in June. It is comparatively resistant to disease as well as bad weather. It is best suited for warmer regions with sunny autumn days where the late blooms can develop well.

'John S. Armstrong', developed by Swim in 1961 as a cross between 'Charlotte Armstrong' and an unknown seedling, is a compact bush only 50 cm (1 ft 8 in) high. Characteristic of this variety is the red colour of the shoots and the very dark, glossy foliage. One stem bears three to nine blooms. The plant is susceptible to mildew. It does best in a rather moist soil. It is used for planting in beds of mixed roses. If one stem bears only a single bloom, or if the side buds are pinched, then it is a beautiful rose for cutting.

John S. Armstrong
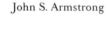

Chrysler Imperial

CLIMBING ROSES

These roses are strikingly decorative. To be at their best they need an adequate support and proper trimming. In winter they should be loosened from the support and the oldest wood cut back to the ground, leaving only young wood on the plant. The young shoots should then be spread out as desired and tied again to the support.

'Firedance', developed by Kordes in 1955, is a cross between *Rosa rubiginosa eglanteria* and *Rosa kordesii*. It is one of the most vigorous of the climbing roses, growing to a height of 5 metres (16 ft), and in warm regions even higher. It is a hardy plant with healthy, pale green foliage that is an excellent foil for the large, scarlet blooms which have a pleasant, faint perfume. It flowers only once, in the second half of June, but profusely, transforming it into a flaming bush. The large hips, appearing after the petals drop, form fan-like cascades. The shoots must be tied and trained over terraces or summer-houses so they do not turn into an unattractive thicket.

Paul's Scarlet Climber

Firedance

'Paul's Scarlet Climber', developed by W. Paul in 1917 as a cross between 'Paul's Carmine Pillar' and 'Soleil d'Or', is an old variety but still the most popular of the climbing roses. This is a healthy plant that withstands bad weather. It grows to a height of 3 to 4 m (10 to 13 ft). Flowering is repeated but the first flowering in mid-June is far more profuse. The blooms have a heavy fragrance. This rose is used to cover tall pergolas, summer-houses, walls and as a solitary subject in parks and large gardens. It is also lovely if grafted on to tall stems of species rootstock to form a weeping standard.

'Heidelberg', developed by Kordes in 1959 as a cross between 'Minna Kordes' and 'Floradora', is one of the loveliest of the red climbing roses. It is very healthy and weather resistant and grows to a height of 2 m (6 ft) (in very good conditions to 2.5 m [8 ft]). The blooms are bright red, large, high centred and have a pleasant perfume. They are pro-duced from June until autumn. 'Heidelberg' is generally used as a freely-growing solitary subject or as a low climber trained over fences, ironwork, and the like. The flowers may also be used for cutting even though the stems are not very long.

'Sympathie' continues to be an unsurpassed modern red climbing rose even though it was developed by Kordes as far back as 1964. It belongs to the *Rosa kordesii* group and is a cross between 'Wilhelm Hausmann' and 'Don Juan'. It has a moderately vigorous growth and reaches a height of 3 to 4 m (10 to 13 ft). The foliage is dark and healthy, resistant to both bad weather and disease. It flowers profusely and continuously until late autumn and has a pleasant fragrance like that of a wild rose. The autumn flowering is exceptionally profuse. This rose is useful as a solitary subject, properly tied to a support, beside the house entrance and between windows. It is the best red rose of the present selection.

Heidelberg

Sympathie

'Danse des Sylphes', developed by Ch. Mallerin in 1959 by crossing 'Danse du feu' and ('Peace' × 'Independence'), is a healthy plant with stems up to 3 m (10 ft) long. The foliage is healthy and dark green, the flowers large and borne in spherical clusters. The first flowering in June is moderately profuse and will be repeated if the blooms are cut as they fade. The blooms are extremely beautiful but are less profuse than those of other red climbing roses. The best use for this rose is as a freely-growing solitary specimen in a park or larger garden, as it spreads symmetrically. The arching shoots touch the ground. It is not so attractive when trained over a support. The blooms are good for cutting and for floral arrangements.

'Golden Climber', also known as 'Mrs Arthur Curtis James', was developed by Brownwell in 1933 by crossing 'Mary Wallace' and an unknown seedling. It is an old variety but still one of the best of the yellow climbing roses, which are not very numerous. It is a healthy, hardy plant of fairly vigorous growth, reaching a height of 3 to 4 m (10 to 13 ft). The shapely, elongated buds open successively so that the plant is continuously in flower until autumn. The blooms have a pleasant perfume. This rose is used to cover pergolas, fences and archways. After 5 to

Danse des Sylphes

Golden Climber

Violet Blue

New Dawn

8 years it needs to be hard pruned, whereupon it will grow and flower for a great many more years.

'Violet Blue', also known as 'Veilchenblau', is an old variety said to be the first *blue* rose. It was developed by G. C. Schmidt in 1909 as a cross between 'Crimson Rambler' and an unknown seedling. A tall plant, reaching a height of 4.5 m (15 ft), it is a vigorous climber and faces bad weather well but, like almost all small-flowered climbing roses, is susceptible to mildew. The small flowers, about 3 cm (1 in) in diameter, are arranged in attractive clusters. This rose is good for covering fences and pergolas; it is better suited for old-type rosaria but may also be used in the modern garden.

'New Dawn' is a very widespread climbing rose developed in 1930 by Somerset as a sport from 'W. van Fleet'. It is a healthy plant and good grower, reaching a height of 3 to 4 m (10 to 13 ft). It forms a thick bush that produces pale pink flowers profusely and continuously until late autumn, except for a brief interval following the first bloom. It is suitable for covering cottages, pergolas and fences, and to ramble down from terraces and banks, and as a solitary, freely-growing specimen, in which case it requires a fairly large space. It is also lovely as a weeping standard grafted on to a tall stem.

Conrad Ferdinand Meyer

Průhonice

SHRUB ROSES

These roses form huge shrubs with lovely, scented flowers and are used as solitary specimens in larger gardens or for freely flowering hedges. In habit they resemble climbing roses but do not need to be tied to a support; all that is usually necessary is to bind the branches so they do not droop under the weight of the blooms.

One of the oldest and most famous shrub roses is 'Conrad Ferdinand Meyer', developed by F. Müller in 1899 as a cross between *Rosa rugosa* and 'Gloire de Dijon'. It is an unusually tall, upright shrub reaching a height of 3 m (10 ft). The flowers are arranged in firm clusters and have a pleasant perfume. This shrub flowers for about four weeks and after a brief

interval once again, but far less profusely. It is best used in parks or for hedges; it is not particularly striking as a solitary specimen because of its straggly appearance.

'Průhonice' is an interesting shrub rose developed in 1972 by L. Večeřa as a cross between 'Message' and 'Eva'. A rose of rather a drooping habit, it grows to a height of 1.8 m (6 ft). The foliage is very healthy, the flowers large and borne profusely and continuously throughout the growing season. They are arranged in clusters of four to six and have a pleasant fragrance. This is a typical solitary specimen that makes a gorgeous display in turf. It is also ideal for hedges and for cutting — whole clusters of flowers are used for decoration.

'Bonn' is a shrub rose resistant to severe frosts that

Cocktail

Bonn

was developed by Kordes in 1950 as a cross between 'Hamburg' and 'Independence'. It is of regular habit and grows to a height of 1.5 m (5 ft). The orange-scarlet flowers, arranged in large clusters, have a slight fragrance and are produced from June until the frost. This shrub is used chiefly as a solitary specimen and for hedges.

'Cocktail', developed by Meilland in 1957 by crossing ('Independence' × 'Orange Triumph') and 'Phyllis Bide', is a fairly small shrub, reaching a height of only 1 m (3 ft) in temperate regions. The crimson flowers with white and yellow centres are single and measure 5 cm (2 in) across. The first flowering is very profuse, the second less so. This is a healthy shrub, though somewhat prone to mildew. It is good for hedges or planted in solitary groups.

103

Maigold

Frühlingsmorgen

'Maigold', developed by Kordes in 1953 as a cross between 'Poulsen's Pink' and 'Frühlingstag', is a large, healthy shrub rose of spreading habit reaching a height of 3.7 m (12 ft). The shoots are short with abundant foliage and a profusion of very fragrant blooms. It flowers only once. 'Maigold' is good for parks and gardens, particularly as a solitary specimen. The yellow colour of its blooms, unusual amongst shrub roses, is very striking.

'Frühlingsmorgen', likewise developed by Kordes, in 1942, by crossing ('E. G. Hill' × 'Catherine Kordes') and *Rosa spinosissima altaica,* is a shrub only 1.5 m (5 ft) high that faces bad weather well but is susceptible to mildew. It flowers only once, though in favourable years it may bear a few late blooms in early September. The flowers are large, pink and single. This is an interesting and very popular variety, good as a solitary subject in the garden and for hedges.

'Nevada', developed by P. Dot in 1927 as a cross between 'La Giralda' and *Rosa moyesii,* is a shrub of vigorous growth reaching a height of 2 to 2.5 m (6 to 8 ft). The shoots are long and covered with abundant foliage and flowers. The buds are a delicate pink, the single, large flowers are creamy-white when fully open. They are without fragrance. The first flowers are borne in profusion; late summer blooms are not as abundant, being somewhat smaller and have a carmine tinge. This rose is widely grown nowadays, particularly as a solitary subject in large expanses of turf in parks. It is also good for hedges.

Handel

Nevada

'Handel', developed by McGredy in 1965 as a cross between 'Columbine' and 'Heidelberg', has become one of the most popular shrub roses in recent years. Of moderately vigorous growth, it reaches a height of 3 m (10 ft) and branches freely. The foliage is a glossy olive green that is an excellent foil for the pale-pink and cream flowers. The shapely, fragrant blooms are borne in clusters on 20 to 30 cm (8 to 12 in) long shoots. The first flowering is very profuse and is followed after a brief interval by another. This rose is resistant to disease as well as bad weather. It is best as a solitary subject in gardens, but should be tied loosely so that the long shoots do not bend to the ground. It is also good for hedges and the flowers can be cut for use in floral arrangements. It was 'Handel' that contributed in great measure to the increased popularity of shrub roses in recent years.

105

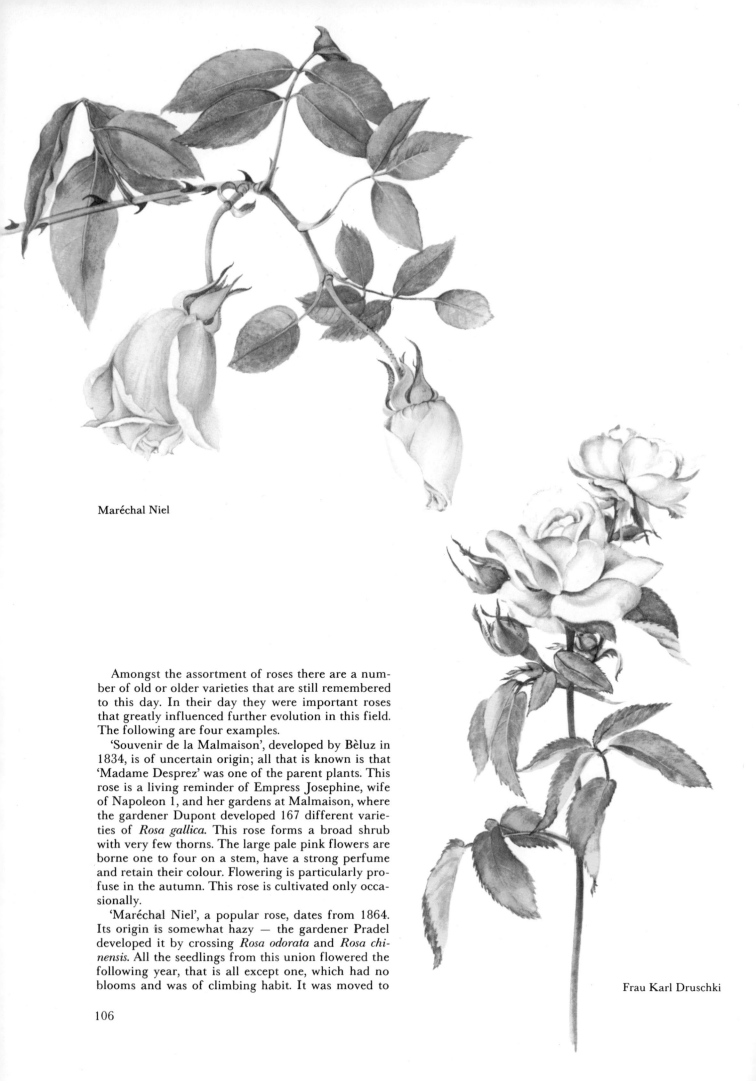

Maréchal Niel

Frau Karl Druschki

Amongst the assortment of roses there are a number of old or older varieties that are still remembered to this day. In their day they were important roses that greatly influenced further evolution in this field. The following are four examples.

'Souvenir de la Malmaison', developed by Bèluz in 1834, is of uncertain origin; all that is known is that 'Madame Desprez' was one of the parent plants. This rose is a living reminder of Empress Josephine, wife of Napoleon 1, and her gardens at Malmaison, where the gardener Dupont developed 167 different varieties of *Rosa gallica*. This rose forms a broad shrub with very few thorns. The large pale pink flowers are borne one to four on a stem, have a strong perfume and retain their colour. Flowering is particularly profuse in the autumn. This rose is cultivated only occasionally.

'Maréchal Niel', a popular rose, dates from 1864. Its origin is somewhat hazy — the gardener Pradel developed it by crossing *Rosa odorata* and *Rosa chinensis*. All the seedlings from this union flowered the following year, that is all except one, which had no blooms and was of climbing habit. It was moved to the glasshouse where it produced masses of magnificent flowers. This, then, is a climbing rose with shoots reaching a length of several metres which is best grown in a glasshouse. It is killed by frost in open ground. Flowering is particularly attractive in the autumn. The blooms have a lovely perfume. The shoots are slender and delicate, the thorns sharp and curved. This rose continues to be a showpiece, and is the pride of many rose lovers to this day.

'Mrs John Laing', developed by H. Bennet in 1887, is a seedling from 'Francois Michelon'. It is a vigorous plant of spreading habit reaching a height of 1.8 m (6 ft). The pink flowers are borne singly on slender, arching shoots and have a strong perfume.

The plant is regularly attacked by mildew. Nowadays this rose is grown only occasionally in older parks.

'Frau Karl Druschki', developed by Lambert in 1901 as a cross between 'Merveille de Lyon' and 'Mme. Caroline Testout', was the most popular rose of its day for a long time. It is the first purely white remontant rose, and is listed by some authorities as a hybrid tea. It is a healthy, hardy and vigorous plant, growing to a height of 1.5 to 3 m (5 to 10 ft). The blooms measure up to 15 cm (6 in) across and are unscented. The buds are slender and pinkish at the tip. This rose is good for parks and large gardens and is also used for cutting. It is grown in many gardens throughout the world to this day.

Mrs John Laing

Souvenir de la Malmaison

In conclusion to this section, six species roses still quite commonly grown in parks and large gardens:

Rosa centifolia muscosa, which translated means hundred-leaved moss rose, is a species rose that continues to be popular and in demand to this day. It has been grown since 1757 and probably originated as a sport from *Rosa centifolia*. This shrub, about 1.5 m (5 ft) high, is upright in youth but later rather spreading. The shoots are slender and flexible. The white flowers are borne in small clusters on short annual shoots growing from the previous year's wood. They are fragrant and open in early June. There is only one flowering. The sepals, stems and part of the leaves are encrusted with hairs of moss-like appearance, hence the name given to this rose. It

Rosa centifolia muscosa

Rosa foetida bicolor

is hardy and suitable for naturalised areas; it is also commonly planted around country cottages and may be attractively combined with climbing roses.

Rosa foetida bicolor, known in England as 'Austrian Copper', is a very old rose. Native to the Near East, it was introduced into Europe as early as the 13th century but its cultivation there dates from 1590. It is probably a sport of *Rosa foetida*, which, however, has all yellow blooms. This shrub grows to a height of 1.5 to 2 m (5 to 6 ft). The shoots are dark chestnut brown with paler thorns. The fragrant flowers, red with yellow centres, bloom during the last week of May; the flowering is not repeated. A hardy plant, it has been grown as a shrub rose in parks for centuries

Rosa gallica   *Rosa moyesii*

and may be seen in newly established, modern-day parks as well. It is very striking when in bloom, especially in groups of three to five shrubs in an expanse of turf.

Rosa gallica, also known as the Gallic or French rose, is one of the oldest roses. Native to central and southern Europe and to western Asia, it may be found growing wild to this day, primarily on warm, limestone banks. Its cultivation in gardens dates from about 1500. The shrub is only 1 m (3 ft) high and makes side shoots from the base. The shoots are reddish, the foliage dark green, the crimson flowers large, 7 to 10 cm $(2^3/_4$ to 4 in) across. They are borne singly at the end of May; the flowering is not repeat-

ed, but is followed by light red hips. This is a hardy rose, used for mass plantings in parks and on banks where it spreads freely by putting out side shoots. It is not good as a solitary specimen because it is too low.

Rosa moyesii, native to central and western China, has been cultivated in Europe since 1894. It is a 3 m (10 ft) high shrub with flexible shoots covered sparsely with thorns. The deep red flowers, which appear at the beginning of June, are distributed thinly over the shrub. They are without fragrance. The flowering is not repeated. This very hardy rose is used in parks as it is too robust for the garden and flowers at the same time as roses of low habit.

109

Rosa hugonis

Rosa omeiensis pteracantha

Rosa hugonis is native to China, whence it was brought to Europe in 1899. This is a spreading shrub up to 3 m (10 ft) high that at first glance does not even resemble a rose. It is one of the first roses to flower, as early as the beginning of May. The blooms are about 5 cm (2 in) across and without fragrance. During the flowering period the shrub is literally smothered with bright yellow, single blooms and hundreds of buzzing bees, for which it serves as food source. A healthy and hardy plant, it is one of the most suitable species roses for parks and large gardens, best planted as a solitary subject.

Rosa omeiensis pteracantha (syn. *R. sericea pteracantha*) is native to central China, whence it was brought to Europe in 1890. This is a spreading shrub growing to a height of 3 to 4 m (10 to 13 ft). The most interesting feature are the lovely, broadly winged red thorns. The single white flowers are rather small, 2.5 to 3 cm (1 in) across, and without fragrance. It is used chiefly in parks and large landscaping schemes as a solitary subject; it may also be used to form an impenetrable hedge.

The hips of many roses are a decorative feature. Their size, shape and colour are characteristic of the given species and varieties and therefore an important means of identification, particularly in the case of species roses.

Rosa rugosa, also known as the Japanese apple rose, has large, globular hips. The shrub grows to a height of 60 to 150 cm (2 to 5 ft), the purple or white flowers are 9 cm (3½ in) across. This is a hardy rose that tolerates acid soil. A great many varieties have been derived from this species.

Rosa multiflora has small oval hips arranged in clusters and resembling beads. The bush grows to a height of about 2 m (6 ft) and in good conditions also attains a great width. The small white flowers are arranged in large panicles.

Rosa canina is most widely used as rootstock. It has many forms and thus the hips are not uniform. The shrub reaches a height of 2 to 3 m (6 to 10 ft) and grows wild throughout all Europe. The flowers are pale pink to whitish. It is very hardy.

Rosa pomifera, known as the apple rose, has pink blooms. The shrub grows to a height of 2 m (6 ft) and has few thorns. The bristly hips are preserved and used as food.

Rosa spinosissima has unique hips which turn black when ripe. This is a low shrub, only 0.5 to 1 m (1$^1/_2$ to 3 ft) high, and very thorny. The flowers are about 6 cm (2$^1/_4$ in) across and coloured whitish yellow to white. It grows in large masses and spreads freely by underground stems.

Rosa moyesii has large, elongate, pear-shaped hips. This rose is described in greater detail on the preceding double-page.

Rosa rugosa (a), *Rosa multiflora* (b), *Rosa canina* (c)   *Rosa pomifera* (a), *Rosa spinosissima* (b), *Rosa moyesii* (c)

BULBS

A garden without bulbs looks bare, cheerless and incomplete in spring and autumn. The bulb is a storage organ containing food reserves and the embryo plant, and was originally a means of surviving in the severe climatic conditions of the plant's native habitat; regions where the summer is either too dry and hot or the growing season too short. A classic example of such behaviour is the snowdrop, which in the wild grows under a bush. It flowers before the shrub puts out leaves and dies down when the shrub is covered with foliage that blocks the sun's rays. Other bulbs also disappear from view after the brief growing period is over and it looks as if nothing were growing in the spot where they had been. In August there is no trace in the garden of the tulips and other bulbs that will flower there in spring. And yet, the bulb that is resting in the ground is basically a complete plant, but strikingly changed in appearance.

Bulbs are the most colourful heralds of spring, unrivalled by any other group of plants at this time. Their beauty, however, may be savoured not only in spring but practically the whole year long if the right kinds are selected for planting and if we include forced narcissi and tulips that bloom in winter.

In the garden these plants are grown only by putting out bulbs. Propagation by means of seeds is a complicated and lengthy process and one used mostly in breeding; propagation by vegetative means is hardly ever used, only some lilies are propagated by bulb scales.

During the growing period the flower uses up all the food stored in the bulb so that in the case of most species the originally planted bulb disappears entirely and a new one grows in its place; this can be lifted and planted out again the following year or left in the ground where it will produce a new plant. Several smaller bulbs, called daughter bulbs or offsets, grow up beside the new bulb and may be used for propagation; however, it takes several years for them to develop and bear flowers. An embryo plant begins forming inside the bulb as soon as it is lifted, during the dormant period. Each healthy bulb will produce a new plant but only large, strong bulbs bear flowers.

Growing bulbs is quite simple. Tulips are planted out in September or October and should be moved every year. They should not be left in the ground for more than three years because then they spread to an unwelcome extent and fewer of them bear flowers. Narcissi are planted in August, together with the roots if possible, and left in the same spot for three to five years so they will form clumps. Lilies are planted in the autumn and left in the ground for several years, as they need to 'settle in'. Small bulbous plants are generally left in the ground longer, even though many may be moved more frequently. Otherwise, all that is necessary is weeding, watering and feeding, and after the flowers have faded the bulbs are left in peace.

There is no general rule as to where bulbs should be planted in the garden. However, one must keep in mind their biological and ecological requirements. Snowdrops, for instance, should not be put in full sun in a dry, warm spot. There is also the aesthetic aspect. Practically all species that flower in spring or early summer die down sooner or later leaving an empty space in their stead within a few weeks. Such bare spots mar the beauty of the garden. In the case of species that grow under shrubs or trees it does not matter, but empty spaces in the middle of the garden should be avoided. How to conceal them for the remainder of the growing season is the question faced by every gardener. It is often recommended to plant crocuses, tulips, colchicums, muscaris and other species in an undercarpet of cushion-forming alpines to heighten the aesthetic effect. Anyone who has tried this, however, has found that the bulbs disappeared after several years, even though they were by no means tender or particularly exacting species. The reason is that in their native steppe regions, bulbs are not accustomed to a cover in summer. Nature in the wild and a garden, however, are two different things. Strong, robust bulbs may be planted in an undercarpet of alpine plants but the latter must not be too vigorous. For example, aubrieta, thymus, *Phlox subulata* and *Cerastium tomentosum* not only make a thick carpet but their root system is very extensive and dense. Such cushions with dense roots catch all the water that falls on the surface and neither moisture nor air and nutrients reach the lower layers of soil where the bulbs are. It must be kept in mind that even in the case of a thin, loose plant cover a heavy rainfall penetrates to a depth of scarcely 15 cm (6 in). If, moreover, such dense cushions are growing in a dry and sunny situation which they find congenial and where they form even more compact and denser mounds and root systems, then any bulbs planted out in their midst are doomed to die. Some rock-garden plants, however, are quite suitable for this purpose and there is no need to fear any serious damage to the bulbs growing in their midst. They include, for example, *Gypsophila repens, Alyssum montanum, Alyssum wulfenianum,* helianthemum, *Sedum sieboldii, Sedum album,* and *Hypericum polyphyllum.*

Places left bare by bulbs that have died down may also be planted with a number of annuals such as *Alyssum maritimum, Dorotheanthus bellidiformis,* dimorphotheca, portulaca and *Gypsophila elegans.* Seedlings that have been grown on are carefully put out between the bulbs as soon as the weather permits, even though the bulbs have not yet faded and withered. They should be tended and watered with care so as not to damage the flowers, stem, leaves and above all the underground parts of the bulbous plants.

Another recommended way of planting bulbs, for instance crocus, *Tulipa kaufmanniana,* muscari and narcissus, is in grass. Here, however, conditions are about the same as in an undercarpet of vigorous alpines. The bulbs look wonderful in the turf but they hardly ever last long because a well-tended lawn is very thick and the bulbs starve, thus making replacement necessary. Another drawback is that the grass must not be cut until the leaves have turned yellow. Leaves are very important plant organs (they synthesise the food the bulb will need to overwinter) and must not be removed prematurely, for this greatly weakens the plant.

Tulips, narcissi and hyacinths may also be grown in separate beds, tulips often together with pansies, forget-me-nots or daisies. It is thus possible to get marvellous colour combinations that make a very striking display in spring. After the flowers haved faded the leaves should be allowed to die down naturally so that the bulbs will ripen as they should. Such bulbs will produce new blooms the following year, be they lifted or left in the ground. If the foliage is reduced prematurely then the bulbs are practically worthless.

Growing tulips and other bulbs together with roses is impractical. When hoeing the soil round the roses the bulbs are often damaged. Also weeding such a bed is difficult and the yellowing bulb foliage is unattractive.

The family of garden tulips is a very large one. The present registered assortment includes some 4000 varieties divided into the following groups according to their characteristics and uses: 1. Single early tulips, 2. Double early tulips, 3. Mendel tulips, 4. Triumph tulips, 5. Darwin tulips, 6. Darwin hybrids, 7. Single late (Cottage) tulips, 8. Double late tulips, 9. Lily-flowered tulips, 10. Parrot tulips, 11. Breeder tulips, 12. Rembrandt tulips, 13. Species tulips. Besides these most important groups there are others such as fringed, multi-flowered, chameleon, green-flowered, and other tulips.

Tulipa. Double and single early tulips grow to a height of 30 cm (1 ft) and bloom as early as mid-April. They are best for beds of a single colour or several colours and most are also valuable for forcing. The flowers are double, irregular, and borne on thick stems. Varieties come in different colours, such as 'Elektra'—carmine, 'Orange Nassau'—orange, 'Peach Blossom'—rose pink, 'Mr Van der Hoef'—yellow, 'Snowstorm'—white. The illustrated variety 'Red Blossom' is also lovely; like most of the tulips of this group, it is derived from the old variety 'Murillo'.

Triumph tulips are varieties resulting from crosses between single early-flowering tulips and single late-flowering varieties. The majority are very good for cutting and early forcing. They are 30 to 50 cm (1 to 1 ft 8in) high and bloom in late April and early May.

Triumph tulip 'Klipfontein'

Double early tulip 'Red Blossom'

The stems are firm and stout and the large firm flowers come in a wide range of colours. Varieties most frequently cultivated are 'Spring Beauty'—white, 'Makassar'—yellow, 'Red Matador'—crimson, 'Edith Eddy'—carmine edged with white, 'Princess Beatrix'—red edged with gold. The illustrated variety 'Klipfontein' is one of the more recent types.

Darwin tulips are very popular and widely cultivated. They are 50 to 70 cm (1ft 8in to 2ft 8in) high and flower in the first half of May. They have ovoid-shaped flowers and stout stems and are used chiefly for cutting. These tulips are very effective planted in a bed in larger or smaller groups of a single colour. This group includes many lovely varieties, such as 'Demeter'—purple, 'William Pitt'—strawberry red, 'Clara Butt'—salmon pink, 'Pink Supreme'—dark pink, 'Duke of Wellington'—white, 'Niphetos'—yellow. The illustrated varieties are: 'Abe Lenstra'—deep pink, 'Queen of Bartigons'—delicate pink, and 'Queen of Night'—deep velvety maroon.

Darwin hybrids are the same height as Darwin tulips but flower earlier, in late April. They, too, have stout stems and large flowers. This is a fairly recent, modern group. These tulips are best planted in larger or smaller groups of a single variety and are also very good for cutting. Noteworthy varieties are: 'Apeldoorn'—light red, 'Golden Apeldoorn'—yellow, 'Diplomat'—red, 'Holland's Glory'—orange-scarlet. A lovely member of this group is the illustrated variety 'Gudoschnik', with large, broad, oval flowers.

Darwin tulip 'Gudoschnik'

Darwin tulips 'Abe Lenstra' (deep pink),
'Queen of Bartigons' (pale pink), 'Queen of Night' (dark maroon)

117

broad mauve-lilac petals with a fringed margin coloured a paler mauve.

Parrot tulips are 35 to 60 cm (14 to 24 in) high and flower at different times from early to late May. They are popular for their large, fringed or laciniate petals but a drawback is that they tend to have a stem too weak for the heavy flower and therefore bend to the ground. Parrot tulips are planted out in beds in small groups, but not together with other tulips, and are good for cutting. A typical representa-

Parrot tulip 'Fantasy'

Fringed tulips 'Swan Wings' (white), 'Burns' (pink), 'Blue Heron' (violet)

The interesting fringed tulips have beautifully coloured flowers with finely fringed edge. Numbering only a few varieties they do not belong to a single, separate group but are included either among the Darwin or single late (Cottage) tulips. They are eminently suitable for cutting because they are very ornamental and last long in a vase. For many years there was only one form, 'Sundew', coloured a deep red. Shown in the illustration are new, modern varieties: 'Swan Wings'—pure white with oblong, slightly open flower with finely fringed edge (classed in the Darwin tulip division); 'Burns'—pink, with thickly fringed edge (classed in the single late tulip division); 'Blue Heron'—a new Darwin tulip variety which has

118

Double late tulip 'Lilac Perfection'

Lily-flowered tulips 'Burgundy' (violet), 'West Point' (yellow)

tive of this group is 'Fantasy'—a sport from the Darwin tulip 'Clara Butt', 55 cm (1 ft 10 in) high with a firm stem and firm flower, salmon pink edged with green. The petals are long, notched, and split in places. Other interesting varieties include 'Black Parrot' almost black, 'Blue Parrot'—violet, 'Orange Favourite'—orange, 'Texas Gold'—deep yellow.

Double late tulips, also called paeony-flowered tulips, are 40 to 50 cm (1ft 4in to 1 ft 8in) high and flower in late May. The flowers are large, compact, double blooms that often break because of their weight. They are very good for cutting and for group planting in beds. Interesting varieties include: 'Pride of Holland'—bright red, 'Golden Nizza'—golden-

yellow edged with red, 'Lilac Perfection'—lilac with white at the base, 'Eros'—soft dusky rose, 'Orange Triumph'—orange-red edged with yellow, 'Mount Tacoma'—white with green markings.

Lily-flowered tulips, 40 to 60 cm (1 ft 4 in to 2 ft) high, flower in late May. This is a modern group popular for its elegant blooms with narrow, recurved petals. The buds are very slender. These tulips are good for mixed beds and also for cutting. The illustrated varieties are 'Burgundy' and 'West Point'. Other interesting varieties are 'Aladdin'—red edged with yellow, 'Red Shine'—carmine, 'China Pink'—pale pink, 'White Triumphator'—white, 'Golden Duchess'—golden-yellow.

Tulipa greigii is a species tulip, one of a large group native to the steppes of central Asia. It has been crossed with *T. fosteriana* and various Darwin hybrids to produce some more beautiful hybrids. Tulips of the *T. greigii* group are distinguished chiefly by the broad, wavy leaves with brownish markings down their length. They are 15 to 30 cm (6 to 12 in) high and flower in early May. The flowers of the type species are large, elegant, purplish-scarlet with black basal blotch margined with yellow. Many beautiful varieties—Greigii hybrids—coloured various shades of yellow, orange, scarlet, pink and salmon-pink, have been produced in the past several decades. The most important ones are: 'Jessica', 'Cape Cod', 'Odessa', 'Oriental Beauty', 'Donnabella', 'Plaisir' and 'Red Riding Hood'. The bulbs need dry conditions and heat during the ripening period.

Tulipa greigii 'Jessica'

Tulipa fosteriana 'Defiance' (pale yellow), 'Cantata' (red)

Tulipa fosteriana is the most important of the species tulips, its beauty far surpassing that of many garden forms. The flowers of the type species, which is 35 to 40 cm (14 to 16 in) high, are broad and fiery-red with black basal blotch rimmed with yellow appearing in mid-April. Many varieties of various

120

Tulipa eichleri

with black basal blotch rimmed with yellow, which appear in late April. The leaves are often longer than the stem. This tulip is demanding in its requirements, which include a sunny and warm situation, and is intolerant of soggy soil in winter. The type species is the one usually grown, though new varieties that are far lovelier are becoming more widespread.

Tulipa kaufmanniana, the water-lily tulip, and its varieties, is the second most important group of species tulips, and one of the most easily grown. They are small, up to 25 cm (10 in) high, and distinguished by a characteristic grey-green colour of the leaves with brownish-purple markings. They flower in late March. The type species is creamy white with pink markings of varying size and intensity on the outside. This tulip has yielded many varieties coloured white or shades of yellow, orange, red, such as 'Alfred Cortot', 'Berlioz', 'Bellini', 'César Franck', 'Heart's Delight', 'Johann Strauss', 'Stresa', 'The First', 'Vivaldi', 'Shakespeare', 'Corona', and 'Ancilla'.

Tulipa kaufmanniana 'Shakespeare' (orange), 'Corona' (yellow), 'Ancilla' (red-white)

colours are cultivated in the garden. Best known is 'Red Emperor'—up to 50 cm (1 ft 8 in) high, vermilion, with flowers larger than the type species. A sturdier variety is 'Princeps' 20 to 25 cm (8 to 10 in) high, which flowers one week later, excellent for a rock garden. The most popular varieties, whose colours include white, yellow, pink, orange and red are: 'Albas', 'Cantata', 'Pinkeen', 'Purissima', and 'Rockery Beauty'.

Tulipa eichleri has a 30 to 40 cm (12 to 16 in) long stem and large, broad flowers, coloured light purple

Tulipa tarda (T. dasystemon), 10 to 15 cm (4 to 6 in) high, is the best known of the dwarf species tulips. It makes a ground rosette of leaves from which rise three to eight snow-white star-like flowers with yellow bases. The perianth segments are greyish-green outside. This tulip flowers in the second half of April.

Muscari. Grape hyacinth, muscari, is a very popular small bulbous plant found in practically every rock garden. Masses of the blue flowers in combination with yellow daffodils make a striking display in spring. It has no special requirements and will grow in any garden soil. It usually spreads freely, although it is recommended to lift and divide the bulbs occasionally. There are many species, some tall, others low, in various shades of blue; some have white flowers but these are less attractive. *Muscari comosum,* flowering in May and up to 50 cm (1 ft 8 in) high, is used for cutting as it lasts well in a vase. *M. armeniacum* has blue flowers edged with white and very long leaves from April to early May. Hyacinthella is very similar and sometimes listed in catalogues under the synonym *M. azureum.* It is a low, resolutely hardy plant which flowers as early as late February or early March, and is suitable for a rock garden.

Hyacinthus. The hyacinth, *Hyacinthus orientalis,* is a beautiful plant flowering in early spring. It is particularly effective planted in groups in the rock garden or bed, or a bowl indoors. Hyacinths are usually grown for forcing. Cultivation in the garden is not

Hyacinthus amethystinus

Muscari armeniacum

Tulipa tarda

Hyacinthus orientalis
'Dreadnought'

'Lady Derby' (pink),
'Jan Bos' (red)

without problems. They require a light soil, sunny situation, and should be put out in October; although no flowers are produced until April.

Hyacinths are grown in the garden in two ways. The bulbs may be left in the ground when the top parts have died down. They will flower again the following year but the flowers will be smaller, decreasing in size with each succeeding year until, after four to five years, the plants cease to flower altogether. Large flowers and lengthy flowering may be achieved only by very large doses of feed to replace as many as possible of the nutrients used up by flowering and required by the bulb for further growth.

The second method is to lift the bulbs after the leaves have withered, clean and dry them, and then store them the same as tulip bulbs. In this case, too, the doses of feed will determine how long and how fine a flower will be produced by the bulb. The only advantage of this method is the possibility of putting the bulb in another spot. Hyacinth bulbs should be planted deeper than tulips (at a depth of 18 to 25 cm [7 to 10 in] depending on the soil). In the eighteenth century the Dutch developed double hyacinths that reached the peak of their popularity in the nineteenth century. Since then, however, it has waned considerably. Illustrated are three old but still widely cultivated varieties: 'Lady Derby' — pink, 'Jan Bos' — red, and 'Dreadnought'.

Hyacinthus amethystinus (synonym: *Brimeura amethystina*) is 25 cm (10 in) high, with narrow, linear leaves and tubelike flowers coloured porcelain-blue. This is one of the loveliest, early-flowering (March-April) bulbs. There is also a white form. This hyacinth grows wild in the Pyrenees.

Narcissus. Daffodils or narcissi, with their lovely, fresh beauty are synonymous with spring. A striking effect is obtained by putting out groups of three to five bulbs of the same variety which will then form a fan-shaped clump that is most attractive, particularly if set off against a backdrop of dark conifers which provide a pleasing contrast. Narcissi are also good as an underplanting for ornamental shrubs and may similarly be planted in grass. Best for this purpose are early-flowering varieties because the grass must not be cut until their leaves have turned yellow.

Narcissi are divided into eleven groups according to the shape of the flower, some are further divided into subgroups according to colour.

The first group comprises the trumpet narcissi. This section includes all varieties that have one flower to a stem and trumpet or corona as long as or longer than the perianth segments ('petals'). They are about 40 cm (1 ft 4 in) high. Of the many varieties

the following are shown in the illustration: 'Beersheba'—pure white with long trumpet and long perianth, 'Content'—trumpet pale yellow, perianth creamy-white, 'Preamble'—trumpet lemon-yellow, long, perianth white.

The second group includes the large-cupped narcissi, with one flower to a stem, the corona more than one-third but less than equal to the length of the perianth segments. They are about 40 cm (16 in) high. Pictured are the following popular cultivated varieties: 'Easter Bonnet'—perianth segments creamy white, slightly wavy and corona pale apricot orange with broad, markedly wavy salmon-pink edge; 'Polindra'—perianth segments smooth, white, and corona yellow with slightly darker edge. 'Belisana'—perianth segments oval, white, and the corona very wavy and coloured yellow with broad, orange edge. 'Signal Light'—perianth segments oval, pointed, creamy white, and corona pale orange, only

Large-cupped narcissi 'Easter Bonnet' (white and orange), 'Polindra' (white and yellow)

Double narcissi 'Hollandia' (orange and yellow), 'Golden Castle' (white and yellow)

slightly wavy on the edge. 'Tannhäuser'—perianth segments broadly oval, smooth, yellow, and corona yellow with faintly wavy, orange-red edge.

The third group includes the small-cupped narcissi 30 to 40 cm (12 to 16 in) high, with one flower to a stem and shallow, flat corona not more than one-third the length of the perianth segments.

The fourth group includes the double narcissi, which are used primarily for forcing. They are not particularly good for bedding because the heavy flowers cause them to bend to the ground, especially after a rainfall, and they often break. Shown in the illustration are 'Golden Castle'—the outside perianth segments creamy white, the inside ones pale yellow, and 'Hollandia'—with lovely double orange corona and pale yellow perianth.

Large-cupped narcissi 'Tannhäuser' (yellow), 'Signal Light' (white and orange), 'Belisana' (white and yellow)

Trumpet narcissi 'Beersheba' (pure white), 'Content' (pale yellow and creamy white), 'Preamble' (lemon yellow and pure white)

Narcissus triandrus hybrid

Narcissus cyclamineus, varieties 'Jumblie' (2—3 flowers to a stem), 'Jenny' (pale yellow), 'Peeping Tom' (deep yellow)

The fifth group comprises the Triandrus Hybrids, all of which have the characteristic features of the type species *Narcissus triandrus,* from which they are derived. These have one to six pendent flowers on a stem, the perianth segments slightly reflexed and rolled, and the corona cup shaped. The plants are 25 to 35 cm (10 to 14 in) high and the flowers of the different varieties vary in size, some being larger, others smaller.

The sixth group comprises the Cyclamineus Hybrids which appear on the following page.

The seventh group includes the Jonquilla Hybrids, all of which have the basic characteristics of the type species, *Narcissus jonquilla,* from which they are derived. The flowers are golden-yellow with longish,

trumpet-like corona and have a very sweet fragrance reminiscent of oranges. There are one to three flowers on a stem. Pictured is the variety 'Tittle-Tattle' with two to three flowers on a stem, the perianth is pale yellow and the corona, a shallow cup, is a deeper shade. Also pictured for purposes of comparison is the type species *N. jonquilla.*

The eighth group includes the Tazetta Hybrids, all of which have the characteristic features of the type species, *Narcissus tazetta,* from which they are derived. There are four to twenty flowers on a stem. They measure 3 to 6 cm (1 to 2 in) across and generally have a pleasant perfume. They are used chiefly for forcing. Recommended for the garden are the varieties shown in the illustration. 'Laurens Koster',

up to 60 cm (2 ft) high and has a flower 9 cm ($3\frac{1}{2}$ in) across. The white, oval perianth segments terminate in a small point and overlap and the corona is flat with a yellow centre edged bright red. This is an excellent form for cutting and for forcing from mid-January.

The tenth and eleventh groups include botanical narcissi type species, forms and varieties that grow in the wild. As with tulips, these are mostly small and low growing species flowering earlier than the large-flowered narcissi and therefore suitable chiefly for the rock garden. They number a great many different kinds which are divided into eight subgroups.

Narcissus tazetta hybrids 'Laurens Koster' (white), 'Scarlet Gem' (yellow)

Narcissus jonquilla hybrid, variety 'Tittle-Tattle', compared with the botanical species

a variety introduced as early as 1906 but still one of the best forms. It has up to seven flowers on a stem, the perianth segments are creamy white and the short orange-yellow corona. 'Scarlet Gem', also an old variety dating from 1910, has four to six flowers on a stem, the perianth is golden-yellow and the short, wavy corona orange. This is an excellent variety for late forcing.

The ninth group includes the Poeticus Narcissi, all of which have retained the essential characteristics of the type species *Narcissus poeticus*. These are the latest to flower and have a pleasant fragrance. There is one flower to a stem. It is pure white with small, short and flat corona and white, oval perianth segments. The best variety is 'Actaea', which is robust,

Narcissus poeticus hybrid 'Actaea'

Narcissus cyclamineus and its hybrids form the sixth group of narcissi. It is one of the loveliest of the small narcissi. The yellow flowers have a long, narrow corona and strongly recurved perianth segments that form a narrow crown at the base of the trumpet. It flowers early and requires a moist situation. It grows wild chiefly in Spain and Portugal. Breeding has yielded many varieties, which grow to a height of 30 cm (1 ft) and have one flower to a stem. They are good for the rock garden. Attractive varieties include those shown in the illustration: 'Jenny' — with a large flower, the corona long, broad and pale yellow; 'Jumblie'—with corona long and bright yellow; this form bears two to three flowers on each stem; 'Peeping Tom'—an excellent variety for cutting; the flowers are very persistent and the corona is long and deep yellow.

Galtonia. This is a lesser known bulb. Only one species, *Galtonia candicans,* sometimes called summer hyacinth, is generally grown in Europe. It is 80 to 100 cm (2 ft 8 in to 3 ft 4 in) high and bears a loose raceme of greenish, bell-shaped flowers that open successively from the bottom up. They appear in August. Stronger bulbs produce two stems. Galtonia will grow in almost any location but does best in light soil and a warm, sunny situation. It requires a light cover of leaves or evergreen boughs for the winter, particularly the first few years after being put out. Fading flowers are unattractive and should therefore be removed. It is propagated by means of seeds which are produced in ample numbers. Seeds are sown in February in trays in a greenhouse and the seedlings planted out in May. As a rule, they do not flower till the second year. They are also good for cutting, opening to the very last flower in the vase.

Scilla. Squill, scilla, is the most widely grown of the small bulbs. This is a large genus with a great many species and varieties. The most popular is *Scilla sibirica,* a small plant 10 to 20 cm (4 to 8 in) high, that bears brilliant-blue, drooping, bell-shaped flowers in March. Some species are larger with a greater number of flowers that may be starshaped and white. Scillas are very adaptable but do best in light soil in a sunny situation. They spread by seeding themselves and in good conditions will form masses in a few years' time which are very striking in the rock garden or as an underplanting to open deciduous shrubs. Illustrated here are the white variety *S. sibirica alba* and the blue 'Spring Beauty'.

Puschkinia. This genus is named after Count A. A. Muschin-Puschkin, Russian chemist and botanist, and includes two species of small bulbous plants native to Asia Minor and the Caucasus. The bulb is small, about 2 cm ($^3/_4$ in) across, globose and white with greyish-brown skin. The leaves are broadly linear, about 1.5 cm ($^1/_2$ in) wide. The bell-shaped flowers greatly resemble those of squill; they are pale porcelain-blue and borne in dense clusters on 15 cm (6 in) high stems in March and April, as a rule. *Puschkinia scilloides,* native to the Caucasus, is about 15 cm

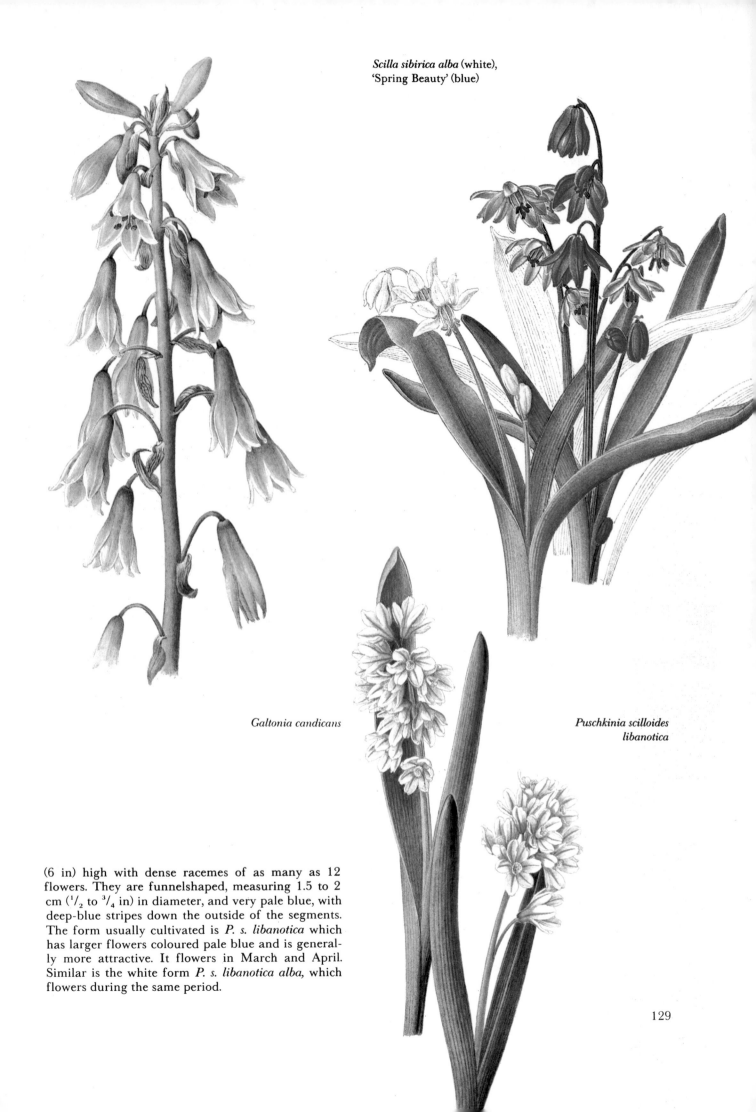

Scilla sibirica alba (white),
'Spring Beauty' (blue)

Galtonia candicans

Puschkinia scilloides
libanotica

(6 in) high with dense racemes of as many as 12
flowers. They are funnelshaped, measuring 1.5 to 2
cm ($^1/_2$ to $^3/_4$ in) in diameter, and very pale blue, with
deep-blue stripes down the outside of the segments.
The form usually cultivated is *P. s. libanotica* which
has larger flowers coloured pale blue and is generally more attractive. It flowers in March and April.
Similar is the white form *P. s. libanotica alba,* which
flowers during the same period.

Leucojum. The snowflake, leucojum, is one of the best known of the spring flowers. It requires partial shade and a moist situation where it will form large masses of lovely flowers, which can be used also for cutting. *Leucojum vernum*, 25 to 30 cm (10 to 12 in) high, grows freely in the wild and flowers in March and April. The flowers, usually one or two on a stem, are about 2 cm ($^3/_4$ in) across and coloured white with a green spot at the tip of each segment. *L. aestivum* is more robust, 30 to 50 cm (1 ft to 1 ft 8 in) high, with clusters of five to nine flowers on a stem, appearing from May until June. *L. autumnale*, native to Spain, Portugal, Sardinia and Sicily, flowers in August and September and also requires a warmer location. The flowers have pale red spots at the base of the segments.

Galanthus. The snowdrop, galanthus, is one of the first flowers of spring, often appearing while snow is still on the ground. *Galanthus nivalis*, commonly growing in the wild, has flowers that measure about 2 cm ($^3/_4$ in). The 'more modern' species *G. elwesii* has globose flowers about twice that size. Both will grow practically anywhere, but do best in light, humus-

Galanthus nivalis

Leucojum vernum

rich soil under deciduous trees where there is plenty of moisture in spring. They spread rapidly, one bulb forming a large clump of lovely snowdrops within a few years. They die back soon after flowering. *G. nivalis* has many varieties: *G. nivalis florepleno* with double perianth segments, *G. nivalis atkinsii*—taller with large green blotches, and *G. nivalis* 'S. Arnott'—pretty, with green blotches on the segments and a pleasant fragrance.

Lilium. *Lilium speciosum* is one of the loveliest of all lilies for planting out. It is 80 to 140 cm (2 ft 8 in to 4 ft 8 in) high with broadly lanceolate leaves arranged alternately on a dark stem. The flowers, about 10 cm (4 in) across, are borne in large, loose racemes. They are white with a raspberry-pink tinge and crimson spots and the edges of the perianth segments are often attractively wavy. This lily flowers in August and has a lovely, sweet perfume. There are several variously coloured forms: *L. s. album*—completely white with a pink tinge on the outside and brown pollen, *L. s. roseum*—with pink flowers more or less like those of the species, *L. s. rubrum*—one of

130

the best known with deep rose flowers and reddish-violet stigma. Commonly cultivated nowadays are the hybrids obtained by crossing *L. speciosum* with other lilies, primarily *L. auratum*. Propagation is by means of bulb scales as well as from seed and in a congenial site this lily is surprisingly undemanding and hardy.

The lily 'Black Beauty' is a cross between *L. speciosum punctatum* and *L. henryi*. It has the typical Turk's-cap flowers, 10 cm (4 in) long, with deep-red perianth segments and large green nectaries. They have unusually long stalks and are arranged in a very loose and tall raceme. This is a hardy and robust variety with no special requirements and is excellent for cutting.

Lilium speciosum

Lilium 'Black Beauty'

The lily 'Nutmegger' belongs to the group of Mid-Century hybrids. This is a very widespread group of hybrids derived from crosses between *L. hollandicum* and *L. tigrinum* in the 1950s, as indicated by the name mid-century. Traits inherited from the parent plants include vigour and in some cases also the ability to form bulbils in the axils of the leaves. They flower in June and are coloured yellow, orange or red. The group is divided into three divisions according to the position of the flowers: 1. lilies with upward-facing flowers 'Enchantment', 2. lilies with outward-facing flowers, 3. lilies with drooping, downward-facing flowers, which includes 'Nutmegger'. This is an attractive, hardy form with very good characteristics. The long stem bears as many as thirty Turk's-cap flowers on long pedicels which are good for cutting. The flowering period is in July.

Another Mid-Century hybrid, 'Enchantment', is one of the best known of the group. It is 80 to 90 cm (2 ft 8 in to 3 ft) high and makes numerous bulbils in the axils of the leaves. The flower is similar to that of *L. tigrinum* but slanting upward. It does very well in the garden and is just as good for bedding as for forcing.

Lilium regale is a very popular and widely cultivated lily. The stems are 80 to 140 cm (2 ft 8 in to 4 ft 8 in) long and bear clusters of as many as 20 white trumpet flowers with a yellow throat and rose-to-red median stripe on the outside. The flowers measure 12 cm ($4^1/_2$ in) across and have a very strong, almost unpleasant fragrance. They appear in July. This is a hardy lily and may be planted in sun but shade should be provided for the ground surface. The soil can contain lime. It is propagated easily and rapidly from seed; some seedlings may not flower until the second year. *L. regale* is often used for breeding pur-

Lilium 'Nutmegger'

Lilium 'Enchantment'

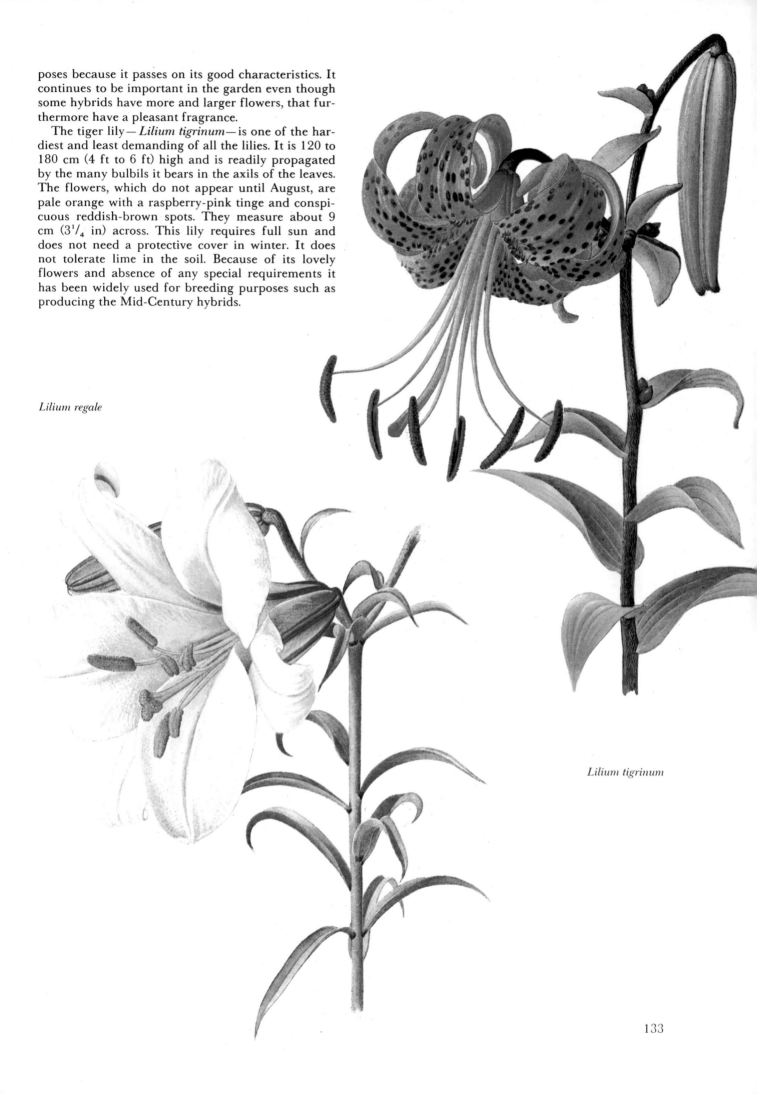

poses because it passes on its good characteristics. It
continues to be important in the garden even though
some hybrids have more and larger flowers, that furthermore have a pleasant fragrance.

The tiger lily—*Lilium tigrinum*—is one of the hardiest and least demanding of all the lilies. It is 120 to
180 cm (4 ft to 6 ft) high and is readily propagated
by the many bulbils it bears in the axils of the leaves.
The flowers, which do not appear until August, are
pale orange with a raspberry-pink tinge and conspi-
cuous reddish-brown spots. They measure about 9
cm ($3^1/_4$ in) across. This lily requires full sun and
does not need a protective cover in winter. It does
not tolerate lime in the soil. Because of its lovely
flowers and absence of any special requirements it
has been widely used for breeding purposes such as
producing the Mid-Century hybrids.

Lilium regale

Lilium tigrinum

133

less often in gardens but even there it is lovely in its own way. It is 80 to 180 cm (2 ft 8 in to 6 ft) high with characteristic Turk's-cap flowers about 5 cm (2 in) in diameter and usually coloured a soft lilac with darker spots. In some varieties or hybrids the colour may be white or red, but never a bright hue. The flowering period is in June and July. *L. martagon* does poorly in sun and should thus be planted in partial shade. It thrives in limy soil and will last many years bedded out in the garden without any particular care. Propagation is by means of offsets; if multiplied from seed it takes a long time for it to grow to flowering size. The fragrance is rather unpleasant.

The lily 'Connecticut Glow' belongs to the group of Connecticut hybrids. These are crosses between *L. flaviflorum* and *L. x hollandicum* showing the pronounced influence of *L. tigrinum.* They come in

Lilium martagon

Lilium henryi

Lilium henryi is a striking lily native to the mountains of central China. It is 150 to 200 cm (5 ft to 6 ft 8 in) high and the drooping flowers on long pedicels, borne in large racemes of 15 to 20 flowers, are coloured pale orange. They are without fragrance and in the centre, round the nectaries, there are prominent, 6 to 7 mm long papillae. The flowering period is in August. *L. henryi* will grow in almost any location; the one requirement is soil containing lime and this plus its late flowering make it a very good solitary subject for parks and gardens. Crossing of the type species with other lilies produced many new forms. The hybrids have larger flowers and come in a wider range of colours so that they are becoming far more popular than the type species. All backcrosses from *L. henryi* are classed as Henryi hybrids.

The Turk's-cap lily, *Lilium martagon,* grows wild in the open woodlands of central Europe. It is seen colours ranging from yellow to red and chestnut brown. 'Connecticut Glow' has a strong stem with dark green leaves and 8 to 10 flowers which generally appear in mid-July. The flowers are borne in an erect umbel on long pedicels; they are dark carmine outside and paler carmine inside. This is a hardy lily that is easy to grow. It requires full sun and good garden soil and is suitable for group planting and also for cutting.

The lily 'Golden Splendor' belongs to the group of Aurelian hybrids, which have revolutionized the growing of lilies in the garden. They are crosses between trumpet lilies and *L. henryi* and there are so many of them that they are divided according to the shape of the flower into several sections: trumpet,

Lilium 'Golden Splendor'

cupped, flat and Turk's-cap. They are 100 to 200 cm (6 ft to 13 ft) high and the flowers, which come in various colours, are produced from July until September. These are robust, hardy lilies needing no special care and most of them tolerate soil containing lime. The flowers are often very large and heavy and should therefore be tied to stakes. They do best in partial shade in good garden soil. 'Golden Splendor' is one of the best varieties of the Golden Clarion strain of the trumpet Aurelian hybrids. It usually bears 8 to 20 broadly trumpet-shaped flowers coloured a warm yellow.

Lilium 'Connecticut Glow'

135

Fritillaria. This is a large genus of bulbous plants, only two of which are generally cultivated: *Fritillaria imperialis* and *F. meleagris*. They differ not only in appearance but also in their requirements. The former has a larger bulb which should be planted at a depth of 15 to 20 cm (6 to 8 in), the latter has a smaller bulb which should be planted 6 to 8 cm (2 to 3 in) deep. The bulbs may be left in the ground for a number of years. The flowering period is in April; in June the plants die down and the leaves disappear. Propagation is by offsets. Crown Imperial, *F. imperialis,* is a tall (about 1 m [3 ft] high) and demanding plant. The strong stem terminates in a whorl of 12 bell-like flowers up to 6 cm (2¼ in)

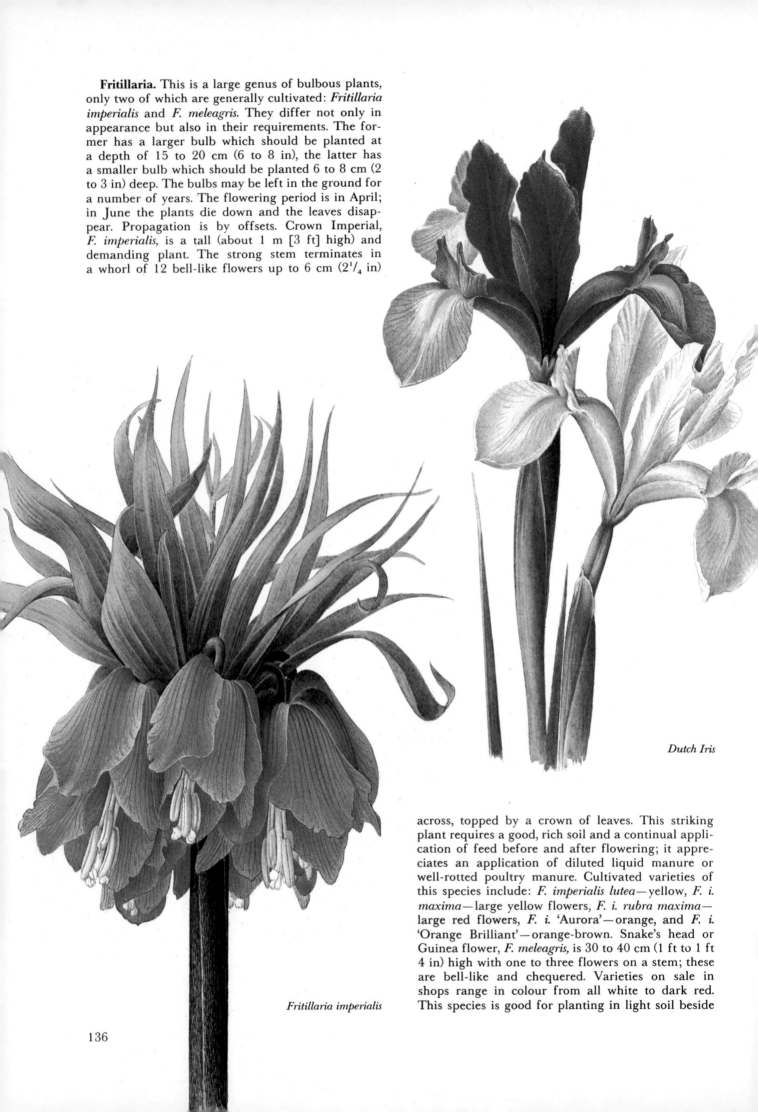

Dutch Iris

Fritillaria imperialis

across, topped by a crown of leaves. This striking plant requires a good, rich soil and a continual application of feed before and after flowering; it appreciates an application of diluted liquid manure or well-rotted poultry manure. Cultivated varieties of this species include: *F. imperialis lutea*—yellow, *F. i. maxima*—large yellow flowers, *F. i. rubra maxima*—large red flowers, *F. i.* 'Aurora'—orange, and *F. i.* 'Orange Brilliant'—orange-brown. Snake's head or Guinea flower, *F. meleagris,* is 30 to 40 cm (1 ft to 1 ft 4 in) high with one to three flowers on a stem; these are bell-like and chequered. Varieties on sale in shops range in colour from all white to dark red. This species is good for planting in light soil beside a pool or stream because it prefers a moist atmosphere. Here it does well and is very striking. Frequently cultivated forms are: 'Artemis', 'Emperor', 'Orion', 'Pomona' and the white form *F. meleagris alba*.

Iris. Of the bulbous irises the Dutch irises (raised from *Iris xiphium praecox* and *I. tingitana*) are used for forcing and sold in shops in spring. The others are very similar. In gardens they are mostly grown for cutting but are also good in beds of perennials.

English irises (forms and hybrids of *I. xiphioides*) are hardy plants, but Dutch irises and Spanish irises (*I. xiphium*) are less hardy. They need sun and well-drained soil. When the flowers have faded and the foliage has died down the bulbs should be lifted and planted out again in October, otherwise they will put out new leaves in autumn and may suffer damage by frost. Irises multiply readily by offsets.

Erythronium. This genus has several species, the one most frequently cultivated is dog's-tooth violet, *Erythronium dens-canis*, which has not only lovely flowers but also very decorative leaves. These are about 15 cm (6 in) long and coloured green with purple marbling. The stems are about 20 cm (8 in) long and terminated by a single, pendent flower resembling the cyclamen. It measures 3.5 cm ($1\frac{1}{4}$ in) across and is coloured violet to purple. The flowering period is March to April. Some varieties are pale mauve, 'Lilac Wonder', others pink, 'Pink Perfection', 'Rose Beauty', and there is also a white form, 'Snowflake'. The bulbs should be planted in light, well-drained soil and a lightly shaded location in August or September. It is best to leave it permanently in one spot, for it takes a number of years for it to become established. Propagation is by offsets. It dies down in summer.

Erythronium dens-canis

Fritillaria meleagris

137

weeks in the vase. It is planted in groups. *A. ostrows-kianum,* only 15 to 20 cm (6 to 8 in) high, with umbels of deep pinkish-red flowers in June and July. It requires a light soil and sunny situation. Also very good for growing in the garden are *A. karataviense* with round umbels of lilac-pink flowers in late April and May, *A. christophii,* one of the loveliest, with large round umbel (as much as 25 to 30 cm [10 to 12 in] in diameter) of violet flowers, the huge *A. giganteum* and the white—flowered *A. neapolitanum.*

Chionodoxa. Glory of the Snow, chionodoxa, is one of the easiest bulbs to grow, reaching a height of 15 to 30 cm (6 to 12 in). It forms clumps of delicate star-like flowers, generally in various shades of blue. *Chionodoxa luciliae alba* is white, *C. luciliae rosea* is pink, 'Pink Giant' has large pink flowers, *C. gigantea* has large, pale-blue flowers, and *C. sardensis* has brilliant-blue flowers with small white centres. The flowering period is in March; the plants die down in May. They spread freely by seeding themselves, making the best clumps in light soil and a slightly shaded position.

Ornithogalum. This is a large genus of plants that are not widely cultivated because many need a warmer climate and are often killed by frost. A hardy species and thus suited for growing in the garden is the Star of Bethlehem—*Ornithogalum umbellatum.*

Chionodoxa luciliae (blue) and its variety 'Pink Giant' (pink)

Allium moly (golden yellow), *A. ostrowskianum* (deep pink)

Allium. This genus, which includes the onion, leek and garlic, embraces a great number of species, many of which are decorative. Their value, however, is lessened by the fact that all have a garlic-like scent, although this disappears when the flowers are cut. Some are lovely plants even after the flowers have faded. Smaller bulbs should be planted at a depth of 6 cm ($2^{1}/_{4}$ in), larger ones 10 to 15 cm (4 to 6 in) deep. They should be left undisturbed in the ground for several years; if they are to be transplanted, then they should be moved in autumn after all the leaves have turned yellow. Illustrated are two species: *Allium moly,* 20 to 25 cm (8 to 10 in) high, with umbels of 10 to 40 golden-yellow flowers which appear in July. When cut it will last about three

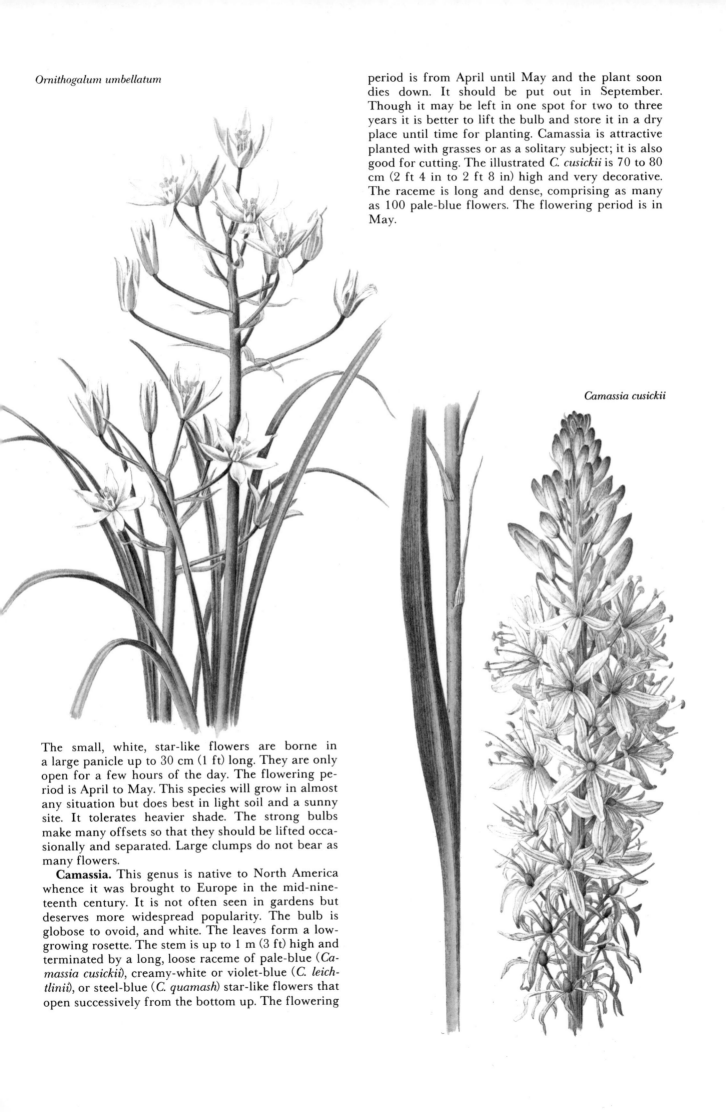

Ornithogalum umbellatum

period is from April until May and the plant soon dies down. It should be put out in September. Though it may be left in one spot for two to three years it is better to lift the bulb and store it in a dry place until time for planting. Camassia is attractive planted with grasses or as a solitary subject; it is also good for cutting. The illustrated *C. cusickii* is 70 to 80 cm (2 ft 4 in to 2 ft 8 in) high and very decorative. The raceme is long and dense, comprising as many as 100 pale-blue flowers. The flowering period is in May.

Camassia cusickii

The small, white, star-like flowers are borne in a large panicle up to 30 cm (1 ft) long. They are only open for a few hours of the day. The flowering period is April to May. This species will grow in almost any situation but does best in light soil and a sunny site. It tolerates heavier shade. The strong bulbs make many offsets so that they should be lifted occasionally and separated. Large clumps do not bear as many flowers.

Camassia. This genus is native to North America whence it was brought to Europe in the mid-nineteenth century. It is not often seen in gardens but deserves more widespread popularity. The bulb is globose to ovoid, and white. The leaves form a low-growing rosette. The stem is up to 1 m (3 ft) high and terminated by a long, loose raceme of pale-blue (*Camassia cusickii*), creamy-white or violet-blue (*C. leichtlinii*), or steel-blue (*C. quamash*) star-like flowers that open successively from the bottom up. The flowering

CORMS
AND TUBERS

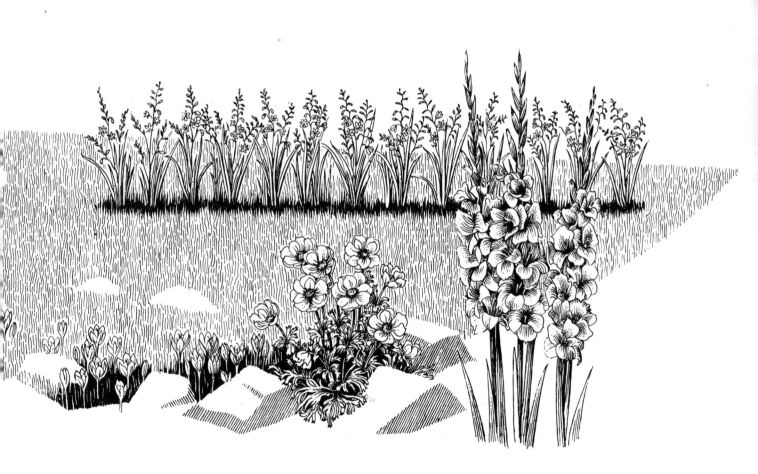

These are generally plants that flower in late summer and autumn. They are grown from corms and tubers which are of varied shape. Corms and tubers differ from bulbs in that they are solid right through instead of being composed of layers or tunics. Physiologically, however, they are the same, with alternating periods of growth and rest when the plant dies back, reflecting the fact that most corms and tubers are native to steppe regions, where this resting stage underground has a survival value. It enables them to live, in a dormant state, through adverse climatic conditions, growth being resumed when conditions are again favourable. Whereas bulbs are planted out in autumn and flower in spring, corms and tubers are put out in spring and flower in summer or autumn.

CULTIVATION

Cultivation of corms and tubers differs. Some are easy to grow, such as gladiolus, while others are more difficult, such as tuberous begonias. All, however, require a lot of food and deplete the soil to a marked degree. For this reason they should be put in a different bed every year and provided with liberal doses of organic fertilizer.

Gladiolus is one of the most popular and widely cultivated flowers of this group and is most useful for cutting. In the vase, gladioli will open to the very last bud; and they should be cut when the first two blooms are just opening. They are not nearly as striking in a bedding scheme, as the plants do not stand upright and there are nearly always some fading flowers to detract from the beauty of those in full bloom.

Gladiolus corms are bought in winter and spring. It is important only to buy healthy ones. Gladiolus has no special requirements and will grow in practically any soil except extremely poor soil. The bed should be in a sunny and sheltered spot, for in an exposed site wind may cause the stems to bend or even break, and in shade they flower poorly. The soil should be deeply dug and well fertilized. Corms should be planted whole, with the basal plate downward (so the buds can grow straight up), about 10 cm (4 in) deep, spaced 8 to 10 cm (3 to 4 in) apart.

If gladiolus is left to flower in the bed, the spike should be removed as soon as the blooms have faded, and weeding and watering continued. The corms should be lifted in dry weather in September or October but preferably sooner because disease may be transmitted from the foliage to the corm, particularly in moist conditions, and will spread when the corms are stored. Before lifting the corm cut off the stem about 10 to 15 cm (4 to 6 in) above the ground and loosen the soil round the corm. Then clean the corms carefully and dry them in a warm, well-aired place for at least three weeks. When they are dry, pull away the remains of the old corm, trim off the roots, break off the remaining top parts and strip off the outmost layer of the new corm. Healthy corms should be stored in a dry room at a temperature of 5° to 10°C (41 to 50°F). It is recommended to sprinkle peat between the corms; this evens out changes in temperature and atmospheric moisture.

Dahlias, perhaps the best known and most widely cultivated of all corms and tubers, are versatile flowers which can be used for many purposes. They are always lovely planted by themselves. Best for this purpose are the decorative dahlias, but only in large gardens. For smaller gardens the cactus, semi-cactus and ball-flowered dahlias are best, and for small front gardens the pompon or collerette dahlias. Dahlias are also attractive planted with ornamental shrubs, forsythia, spiraea, weigela and any of those that have decorative fruit or foliage in the autumn. Small, single dahlias are suitable for the rock garden where they make a bright, colourful display in the autumn when little else is in flower there; they are particularly attractive associated with ornamental grasses. All dahlias, excepting the decorative and single forms, can be used for cutting.

Dahlias are easy to cultivate and will grow practically anywhere. They do best, however, in a sunny and sheltered situation. Any soil, except an extremely dry or soggy one, will do, but it must be well fertilized. The tubers should be planted about 10 cm (4 in) deep from May onwards and will sprout in about 20 days. During the growing period they should be watered and solitary specimens tied to a stake. Flowers should be removed as soon as they fade. The tubers are usually not lifted until after the first frost has killed the foliage. Before lifting the tubers, cut the stems down to about 10 cm (4 in), then place the tubers stem downwards on slats and spread a layer of peat in between. They may be stored together with gladiolus corms. Dahlias are usually propagated by dividing the tubers. Strong tubers should always be divided before planting so that they do not make too many shoots, which results in fewer flowers. This should be done in spring, a few days before planting. As with most decorative flowers dahlias should be put in a different bed each year and only healthy tubers used.

Tuberous begonias are striking plants grown mostly in city parks. Large-flowered and multi-flowered begonias may be used in gardens in partially shaded locations. They are pretty as edging plants for beds and are lovely planted in grass in small groups. They can also be used for floral decoration in bowls and jardinières, hanging down over the sides, or in window boxes that face north.

Begonias are planted out in beds as young seedlings which can be purchased from a nursery with flowers about to open or else they are grown from tubers. Tubers should not be dried out or damaged by careless removal of the roots as this results in loss of vigour. They should be planted in the first half of April in pots or boxes containing peat or light soil, put in a light place at normal room temperature and watered moderately. Large seedlings are put out in beds at the end of May, after they have been hardened off, spaced about 20 cm (8 in) apart. The soil should be free draining, rich and slightly acid. A mixture of peat and well-rotted compost is best. Liquid feed should be applied once every two weeks and faded flowers should be removed regularly. In autumn watering should be decreased so that the top parts die down. Tubers may also be put out directly into beds of light soil, in May, but then they will flower later. It is better for begonias to be grown on and kept flowering for as long as possible until well into autumn.

As soon as the top parts start to dry the plants should be lifted with a small trowel, the soil carefully removed and the stem broken off about 2 cm (¾ in) above the tuber. The tubers should then be placed beside each other in a box and stored in a well-aired room. When the soil has dried sufficiently and the remaining stem can be removed with ease then the tubers should be cleaned thoroughly. Roots should be removed with care so as not to damage the tubers. This is best done with sharp secateurs. Begonia tubers are stored in the same way as those of gladioli and dahlias.

Other corms and tubers exhibit marked differences. Their cultivation and use are not nearly as uniform as that of bulbs. Some are hardy, others require a protective cover in winter, and still others need to be stored in a frost-proof place for the winter. Crocuses and colchicums include several species that are cultivated in the same way as bulbs—being planted in autumn and flowering in early spring. All, however, are amongst the loveliest of garden flowers and therefore deserve the extra care and effort required to grow them.

Cactus dahlia, spider-like type

Ball dahlia

Semi-cactus dahlia

144

Dahlia. The dahlia is called the queen of late summer. No other flower can match dahlias for their wide range of brilliant colours (from white to almost black), and wide variety of sizes and shapes (reminiscent of chrysanthemums, asters, water-lilies and peonies). The only things these beauties lack are fragrance and the colour blue.

Dahlias are quite easy to breed and have given rise to countless new varieties. Their classification into different groups is extremely difficult and there is none that is universally accepted so that their division in different countries varies. Also new shapes that cannot be put in any of the groups are being produced all the time—these are relegated to the 'miscellaneous' section. Nevertheless, there are several basic groups into which dahlias can be divided. The classification most commonly used nowadays is the garden classification adopted at the symposium in Brussels in 1962 which includes the following ten groups:

1. *Single-flowered dahlias.* This group has a single row of ray petals surrounding an open yellow central disc. These include all single-flowered varieties ranging in size from dwarf to 50 cm (1 ft 8 in) and more in height. They are usually grown in mixtures in the garden and are fairly easy to propagate, even from seed.

2. *Anemone-flowered dahlias.* A more recent group that is becoming increasingly popular. In these the flowers have a single row of flattened ray petals surrounding a raised centre with tubular petals round the rim. They are of medium height and good for mass planting.

3. *Collerette dahlias.* A similarly recent popular group; the plants, about 1 m (3 ft) high, are smothered with flowers that have a single inner row (collar) of small petals, usually of a different colour from the outer row of petals. In other words, the flower has three rows: a row of flattened ray petals, a row of small petals, and a yellow central disc.

4. *Peony-flowered dahlias.* This is a less widely grown group. The flowers are semi-double with central disc visible when they are fully open. They consist of two or more rows of flattened or slightly wavy ray petals. The plants grow to a height of 120 cm (4 ft).

5. *Decorative dahlias.* This is one of the main groups and the most popular in Europe. The plants are robust, growing to a height of 2 m (6 ft) or more and the flowers measure as much as 30 cm (1 ft) in diameter. They are fully double with no central disc. The petals are broad, more or less flat and pointed.

6. *Ball dahlias,* also called large pompons. A popular group growing to a height of 100 to 120 cm (3 ft 4 in to 4 ft) with fully globular or slightly flattened flowers, more than 10 cm (4 in) across. The petals have more or less incurved edges and are arranged in regular formation.

7. *Pompon dahlias.* These are great favourites in the small garden. According to international standards the flowers must not be more than 5 cm (2 in) in diameter, though so called medium-size pompons

Pompon dahlias

measuring 5 to 10 cm ((2 to 4 in) across are admitted. The flowers are fully double, perfectly globular, and the petals tubular, short and blunt. They are usually brightly coloured.

8. *Cactus dahlias.* This is the second main group as regards number of cultivated species. The plants are 120 to 180 cm (4 ft to 6 ft) high, the flowers 10 to 15 cm (4 to 6 in) in diameter. This group is divided into three slightly-different types: the classic, fully double type with pointed, rolled petals, the spider-like type with rolled petals curving inward, and the so-called fimbra or antler-like type with petals forked at the tip.

9. *Semi-cactus dahlias.* A very popular and attractive group. The plants are about 150 cm (5 ft) high, the flowers 12 to 15 cm (5 to 6 in) across. They are halfway between the decorative and cactus dahlias with ray petals broad at the base and rolled at the tip, which is pointed.

10. *Miscellaneous.* This group includes all those dahlias which cannot be fitted into any of the other groups. They include the chrysanthemum-flowered, water-lily-flowered and botanical peculiarities.

Decorative dahlia

146

Cactus dahlia

Cactus dahlia, type
fimbra

Dahlias with
simple flowers

147

Gladiolus. Most often cultivated are the following varieties: 'D'Artagnan', one of the large-flowered varieties that are very popular in the garden for the beauty and size of their blooms. It is a fairly early form with large expanded florets that have a blotch on the lower petals. It is healthy, not particularly demanding in its requirements, easy to multiply and easy to grow. As with all gladioli the corms must be lifted in autumn and stored in a frost-proof room at a temperature of 6° to 10°C (43° to 50°F) for the winter.

'Blue Diamond', one of the blue forms of gladiolus that are very popular even though they are usually

Gladiolus 'Blue Diamond'

Gladiolus 'D'Artagnan'

148

difficult to propagate. It belongs to the large-flowered early-flowering group. The stem bears up to 18 florets with as many as 5 open at one time.

'Pink Sensation', a late-flowering form of the large-flowered group. The florets are big with a large blotch marked with purple.

'Mexico', a large-flowered variety with 18 florets to a spike. Often as many as 8 open at the same time.

The gladiolus varieties cultivated nowadays are of very complex origin, being derived from a great many African and European species, and breeders continue their efforts thus adding ever new forms to the existing assortment. In 1880 there were about 2,000 varieties and today there are more than 100,000. The most numerous group are the large-flowered gladioli. They are robust with strong, firm stems and a dense spike about 50 cm (1 ft 8 in) long with 15 to 20 flowers. Early varieties usually flower in July, mid-season ones in August and late varieties in September. From the very first breeders have been trying to obtain varieties that are resistant to frost but so far without success. They are also unable to breed scented varieties. When breeders succeed in producing large-flowered, fragrant varieties with all the existing good features then gladiolus will be the most popular of all flowers in the garden.

Gladiolus 'Pink Sensation'

Gladiolus 'Mexico'

149

Primulinus gladioli. This popular modern group of large-flowered varieties are derived from the type species *Gladiolus primulinus,* which grows wild in tropical Africa. It was selected for breeding purposes for the characteristic hooded shape and yellow colour of the flowers, both of which are inherited by the offspring. Breeding has yielded very attractive varieties, one of which, Jan Voerman, is shown in the illustration. The flowers have the characteristic hooded shape with as many as seventeen on a stem, at least four of which are always open at the same time.

Convallaria majalis. Lily of the valley is a universal favourite in the garden and very easy to grow.

The spot selected should be one where its tendency to spread by its tubers does not matter. Sprouting tubers, two or three years old if possible, should be planted out fairly close together and watered. Until the plants spread it is necessary to eliminate weeds; later they will cover the soil with their leaves and will require no further care. A fine compost should be applied every autumn and lime every second year so that the plants do not deplete the soil of nutrients. Garden forms with larger flowers and longer stalks are cultivated in addition to the type species. There is also a form with pink flowers and one with double pink flowers.

Gladiolus primulinus variety 'Jan Voerman'

Convallaria majalis

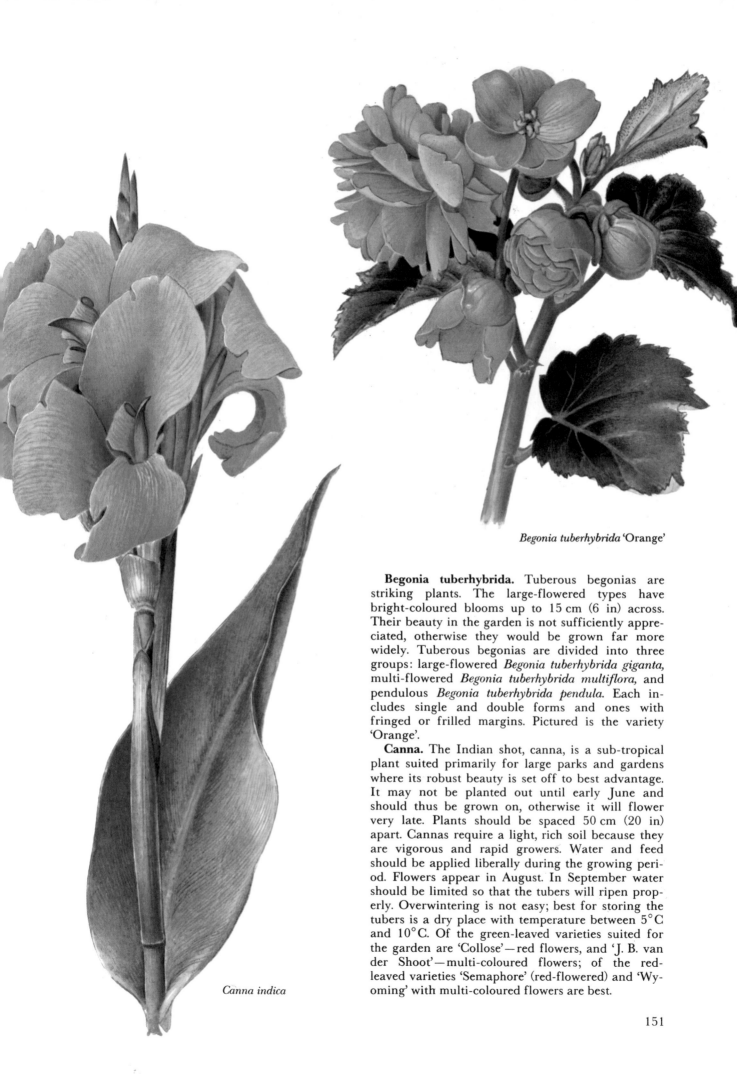

Begonia tuberhybrida 'Orange'

Begonia tuberhybrida. Tuberous begonias are striking plants. The large-flowered types have bright-coloured blooms up to 15 cm (6 in) across. Their beauty in the garden is not sufficiently appreciated, otherwise they would be grown far more widely. Tuberous begonias are divided into three groups: large-flowered *Begonia tuberhybrida giganta,* multi-flowered *Begonia tuberhybrida multiflora,* and pendulous *Begonia tuberhybrida pendula.* Each includes single and double forms and ones with fringed or frilled margins. Pictured is the variety 'Orange'.

Canna. The Indian shot, canna, is a sub-tropical plant suited primarily for large parks and gardens where its robust beauty is set off to best advantage. It may not be planted out until early June and should thus be grown on, otherwise it will flower very late. Plants should be spaced 50 cm (20 in) apart. Cannas require a light, rich soil because they are vigorous and rapid growers. Water and feed should be applied liberally during the growing period. Flowers appear in August. In September water should be limited so that the tubers will ripen properly. Overwintering is not easy; best for storing the tubers is a dry place with temperature between 5°C and 10°C. Of the green-leaved varieties suited for the garden are 'Collose'—red flowers, and 'J. B. van der Shoot'—multi-coloured flowers; of the red-leaved varieties 'Semaphore' (red-flowered) and 'Wyoming' with multi-coloured flowers are best.

Canna indica

151

Crocus chrysanthus

Crocus biflorus

Crocus. Crocuses are favourite spring flowers that have been cultivated for thousands of years. The genus numbers almost a hundred species growing wild primarily in the Mediterranean region. They are popular for planting in the rock garden, in grass, under shrubs and in various odd spots where they flower in spring and then die down. Crocuses are divided into two groups—those that flower in spring and those that flower in autumn. The autumn-flowering crocuses are not widely grown; some of them are *naked* in autumn like colchicums. Spring-flowering crocuses include a great many species and varieties in various colours. Most widely grown are the large-flowered hybrids. Even though they have corms their cultivation is the same as for the bulbous plants, tulips and narcissi.

Crocus chrysanthus grows wild in Greece and Asia Minor. It is one of the most important species in gardening for it has been used to produce many noteworthy varieties such as the white forms 'Snow Bunting', 'Warley White' and 'Lady Killer', the yellow forms 'Advance', 'Cream Beauty', 'E. A. Bowles' and 'E. P. Bowles', 'Mariette' and the blue forms 'Blue Bird', 'Blue Pearl', 'Blue Giant' and 'Princess Beatrix'.

152

Crocus biflorus grows wild in Italy, the Balkans and Asia Minor as far as Iran. The flowers are medium-sized and very variable in colour. The leaves appear at the same time as the flowers. Many varieties are grown in gardens, notably *C. biflorus adamicus*—pale violet, deep violet outside, *C.b.alexandrii*—pure white inside, dark purple outside, *C.b.argenteus*—very pretty, violet, striped purple, and *C.b.weldenii albus*—one of the loveliest crocuses of all with pure white flowers.

Crocus vernus

Crocus speciosus

Crocus vernus is the term embracing all the garden varieties, which have much larger flowers than the wild species. They flower in spring. Most frequently cultivated varieties include: white—'Jean d'Arc', 'Peter Pan' and 'Kathleen Parlow', blue to deep purple—'Early Perfection' and 'Queen of the Blues', blue-white or striped forms—'Cinderella', 'Pickwick' and 'Striped Beauty', and the yellow, very early form 'Dutch Yellow', known also as 'Large Yellow' or 'Yellow Giant'.

Crocus speciosus belongs to the group of autumn-flowering crocuses. It flowers in September, October and sometimes November. The flowers are large and pale blue with dark veins. The leaves appear after the flowers have faded. In congenial conditions it soon forms complete carpets of pale-blue delicate flowers.

Colchicum hybridum 'Violet Queen'

Iris reticulata 'Harmony'

Colchicum autumnale

Iris. Two species of dwarf iris found in Europe are *Iris reticulata* and *I. danfordiae*. They are small plants flowering very early in spring, with foliage dying back in summer. The size of the plants, flowering period, growth of leaves as well as period and manner of dormancy are similar to spring-flowering crocuses. Cultivation of dwarf irises is not easy. Usually it flowers only after the first, and sometimes also the second year after it is put out, then the corm weakens and breaks up into many cormlets, from which it is very difficult to grow new seedlings. How long dwarf iris will flower depends on the site. Best is a light, well-drained and nourishing soil and a sunny spot in the rock garden.

Crocosmia. Montbretia — *Crocosmia crocosmiiflora* — has flowers which look like small gladioli, usually coloured orange to brownish red. The corms sprout in spring and the plants bear flowers from July until the frost. They require a light, well-drained soil and warm, sunny situation. Corms are damaged by winter damp and therefore the soil surface should be covered with peat or a layer of leaves in winter. The corms should not be left in the same spot more than three years. They can be lifted every year in autumn, overwintered like gladioli corms and planted out again in spring. Propagation is by cormlets which are produced in abundance.

Colchicum. This genus numbers more than 50 species widespread in Europe, Asia and North Africa. They are small plants suited primarily for the rock garden or for planting in grass. The tubers should be planted in August about 10 cm (4 in) deep. The large leaves appear in spring and soon die down. They are followed in autumn by lovely violet-blue flowers, greatly resembling crocuses. In heavy, rich, moist soil in sun they soon spread and form profusely flowering clumps. They may be left in the same spot for many years. If the plants need to be moved the tubers should not be kept out of the ground for long. Propagation is by offsets, which generally reach flower-bearing size in the second year. A word of warning — colchicums are poisonous!

Crocosmia crocosmiiflora

Colchicum hybridum is the name under which are classed many lovely varieties produced by crossing *C. latifolium* (syn. *C. sibthorpii*) and *C. speciosum*. The illustrated 'Violet Queen' is deep lilac-pink, 'Autumn Queen' is dark violet with purple mosaic markings, 'The Giant' has large lilac-pink flowers, 'Lilac Wonder' is violet-blue and late-flowering, 'Princess Astrid' is dark pink with purple chequered markings and 'Water Lily' has large, double, lilac-pink flowers resembling a water-lily. Some of the less important colchicums do not flower until spring and are cultivated in the same manner as spring-flowering crocuses.

155

Anemone blanda

Anemone coronaria
'St. Brigid'

Anemone. Windflower, whose generic name, anemone, is derived from the Greek word *anemos* meaning wind because the petals, which are easily shed, become a plaything toyed with by the wind. The genus numbers 60 species that grow wild throughout the moderate regions of the northern hemisphere. Of those that have tubers and flower in spring, (from March to April), gardenworthy is the small *Anemone blanda,* growing wild in the Balkans and Asia Minor. It slightly resembles *A. nemorosa,* also growing in the wild, but the flowers are almost twice as large. Most popular for garden cultivation is *A. coronaria,* grown mainly for cutting. It is lovely in the rock garden, in

perennial beds and also in rough grass, to which it adds a bright spot of colour. The tubers are hard and if stored in a dry place will last as long as three years. Before they are planted out they must be soaked in lukewarm water for about one day. They should be planted about 5 cm (2 in) deep and 10 cm (4 in) apart, right side up, in March or April. They flower in late May and June. The tubers should be lifted in autumn after the plants have died down and stored like gladiolus corms. These anemones are sold in a mixture of colours, ones with single blooms under the name *A. coronaria* 'De Caen' and ones with double blooms under the name *A. c.* 'St. Brigid'.

156

Eranthis. Winter aconite is one of the earliest of all flowers. Its botanical name is derived from the Greek words *er,* meaning spring, and *anthos,* meaning flower. It is a small plant, native to southern Europe, with an irregularly formed tuber. The leaves appear after the yellow flowers have faded. The flowers close in the evening and in cloudy weather. *Eranthis hyemalis* is about 10 cm (4 in) high with pale yellow flowers which appear from February to March. Eranthis has no special requirements; it is ideal for the rock garden, in groups with other small early-flowering species and as an undercarpet to deciduous shrubs. It will grow many years in one spot, forming large clumps in time.

Tigridia. The tiger flower, tigridia, is a striking exotic flower native to Mexico, Guatemala and Peru. About 12 species grow in the wild but only *Tigridia pavonia,* and its hybrids, is widely grown in gardens. They are small, striking plants with brightly coloured

Tigridia pavonia

Eranthis hyemalis

flowers, measuring 10 to 15 cm (4 to 6 in) in diameter, and are the pride of every gardener when in bloom. The flowering period is from mid-July until September. Tigridia grows best in well-drained, humus-rich soil, a warm, sheltered site and full sun. It must be watered liberally during the growing period. The corms should be planted out in late April or early May about 10 cm (4 in) apart and 5 to 10 cm (2 to 4 in) deep, and the ground covered with a layer of peat or compost. The corms should be lifted in the second half of October, allowed to dry slowly, cleaned and stored in a frost-proof room.

autumn are planted in August. They appreciate a winter cover. Cyclamens are excellent for sheltered and shaded spots in the rock garden. They may also be planted in groups under tall trees or shrubs. Usually they do not reach their full glory until they have become established, which takes several years. *C. europaeum* (syn. *C. purpurascens*) grows wild throughout Europe. It is a hardy plant. The leaves are green with silvery markings on the upper surface and dark red below. The flowers, coloured purplish-pink with a small dark mouth, appear in August and September and have a very pleasant fragrance. *C. neapolitanum* (syn. *C. hederifolium*) grows throughout the Mediterranean region. It should be planted deep in the ground, as much as 20 cm (8 in), and flowers in late summer, later than the preceding species. The flowers are pink and without fragrance.

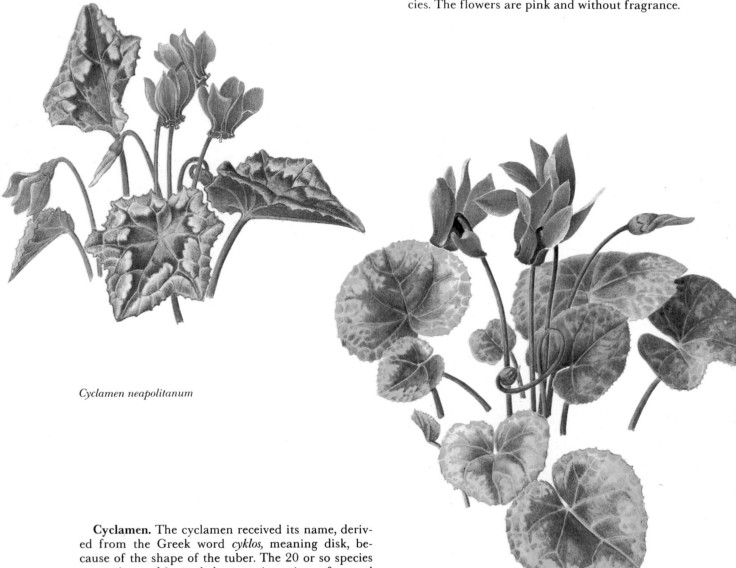

Cyclamen neapolitanum

Cyclamen europaeum

Cyclamen. The cyclamen received its name, derived from the Greek word *cyklos,* meaning disk, because of the shape of the tuber. The 20 or so species are native to the wooded mountain regions of central Europe and the Mediterranean. They make a ground rosette of firm, heart-shaped or kidney-shaped leaves from which rise long stems terminated by pendulous flowers with recurved petals. Most species die back during the resting period. The hothouse cyclamen *Cyclamen persicum* is the most well known. Species grown outdoors flower in spring or autumn and some have a pleasant fragrance. Those that flower in spring are planted in September, those that flower in

Eremurus. Foxtail lily, eremurus, produces a long stem, as much as 2.5 m (8 ft) long, with a large raceme of flowers that come in various colours and open successively from the bottom up. This is an exotic plant which is particularly good as a solitary subject in grass or in a group of smaller perennials. In central Europe all species flower in May and die back in summer, when the plants disappear from sight. The tuber is rather large and star-shaped. It should be planted in early autumn in a hole at least 40 cm (1 ft 4 in) deep with a layer of draining material, such as sharp sand, on the bottom. In normal winters there is no danger of its being killed by frost but still it is recommended to cover the ground with a layer of peat or leaves to protect the tuber from winter damp. In spring it soon sprouts and grows rapidly. The more it is fed the better it flowers.

Trillium grandiflorum roseum

Eremurus robustus

Trillium. The generic name of wake robin, trillium, is derived from the Latin word *trillix,* meaning triple, because almost all its parts are arranged in threes. The genus numbers some 30 species native to the wooded regions of North America and Asia. They require a semi-shaded location, best of all under thin, open trees. They do not tolerate a dry, warm situation, nor soil containing lime. *Trillium grandiflorum* is 30 to 45 cm (1 ft to 1 ft 6 in) high and flowers in May. The illustrated *T. grandiflorum roseum* has pinkish-red flowers; some forms have white petals shaded reddish-purple.

159

PERENNIALS

Perennials are plants that are long-lived and produce flowers and seed from the same root structure year after year. They are the largest group of garden plants and embrace a vast number of genera, species and varieties. These include dwarf species only 5 cm (2 in) high as well as giant plants 3 m (10 ft) high or more, plants that are difficult to grow as well as ones that are unpleasantly invasive, plants that are beautiful as well as ones that are of little aesthetic value. The small perennials grown in the rock garden are a special group.

Perennials generally give the garden a natural look and are therefore unsuitable for a formal scheme, but lovely in gardens with an irregular, informal layout.

The wide range of available perennials affords numerous possibilities for their use in the garden. Some flower very early, before the onset of spring, such as helleborus, others not until late autumn, such as chrysanthemum, some are decorative even in winter, such as grasses, stonecrop (sedum), and houseleek (sempervivum). Most perennials should be moved about every five years or so and at the same time divided. The gardener thus has the possibility of continually changing the make-up of the bedding schemes. Beds of perennials should always include several species that flower at different times so that there is colour from early spring

until autumn. Use should also be made of the fact that some have ornamental foliage.

When selecting plants for the perennial bed one should choose species and varieties that will create an attractive, harmonious effect and have similar requirements. The outline of the bed should be irregular, the same applying to the grouping of the individual species. There are, however, certain rules which should be kept in mind when planning the layout of the bed. First to go in should be the plants that will form the corner-stone of the bed—a perennial of striking habit or with striking flowers. These basic plants should not be placed in the middle of the bed but to the side, at about one-third its length or width, and there should be from one to four of them, depending on the size of the bed. Next come the companion plants that balance and brighten the bed and those that flower successively, producing ever-new colour combinations. They should not be placed in a row but in smaller or larger groups arranged in an irregular pattern so that the bed has a certain colour rhythm from spring until autumn. Plants with decorative foliage and ornamental grasses are then planted and last of all plants with a short flowering period for additional variety.

Perennials may also be combined with garden plants from other groups, such as bulbs and tubers. The former brighten beds of perennials that flower in summer and autumn and the latter brighten beds of spring and summer flowering perennials. Perennials are also attractive with annuals, particularly if they have a similar habit of growth, as well as with woody plants, especially low conifers. Perennials for cutting should be planted in an inconspicuous spot where their removal will not mar the bed. Flowers can also be cut from large tufts in the mixed bed, as usually they are produced in sufficient number.

Perennial beds in the garden should not be isolated. They should be backed by conifers, which heighten the colour effect, a green hedge, wall, pergola or building. In the front of the bed and near paths, benches and patios, the more delicate subjects should be planted, whereas those of more robust habit and more brightly coloured should be put at the back and in greater numbers.

There are many perennials suitable for the edge of the bed. They include rock cress (aubrieta), thrift (armeria), low-growing asters (callistephus), bellflowers (campanula), spurges (euphorbia), coral flowers (heuchera), St John's wort (hypericum) and primroses (primula). Some can be used as a substitute for turf, particularly in extremely dry locations, such as low-growing milfoil (achillea), alyssum and cerastium, low-growing chalk plants such as gypsophila and phlox. Plants good for this purpose in shade include bugle (ajuga), pig squeak (bergenia) and hepatica.

Perennials will grow and flower in the same spot for several years. Proper preparation of the site before planting, even for subjects with no special requirements, will save work in ensuing years. The soil should be dug thoroughly to a depth of at least 30 cm (1 ft), weeds eliminated, and compost or peat dug in to improve the soil. If the soil is heavy clay, sand, wood ashes and compost should be added with peat to increase drainage; if it is a light soil then heavier compost such as well-rotted manure should be dug in, in addition to peat.

The edge of the perennial bed requires constant care. Usually the bed is flanked by a grass lawn, the edge of which should always be evenly trimmed. It is helpful if a 20 cm (8 in) wide strip of tin sheet is inserted in the ground so that the top is level with the surface and does not show. The grass roots cannot penetrate this barrier, nor can those of the perennial plants, and the edge is kept neat and tidy with little effort.

Perennials are planted in beds generally in the autumn or spring. Spring-flowering species are planted in autumn, summer and autumn flowering species in spring. Exceptions are irises and peonies, which are planted in August. Young plants put out later in the autumn may need to be provided with a protective cover the first winter.

It is worthwhile to apply mulch (a layer or top-dressing of bulky organic matter which conserves moisture) to perennial beds and borders. Sterilized peat is best for this purpose, which also prevents the growth of weeds.

The perennial bed requires greatest care the first year; later, as the plants spread, they need less attention. For good growth the plants need moisture and a loose, open-soil surface, free of weeds. It is not necessary to apply feed the first couple of years after planting if the soil has been well prepared beforehand and a little compost put between the clumps for the winter. This provides good protection against frost as well as adequate additional nutrients, for the object is not luxuriant growth but profuse flowering. Weeds should be eliminated as necessary.

When they have faded the flower heads should be removed for they mar the beauty of the bed and the production of seeds weakens the plants. Some species become undesirably invasive by seeding themselves, in the case of others prompt removal of faded blooms promotes repeated flowering (especially in lupins and delphiniums). Leaves should be cut back to ground level when the plants die back, during summer and autumn, depending on the species. Some perennials are attractive in winter and may be left until spring to be cut back.

Perennials should be bought from a reliable nursery to ensure that the species and varieties purchased will come true and the plants be strong and healthy, or they may be propagated at home by division of the clumps, by offshoots, or from seed. Most species are propagated easily but the best, most developed, earliest and healthiest specimens must be used, otherwise the resultant plants will be of inferior quality.

Some species are quite invasive and in time eliminate the others. These should be kept within bounds by reducing the size of the root ball, cutting off rootlets, removing faded flowers so that the plants will not seed themselves, and if they do, by pulling up all young seedlings. Every plant is lovely only if it is in proper proportion to the others in the bedding scheme, otherwise it loses its value.

Gypsophila. Baby's breath or chalk plant— *Gypsophila paniculata*—is an unusual perennial which forms an airy mound about 1 m (3 ft) high bearing clouds of small flowers. Hence its use as a complementary feature to bouquets of cut flowers.

Baby's breath is native to south-eastern Europe and western Asia where it grows in sandy soil. There are about 80 species of both perennials and annuals, some of which are low and good for the rock garden. Of the taller species suitable for bedding and cutting the only one generally grown is *G. paniculata* and its varieties.

It is a suitable plant for dry, sunny spots. The flowers are white or pink and appear in July and August. It does not thrive in damp locations and tends to decay there in winter. Dry conditions should be provided even after the flowers have faded. Single varieties are propagated in spring from seed, double varieties, which are much prettier, are best propagated by grafting in summer. Double forms may also be propagated from seed but many of the resulting plants are single. The double varieties 'Bristol Fairy', 'Flamingo', and the small 'Rosy Veil', have to be grafted on to young seedlings of the species.

The clouds of small, dainty flowers add a light and airy touch to every floral arrangement and that is why *G. paniculata* is used almost exclusively for cutting. It is particularly good in bouquets of Sweet William *(Dianthus barbatus)*, Chabaud carnations *(Dianthus caryophyllus)*, bellflowers *(Campanula glomerata)*, tickseeds (coreopsis), blanket flowers (gaillardia), coral flowers (heuchera), or globe flowers (trollius). In floral arrangements consisting of two or more colourful species of perennials, baby's breath is excellent for softening the contrasts. It does not go well with roses. The flowers can be dried and retain their colour in this condition.

Astilbe. False goat's beard, astilbe, is an interesting perennial with feathery plumes of tiny flowers on tall stems. Various parts of the plume are often a different shade or even a different colour. Astilbe is native to south-eastern Asia, chiefly China and Japan, where there are some 35 species. These have interbred to such a degree that only hybrids are grown in today's gardens, some only 30 cm (1 ft) high, others as much as 2 m (6 ft) high. Best known is the *Astilbe arendsii* group which includes moderately-tall to tall plants that flower in from June until August and are excellent for cutting.

Astilbe arendsii is a typical perennial for cool, rather moist, sites in partial or full shade. It thrives in damper regions, particularly near bodies of water, and succeeds even in sun. The soil should be fertile, loamy and acidic. In such a situation the plants will do well for many years without any particular care. The roots of older plants generally surface and thus it is recommended to cover them with peat or compost. It is readily propagated by division in autumn or in spring.

Of the many cultivated varieties recommended for the garden are: the white 'Deutschland' and very ear-

Gypsophila paniculata

ly 'Irrlicht', with thick spikes, the pink very early 'Federsee' and summer-flowering 'Düsseldorf', the early red 'Fanal', with young leaves red later changing to green, the pink 'Cologne', the lilac-rose 'Amethyst', salmon-red 'Fire' and brick-red 'Red Sentinel'. Further attractive forms available include the *A. chinensis* group—moderately tall, very early, with broad, upright panicles, the *A. simplicifolia* group—short, early with fewer panicles slightly pendent at the tip, and the *A. thunbergii* group—tall, late, with broad, pendent panicles.

Astilbes are little used in gardens. They are more often seen in large groups in parks or by the waterside. They are striking as soon as they begin putting out leaves, for these may be red, green, brownish or brownish-red, depending on the variety. The foliage is attractive even after the flowers have faded and also when cut.

Astilbe is an excellent flower for cutting, lasting as long as fourteen days in a vase. Combinations with other flowers require careful consideration. Astilbe has the look of a striking wild flower and therefore should not be put together with flowers that have

elegant blooms such as roses and carnations. Various colour combinations with aruncus, primula, aconitum, iris and trollius are suitable. Astilbes are loveliest by themselves, either in one colour or a combination of all their pastel hues.

Aruncus. Goatsbeard—*Aruncus dioicus* (syn. *A. sylvester*)—resembles astilbe in appearance, but botanically it belongs to a different family. It is distributed throughout the moderate regions of the northern hemisphere, growing wild in damp situations in many European countries. It makes a splendid solitary specimen in the lawn.

Aruncus requires a damp, partially shaded situation and acid, humus-rich soil; it does poorly in sun and will not grow in dry conditions. It grows up to 150 cm (5 ft) tall and flowers in June. The foliage is handsome throughout the growing season, even after the flowers have faded. In the garden it is planted with astilbe, delphinium, eryngium, polygonatum and trollius; in the vase it is very effective in a large bouquet or with peonies or delphiniums. A large bouquet of white aruncus plumes in a large, light room is also lovely.

Astilbe arendsii

Aruncus dioicus

165

Iris. This is one of the most popular and most widely grown perennials. The genus is a large one and its botanical division is very complex. Irises are distributed throughout the moderate regions of the northern hemisphere.

The most widely grown large-flowered garden varieties are mostly hybrids derived from many botanical species, such as *Iris germanica, I. sanguinea, I. sibirica* and *I. kaempferi.* Irises should not be selected solely according to the beauty of the flower but also according to the length of the flowering period and the number of years they will grow in one spot. The loveliest varieties tend to be quite tender and soon die. Large-flowered irises require a warm, sunny site and well-drained soil; most are fairly tolerant of dry conditions but those derived from *I. kaempferi* are moisture loving. In shade and in soil with too much nitrogen they suffer from various diseases, chiefly bacterial rot of the rhizomes. Every three to five years they should be lifted and divided and then planted out again at a shallow depth. Old clumps produce fewer flowers. Irises should be moved and divided in August; if put out later in the autumn they generally do not flower the following year.

Large-flowered irises may be used in many ways, for bedding, for the rock garden, and for cutting. Irises should be cut while in bud, a short while before they open; however, they do not tolerate transport. The pure colours are loveliest—for instance, yellow irises in a dark Chinese vase, or brightly-coloured irises in a white vase. They can be combined with daisy-like plants such as doronicum, chrysanthemum and *Pyrethrum roseum,* but additional greenery is generally not necessary.

Aquilegia. Columbine, *Aquilegia hybrida,* is a perennial with spurred flowers. It grows wild throughout the moderate regions of the northern hemisphere. Generally only hybrids are grown in the garden; the loveliest and most brightly coloured are the so-called American hybrids.

They make strong clumps, 50 to 80 cm (1 ft 8 in to 2 ft 8 in) high, covered with a profusion of flowers in June and July. These may be a single colour or mixture of colours; however, they are generally grown in a mixture. Columbines have no special requirements but do best in a rather moist situation and partial shade. Propagation is only from seed; sometimes they seed themselves but then they are not as lovely. Only seed from the nursery should be used for this purpose. Columbines are used for mixed herbaceous borders and for larger rock gardens. They are also good for cutting and make attractive airy bouquets. They are lovely combined with baby's breath; other good companions are leopard's bane (doronicum), rock cress (arabis) and candytuft (iberis). Faded flowers should be cut off with secateurs.

Hemerocallis. The day lily, hemerocallis, is an interesting perennial with lily-shaped flowers. It is native to eastern Asia. The flowers of the original species were small and coloured yellow or orange. Breeding has yielded large-flowered hybrids in other colours—red, violet, pink and brown. They make fairly large clumps from which rise long stems terminated by lily-shaped blooms lasting only one day. The plant flowers a long time, however, for it has as many as 40 buds which open successively one after the other.

Border Iris

Day lilies are not particularly demanding in their requirements and will last a number of years in one spot. They succeed best when planted in full sun in deep, fertile soil. The plants should be spaced 50 cm (1 ft 8 in) apart and moved as little as possible because they are at their best after a few years when they have spread. Propagation is by division of the clumps in the autumn. Day lilies are used primarily in mixed perennial beds. A bed consisting only of day lilies of different kinds is beautiful in the flowering season (May until August). The foliage is also decorative and serves much the same function as ornamental grasses — the leaves appear early and are a fresh green throughout the entire growing period, even in summer; the plants do not die back until late autumn. The flowers can also be used for cutting; faded ones should be removed immediately.

Aquilegia hybrida

Hemerocallis citrina

(4 in) across; these appear a month later but there is no repeat flowering. Plant breeders have come up with several outstanding varieties.

To grow well these daisies require sun, fertile soil and regular watering. They are multiplied by division of the clumps in spring. As a rule they should be moved and divided every three years.

The second large group of this genus includes the true chrysanthemums, *Chrysanthemum hortorum*, produced by the crossing of the east Asian species *C. indicum* (first in order on this double-page), *C. koreanum* and others. This group embraces a vast number of varieties grown in nurseries for the cut-flower trade. They include single, semi-double and double forms, low growing as well as tall ones, in a wide range of colour. Those selected for bedding schemes in the garden should be early-flowering forms that

Chrysanthemum maximum

Chrysanthemum indicum 'Burgunder'

Chrysanthemum. This is a very large and garden-worthy genus, which includes perennials, annuals as well as greenhouse plants. Of the perennials the one most widely grown in gardens is the native European white oxeye daisy, *Chrysanthemum leucanthemum*, which flowers in late May (some varieties flower again in August). In recent years it has given way to the increasingly popular shasta daisy, *C. maximum*, which is much larger, with flowers more than 10 cm produce blooms in September or October for later they might be damaged by frost. These chrysanthemums, native to the warm regions of China, require a warm, sheltered site, loose soil, regular watering in summer, and dry conditions plus a light protective cover in winter. Propagation is fairly difficult and is not a task for the amateur.

Another important group includes the pyrethrums, *Chrysanthemum coccineum*, better known as *Pyrethrum roseum*. These are pink to red, daisy-like flowers with a pale centre, that bloom in June and after a brief rest again in July if well watered. For good growth they require full sun, fertile soil and regular watering. They do not like to be moved. Propagation is by division, the greatest success rate is achieved if this is done immediately after flowering; they may also be raised from seed.

Echinacea. Purple cone flower, *Echinacea purpurea*, also known as *Rudbeckia purpurea*, resembles daisies but is related to the genus rudbeckia, which, like itself, is native to North Africa. It is a strong growing plant up to 1 m (3 ft) high that flowers in July and August. It is easy to grow and readily propagated by division as well as from seed.

All chrysanthemums, daisies and echinacea are lovely in bedding schemes if put out in large groups. Because most tend to flop it is recommended to plant them close together and provide them with a support so they stand upright. They are first and foremost ideal as cut flowers for floral arrangements. They are used separately or in mixture as well as with other flowers. Loveliest, however, are attractively arranged blooms of the same colour and same variety. They are very long lived in the vase.

Chrysanthemum coccineum

Echinacea purpurea

Rudbeckia. Cone flower, rudbeckia, is a large genus of popular flowers, most of which are yellow. They are native to North America. Some are annual, but most are perennial. All are very easy to grow and have no special requirements, but prefer a rather moist, humusy soil. Most widely grown is *Rudbeckia fulgida,* 60 to 70 cm (2 ft to 2 ft 4 in) high, which produces large, golden-yellow flowers with brownish-black centres from August to September. *R. fulgida sullivantii* is the best of the several varieties. One of the most popular flowers in country gardens is *R. laciniata,* which is up to 2 m (6 ft) high and bears a profusion of dark yellow flowers from July to September. *R. nitida,* of the same height, has yellow daisy flowers with a darker centre and is of less spreading habit. Gaining in popularity in recent years is the variety 'Gloriosa Daisy' with large, single, brownish--red and yellow flowers of varying shades. It requires

Rudbeckia fulgida

Doronicum caucasicum

Doronicum. Leopard's bane, doronicum, native to the mountains of Asia, is a very popular spring-flowering plant in the garden. Generally cultivated are the two species, *Doronicum caucasicum,* which is small (30 cm [1 ft] high), producing yellow flowers in April, and *D. columnae,* taller, flowering in early May. They do best in heavy, fertile, humus-rich soil, that is rather moist, and in a spot that is sunny but shaded from the midday sun. Propagation is by division. They will make a bright display in the same spot for many years and are lovely in mixed perennial beds and suitable for cutting.

170

Coreopsis grandiflora   *Centaurea dealbata*

a rather warm situation and dryish soil. It is perhaps the best perennial for cutting because it is very long-lived in the vase. All cone flowers are generally multiplied by division and all are suitable for cutting.

Coreopsis. Tickseed, coreopsis, is native to the prairies of North America. Of the many species *Coreopsis grandiflora* has the largest and loveliest flowers. It is 70 to 90 cm (2 ft 4 in to 3 ft) high. For good growth it requires a sunny site and fertile soil and should be divided and transplanted every three years or so. The flowers last long on the plant, and in the vase partly opened buds will open fully. Faded flowers should be removed promptly to prevent the formation of seed, which saps the plant's strength, and promotes spreading.

Centaurea. Cornflower or knapweed, is a very widespread genus of annuals, biennials and perennials. The perennial species tend to be overlooked by gardeners even though they have a long flowering period and large, interesting flowers in a wide range of colours, pure blue, rosy-violet, yellow and white. They tolerate both drought and heat. The two species mainly cultivated in gardens are the blue *Centaurea montana*, which is up to 50 cm (1 ft 8 in) high and flowers in May and June, and the rose-coloured *C. dealbata*, native to Asia Minor and the Caucasus, which is 80 to 90 cm (2 ft 8 in to 3 ft) high and flowers in June and July. They are easy to grow and in deep, moisture-retentive soil do not even need watering. Propagation is by division.

171

Heliopsis. Orange sunflower, heliopsis, is a very rewarding perennial native to North America. It grows to a height of 130 cm (4 ft 4 in) and has a long flowering period, from June until September. The flowers open successively one after the other and are slow to fade. They last a long while in the vase and therefore are excellent for cutting. This plant is easy to grow; it is not damaged by drought nor is it prone to disease, it does not need a support and is not invasive, but it will not tolerate wet conditions. Propagation is by division of clumps.

Orange sunflower has many uses. It is best suited for the informal, natural sections of the garden and for parks in larger groups. It may be combined with bergamot, monarda, dark species of sneezeweed, helenium, and tall grasses, and in the vase with delphinium, rudbeckia, liatris and gypsophila.

Anemone. Windflower, *Anemone japonica,* is a perennial belonging to the vast genus anemone, which includes mostly tuberous plants. These taller, autumn-flowering anemones, native to central and western China, are for the garden among the most important members of the whole genus. They are 80 to 110 cm (2 ft 8 in to 3 ft 8 in) tall and produce white, pink or red flowers from August to October. They do best in partial shade and acid soil rich in humus and with sufficient moisture. It is recommended to provide a protective cover for the winter because they may be damaged by frost. Propagation is fairly difficult, mainly by taking root cuttings. They are good in bedding schemes in groups with ferns, rhododendrons and plants with similar soil requirements. They are attractive associated with ornamental grasses. They are not good for cutting but splendid for dish arrangements.

Scabiosa. Scabious is a widespread genus of annuals and perennials native to the Mediterranean region. The most widely grown, the perennial *Scabiosa caucasica,* however, is native to the Caucasus. It is a tall plant, 60 to 100 cm (2 ft to 3 ft 4 in) high, that bears a succession of blue, white or violet flowers from June to September. It requires a warm, sunny

Heliopsis scabra

Anemone japonica

172

Scabiosa caucasica

Heuchera sanguinea

location, light, limy soil, and watering in periods of drought. It dislikes wet conditions, particularly in winter. Propagation is by division in spring, but it can also be raised from seed. Scabious should not be moved in autumn as then they may not survive the winter.

Scabious may be used in a great many ways: in mixed perennial beds, as a solitary subject, and best of all as a cut flower for the vase. It is excellent combined with any of the daisy-like flowers such as chrysanthemum, coreopsis, rudbeckia, gaillardia, and is also very lovely by itself, either in one colour or a mixture of colours.

Heuchera. Alumroot or coral bells, *Heuchera san-guinea,* is an unobtrusive perennial native to North America. The genus numbers a great many species but only hybrids, 30 to 60 cm (1 ft to 2 ft) tall, are grown in gardens nowadays. They flower in early June and may continue to produce blossoms well into summer. Some varieties have a repeat flowering in August. They do best in partial shade and soil rich in humus; if watered regularly they will flower in sun. Propagation is by division, but this is not a simple task, for the roots are woody and must be cut. They are ideal in the rock garden and as edging for larger beds. They are also good for cutting making delicate bouquets, chiefly together with baby's breath, *Lychnis viscaria,* doronicum and arabis.

173

Sedum spectabile

Euphorbia polychroma

'Russell' lupin

Sedum. Stonecrops are fleshy-leaved plants that are great favourites in the rock garden. They are mostly low, evergreen plants, some of which form mats. Somewhat different in character from the other members of the genus is the tall, upright, 40 to 50 cm (1 ft 4 in to 1 ft 8 in) high, herbaceous *Sedum spectabile* of China and Japan, which flowers in August and September. It requires fertile soil and ample but not direct sun. Propagation is by division in spring or early autumn. Older clumps should be divided from time to time, otherwise they will produce fewer flowers. Some varieties have yellow markings on the leaves.

Stonecrop is used in perennial beds, in the natural, informal garden, or in the rock garden, where it makes attractive clumps at a time when there is little colour in the rockery. It is also planted in window-boxes.

Lupinus. Lupin is a striking and popular perennial, native to the western parts of North America. The species have been crossbred to such a degree that nowadays only hybrids are grown. Best known are the Russel lupins, which come in a wide range of colours including yellow, pink, red, blue and white. Some varieties have bicoloured flowers. They are 70 to 100 cm (2 ft 4 in to 3 ft 4 in) high and flower in May and June. They may be raised from seed and will produce a profusion of flowers in the second year. If the seed is not to be harvested the flowers should be removed as soon as they have faded; there will be a rich second flowering.

Coloured varieties require deep, fertile, lime-free soil and a sunny situation, but not full sun or drought. Lupins are loveliest in large groups in a mixture of colours, but they can also be used as solitary subjects in the lawn in spring as well as in mixed perennial beds. They are also good for cutting but do not last long in the vase.

Euphorbia. Spurge, euphorbia, is a vast genus numbering some 1,600 species but only one, *Euphorbia polychroma,* is discussed here. It is a 30 to 35 cm (1 ft to 1 ft 2 in) high sub-shrub which produces heads of bright sulphur-yellow bracts in May and June. The flowers themselves are inconspicuous and surrounded by the bracts. It does best in well-drained, limy soil in sun or partial shade. In a sunny situation the shrubs are more compact and the leaves turn red in autumn. After a number of years they should be divided because they grow very large. The plants may also be propagated from seed.

Euphorbia is planted as a solitary subject in a larger rock garden and in beds with lower plants, but always in parts of the garden that have a natural, informal character. It is also attractive by the waterside.

Solidago hybrida

Solidago. Golden rod, solidago, is a well-known plant native to North America that is often found in large masses. It is not particularly welcome in the garden because the plants, be they only 30 cm (1 ft) or 2 m (6 ft) high, spread readily and can become invasive. They also seed themselves freely, thus producing thousands of young plants that form a carpet. Modern varieties are less invasive but must not be allowed to seed themselves. They are very easy to grow and will thrive practically anywhere, often to an unwelcome degree. They are good for rapid masking of an unattractive spot or as a quick gap filler. They are also used in large bouquets of cut flowers.

175

Primula. Primrose is a very large genus of garden plants, native mostly to western China, Tibet and the Himalayas. Some species are very tender and can be grown only in the greenhouse, others are collector's items. Of the ten or so gardenworthy species, pictured are two of the most popular. *Primula denticulata* makes ground rosettes of leaves from which rise 25 cm (10 in) long leafless stems topped in March and April by large rounded heads of flowers. *P. vulgaris* is a cushion-like plant only 10 to 15 cm (4 to 6 in) high with flowers borne singly on each stem.

The type species is yellow, hybrids are blue, red, white, or pink, usually with a yellow eye. The flowers are quite large.

Both of these primulas thrive in ordinary garden soil with sufficient moisture. Propagation is by division or from seed, mainly in the summer after flowering. Primulas are used mainly in the rock garden or as edging plants for beds, also amidst spring-flowering bulbs as an underplanting to deciduous shrubs. They may be put in pots and used as house plants.

Primula vulgaris

Primula denticulata

Adonis vernalis

Geum chiloense

Adonis. Pheasant's eye, adonis, is a favourite flower for the garden and rock garden. The two most widely grown species are *Adonis amurensis* from Manchuria and Japan, which flowers as early as January and February, does not put out leaves until the flowers are fading, and dies back in June, and *A. vernalis,* from central and southern Europe, Siberia and the Altai, which is also yellow and flowers from March to May, dying back in summer. At first it grows slowly but later it makes a nice clump and survives in the same spot for many years. These plants like a sunny situation and well-drained, limy soil. They are propagated chiefly by means of seeds, which should be harvested just before they are ripe and sown immediately afterwards.

Geum. Avens, the species and hybrids of geum, are perennials found in the moderate regions of both hemispheres. They are 30 to 60 cm (1 to 2 ft) high and the branching, prostrate stems bear pretty, mostly orange but sometimes also red or yellow flowers in May and June; some varieties flower until July. They have no special requirements and although they prefer damp, they will grow in dry soil. Propagation is by division. Avens is suitable for the larger rock garden and for beds of low-growing perennials.

Gaillardia. Blanket flower, gaillardia, are popular garden flowers chiefly because of their bright colours. They include perennials as well as annuals native to Central and North America. Of the perennials there exist two types mainly grown in the garden. The first type includes species that are 70 to 80 cm (2 ft 4 in to 2 ft 8 in) high with floppy stems. These are also good for cutting, particularly for various modern dish arrangements. The second group is represented by plants only 20 to 30 cm (8 in to 1 ft) high, making large clumps that are suitable for mixed borders of perennials and shrubs. For good growth they require sun, a warm situation, and well-drained soil. They can be propagated from seed and by division. The plants do not last long in the bed, only two to three years, after which they must be replaced.

Lychnis. Campion or catchfly are perennials related to carnations and not as popular in the garden as they once were. The genus includes two species that are quite different in appearance.

Lychnis viscaria, shown in the illustration, grows naturally in meadows and on hillsides throughout Europe. Only the double form, with thick racemes of bright pink flowers borne on 30 to 40 cm (1 ft to 1 ft 4 in) long stems in May and June, is of value as an ornament for the garden. It likes a sunny situation but not full sun. It may be propagated only by division. It is lovely as a bedding plant, particularly with *Aster alpinus,* iris and veronica. It may also be used for cutting and is best by itself in a small vase together with one of the ornamental grasses such as festuca, avena or phalaris.

Gaillardia hybrida

Lychnis chalcedonica

Lychnis chalcedonica, known as the Maltese cross, is an old flower of country gardens. It grows to a height of 70—100 cm (2 ft 4 in to 3 ft 4 in) and flowers in late summer. It is easy to grow and often seeds itself. The intense colour of the flowers is particularly striking in a bed with white Shasta daisies *(Chrysanthemum maximum),* erigeron, delphinium and achillea; it may also be put together with plants which tolerate dry conditions such as nepeta, stachys and inula.

Erigeron. Fleabane, erigeron, is a large genus of garden plants distributed throughout the world excepting Africa. Few species are gardenworthy as ornamentals in themselves but cross-breeding has yielded the lovely and popular varieties. Fleabane greatly resembles asters but flowers as early as June, whereas asters do not flower until autumn. It is dis-

tinguished from spring-flowering asters by having finer ray petals which are furthermore usually arranged in several rows. Fleabane is 50 to 80 cm (1 ft 8 in to 2 ft 8 in) high and generally blue, although there are pink as well as silvery-violet forms. Some are double, but these are not as attractive. Fleabane has no special requirements, needing only good garden soil, sun and regular watering. The flowers should be removed as soon as they have faded; early varieties will then flower again in autumn. Propagation is by division in spring.

Fleabane is used in mixed perennial beds and low-growing forms also as edging plants. They are good for cutting and will last 10 to 14 days in a vase. Buds will not open but open flowers will remain fresh a long time.

Lychnis viscaria

Erigeron hybridus

179

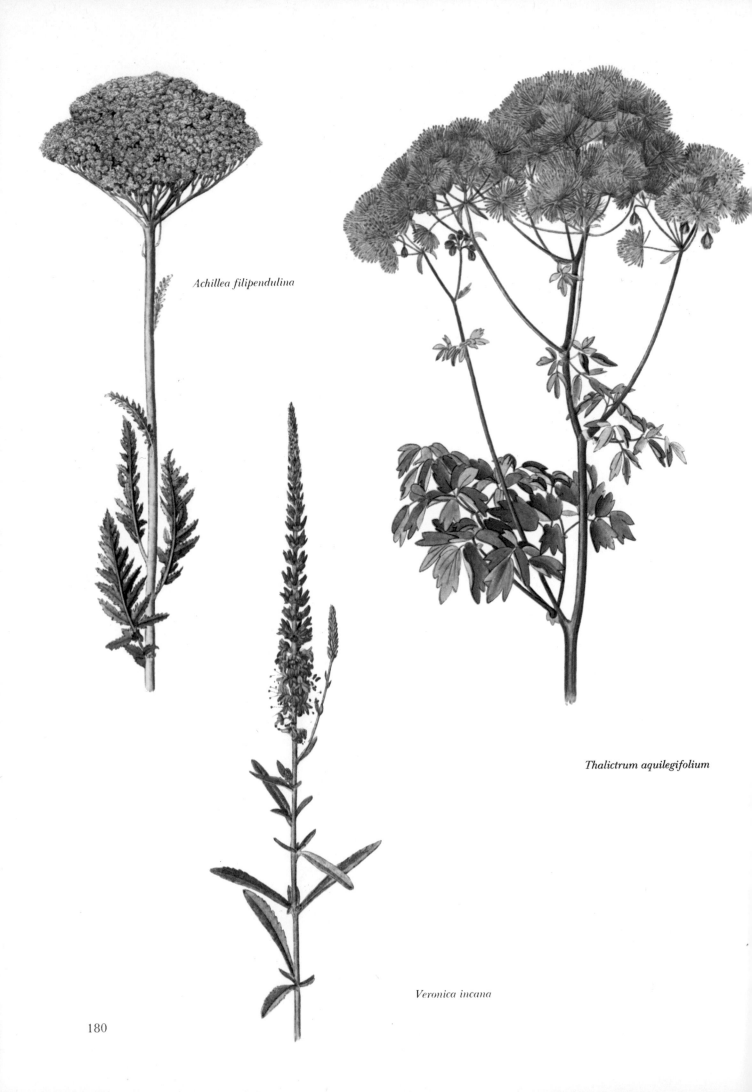

Achillea filipendulina

Thalictrum aquilegifolium

Veronica incana

180

Achillea. Yarrow or milfoil, is a widespread genus of perennials distributed throughout the northern hemisphere, chiefly in Europe and Asia. It includes many species ranging from very small to tall plants. They are also widely grown in gardens, particularly in informal schemes. *Achillea filipendulina,* from the Caucasus, is a very handsome perennial, 100 to 150 cm (3 ft 4 in to 5 ft) high, which produces large flat heads, up to 10 to 15 cm (4 to 6 in) across, of bright yellow flowers in July and August. It is easily grown in any situation and needs the minimum of attention, surviving even without regular watering. Propagation is by division in the autumn.

It is used in natural parks, in large groups, in front of ornamental trees and shrubs and in the garden only at the back of the border. Attractive companions are *Lychnis chalcedonica,* nepeta, *Salvia nemorosa* and perennials that have similar requirements. It is also useful for cutting, being long-lasting in a vase, and can be dried for winter decoration, retaining its colour quite well.

Thalictrum. Meadow rue, thalictrum, is a rather unusual flower. Of the many species distributed throughout the world practically the only one grown in the garden is *Thalictrum aquilegifolium,* distributed from Europe through the whole of Siberia to Japan. It is 80 to 120 cm (2 ft 8 in to 4 ft) high with foliage resembling that of columbine (aquilegia), and fluffy flower heads, violet or white, in May and June. Thalictrums do best in partial shade in fresh, humus-rich soil. In a less congenial, particularly dry, situation they are often attacked by aphids. Meadow rue is easily raised from seed.

These flowers are best suited for the natural, informal garden. In the wild they grow in woodland clearings and are most effective in the garden in front of darker trees and shrubs. *Achillea filipendulina,* columbine (aquilegia), poppy *(Papaver nudicaule)* and Solomon's seal (polygonatum) are suitable companions.

Veronica. Speedwell, veronica, is a very large genus of perennials that differ greatly in appearance as well as method of cultivation. Best for the garden are the low, prostrate species; shrubby forms are less attractive and less widely grown. Of the latter the one most commonly seen in cultivation is *Veronica incana,* which grows wild in south-eastern Europe and northern Asia. The broadly lanceolate leaves are arranged in a ground rosette from which rise upright stems 30 to 40 cm (1 ft to 1 ft 4 in) long. The blue flowers open in succession from June to August. The whole plant is silvery-felted. It does best in well-drained, rather acid soil and full sun, and is readily propagated by division.

It is best suited for the rock and heath gardens or sections devoted to perennials which need dry conditions. Given proper care it grows into large masses.

Helenium. Sneezeweed, helenium, is a versatile perennial that is not included in the garden scheme as often as it deserves. Old species of this genus, native to North America and Canada, are tall and sparsely leaved and suitable for natural, informal gardens. They generally do not flower until late summer. In recent years, however, breeders have come up with a new group of varieties that flower earlier and look quite different. They are more branched,

lower and broader, and of looser habit. The individual flowers are borne on longer stems. They are coloured red, yellow, or reddish-brown and most have a dark centre. The flowering period begins as early as July and lasts until late autumn. These new varieties deserve to be more widely cultivated. They are easy to grow, requiring only sun and regular watering; they do not tolerate dry conditions. Propagation is by division but only in spring; if moved in autumn they may not survive the winter.

Heleniums are used in large, brightly-coloured, mixed groups, in beds by themselves, as solitary subjects in grass, and above all for cutting. In the vase they are used by themselves or with baby's breath, early-flowering varieties with fleabane. They are also attractive with white daisies (chrysanthemum), yellow African marigolds (tagetes), or pink scabious.

Helenium hybridum

Campanula. Bellflower, *Campanula persicifolia*, is a beautiful flower belonging to the large genus campanula, which numbers 250 to 300 species distributed throughout the northern hemisphere, chiefly in Europe. They are divided according to height into low species best for the rock garden, such as *Campanula portenschlagiana*, described in the chapter on rock garden plants, and tall species, such as the commonly grown *C. medium*, a biennial which is described in the section on annuals and biennials, and *C. persicifolia*, a perennial, selected because it is probably the best-known and most widely cultivated of the perennial bellflowers. It grows wild in Europe and also in large numbers in Siberia. It is 50 to 80 cm (1 ft 8 in to 2 ft 8 in) high and flowers in June and July. The bell-shaped flowers are arranged in loose racemes on leaved stems rising from a ground rosette. The type species is pale blue but more widely grown in gardens is the white variety *C. p. alba*. There are also double forms but these are not as

beautifully light and airy. The white double form is called *C. p.* 'Moerheimii', and good blue forms are 'Telham Beauty' and 'Blue Belle'.

This bellflower thrives in moist, loamy garden soil in both sun and partial shade. It tolerates slightly dry conditions for quite a long time. Propagation is by division; the type species and the white, single form may also be multiplied by means of seed. Double forms do not produce seeds. It is used in mixed perennial beds, in unstructured groups of perennials, and in the wild parts of the garden. Also suitable for cutting, it is loveliest in a vase by itself with only white or pink baby's breath to offset it. It is also attractive with daisies *(Chrysanthemum leucanthemum)*, Sweet William *(Dianthus barbatus)*, and tickseed (coreopsis), which makes a striking contrast.

Other tall species that are excellent for the garden are *C. glomerata*, about 50 to 60 cm (1 ft 8 in to 2 ft) high with terminal clusters of dark violet flowers in June and July and very good for cutting, which in

Papaver orientale

Campanula persicifolia

congenial conditions, sun and fertile soil, spreads by underground stems to an undesirable degree, and *C. latifolia,* up to 130 cm (4 ft 4 in) high with large violet-blue bells borne from July until August. It is also good for cutting.

Papaver. Oriental poppy, *Papaver orientale,* belongs to the large group of ornamental poppies widespread in the moderate and sub-tropical regions of the Old World. They include annuals as well as perennials and all exude a milky sap when bruised. There are tall as well as dwarf species; one of the latter, *P. kerneri,* is described in the chapter on rock garden plants. Best known and most widely cultivated of the tall poppies is *P. orientale,* which is up to 1 m (3 ft) high and flowers in June. The type species is red, cultivated varieties include orange-scarlet 'Marcus Perry' and salmon 'Salmon Glow'. After flowering the whole plant dies back, and new leaves appear in the autumn, which survive the winter.

The oriental poppy needs a sunny situation and fertile soil. It can be raised from seed but the colour cannot be predicted. Varieties are therefore propagated by vegetative means, by root cuttings. This is not an easy task; young plants must be grown on in pots and moved together with the root ball so as not to disturb the roots. If they become established they will survive and flower profusely in the same spot for many years. Poppies are planted in mixed perennial beds, not in groups but singly, for the size of the flower and brilliance of colour make the plant a striking feature. It may also be planted as a solitary specimen in grass; varieties with firm, upright stems are best for this.

Phlox. *Phlox paniculata* also belongs to a large genus that includes annuals and perennials, both dwarf and tall. An annual species is described in the chapter on annuals and a dwarf form in the chapter on rock garden plants. The tall *P. paniculata,* native to the eastern United States, is 60 to 120 cm (2 ft to 4 ft) high and has a long flowering period, from June until September. There are many varieties coloured white, pink, violet or red, some flowering earlier, others later.

Phlox is demanding in its requirements as to location. It does best in its native piedmont regions

Phlox paniculata

where it has rich, naturally moist soil that does not dry out, fresh air and partial shade. It can be propagated by division of the clumps but because of the danger from eelworm, a common pest of this species throughout Europe and one which can destroy the plant in an unsuitable location, it should be propagated only by root cuttings early in the year or by seed. *P. paniculata,* with its bright glowing colours, is most effective planted in large numbers. Some varieties have a repeat flowering in congenial conditions, bearing a profusion of flowers in lateral panicles after the top has been cut off. The flowers may be used also for cutting but they have a characteristic smell that some people find unpleasant.

Incarvillea grandiflora

Stachys lanata

Stachys. Lamb's tongue, donkey's ears, *Stachys lanata,* native to the Caucasus and Iraq, is of lesser importance for the garden, even though it is charming. It is not grown for the flowers but for its lovely, soft, white-felted leaves. The stems, up to 50 cm (1 ft 8 in) long, bear spikes of small flowers from June to August, but these have little ornamental value, tending rather to mar the beauty of the foliage.

This is a plant for dry, sunny locations, where the leaves are a beautiful silvery colour. In damp conditions the leaves rot, in shade they are a dingy grey.

The plant makes numerous offshoots and in time forms whole carpets. It needs to be kept in check rather than multiplied. Its chief use is as ground cover in dry and stony positions, best as an underplanting in which more striking plants such as verbascum, echinops, echinacea, achillea and salvia are put out singly. It is also attractive in the rock garden.

Incarvillea. Chinese trumpet flower, incarvillea, is also of less importance in the garden, which is a pity, for it has a special beauty of its own with its exotic-looking flowers and handsome foliage. There are

Platycodon grandiflorum

some 15 species, native to Tibet, Turkestan and China. The one most often grown in the garden is *Incarvillea grandiflora*, which is only 20 to 30 cm (8 in to 1 ft) high and flowers in May and June, usually with 3 blooms on a stem. *I. delavayi* is similar but up to 80 cm (2 ft 8 in) high and bears five to six gloxinia-like flowers on a stem a week or two later. Both have a tap root.

This plant requires a sheltered and sunny or slightly shaded situation, fertile, well-drained and a limy soil with sufficient moisture. Perhaps these

requirements are the reason why it is so little grown in the garden. Propagation is mainly from seed. It is used in beds by itself or as edging for beds, in a border of perennials, and also in the rock garden.

Platycodon. Balloon flower, *Platycodon grandiflorum,* is another perennial not often grown in the garden, which is a pity because of the unusual shape of the flowers in the stage when the buds expand and form a hollow globe before opening into a wide bell. This genus is widespread in eastern Asia, China, Manchuria and Japan. Platycodons have white, fleshy roots and greatly branched stems that usually spread out. When bruised they exude a milky sap. The plants are 40 to 70 cm (1 ft 4 in to 2 ft 4 in) high and flower in July and August. The type species is blue, but there are also pink and white varieties. The form 'Mariesii' is low-growing, dense and has a long flowering period.

Platycodon needs a sunny situation, good, well-drained soil and dry conditions in winter. Otherwise it has no special requirements and is long-lived. Propagation is only from seed. Older plants cannot be divided and so are moved with difficulty, because they have thick, deep roots. It is most useful in larger rock gardens, on dry walls or scattered in a carpet of perennials so that the beauty of the individual flowers stands out. In its native lands it grows with *Dianthus chinensis, Delphinium grandiflorum, Paeonia lactiflora* and *Physalis alkekengi*. Bedding schemes incorporating these combinations are particularly lovely.

Echinops ritro

Echinops. Globe thistle, echinops, is a well-known plant with round, thistle-like flowers. In Europe it grows wild in the warm regions of the south. It is about 80 to 100 cm (2 ft 8 in to 3 ft 4 in) high, with pale blue to violet-tinged flower heads, 2 to 4 cm ($^3/_4$ to $1^1/_2$ in) across, in July and August. The leaves are stiff, toothed and spiny. These are undemanding plants that require sun and tolerate dry conditions. They thrive even in stony soil. Propagation is by division or from seed; in congenial conditions they are invasive and sometimes form large masses. They make lovely bouquets for winter decoration and are very attractive with yellow flowers such as solidago and heliopsis. In bedding schemes good associates are species such as stachys, anaphalis, nepeta and helichrysum.

Aster. This is a very large and important genus numbering more than 600 species and commonly known as Michaelmas daisies. Several flower in spring but these are mostly low plants suitable for the rock garden. The most widely grown are the autumn-flowering species which have smaller blooms than the spring-flowerers but are taller and of thicker habit with greatly branching stems.

Michaelmas daisies are mostly native to North America, although some are found in the moderate regions of Europe. Propagation is by division, which is usually quite easy, and by cuttings. Although they produce a great number of seeds this form of propagation is rarely used because the seedlings are of poor quality. One of the most important species is *Aster dumosus*. Only the cultivated varieties are grown nowadays, some only 20 cm (8 in) high, others up to 70 cm (2 ft 4 in) high, with flowers coloured blue, white, violet, pink or carmine red, in August and September. They make thick clumps and produce a great many offshoots, thus crowding out less vigorous plants. They have no particular requirements, apart from sun. They tolerate quite dry conditions, needing only occasional watering before and during the flowering period. They are susceptible to mildew and verticillium; spraying is relatively ineffective and it is better to grow hardier varieties, even though they are not completely resistant. *A. dumosus* is best planted in small beds, as edging, or in the rock garden.

Another important species is *A. amellus,* which is 50 to 70 cm (1 ft 8 in to 2 ft 4 in) high and has flowers 4 to 7 cm ($1^1/_2$ to $2^3/_4$ in) across in August and September. Cultivated varieties include many blue-violet and pink ones. In the wild it grows on sunny limestone hillsides and in open woodland groves in central and south-eastern Europe. Requirements in the garden are fertile soil, light and warmth; it tolerates lengthy periods of drought. Seedlings must have good root balls when they are put out, otherwise they root poorly. They require greater attention at this time. Propagation is difficult; division does not yield good results and cuttings root poorly. Seedlings from seed are of poor quality. In bedding schemes *A. amellus* is associated with iris, coreopsis, heliopsis, rudbeckia, chrysanthemum and ornamental grasses.

Aster novae-angliae is the most robust of the Michaelmas daisies, growing to a height of 100 to 150 cm (3 ft 4 in to 5 ft), with small flowers in September

and October. These close in rain and at dusk. The entire plant is slightly hairy. Requirements are the same as for *A. dumosus,* but it is not prone to disease. The leaves on the lower, shaded parts of the stems are soon shed and so it is best to put this plant behind smaller plants that retain their foliage until autumn, for instance centaurea, paeonia, coreopsis and *Aster dumosus.*

Aster novi-belgii is a more important group than the preceding one. The plants are similar but not so tall (80 to 110 cm [2 ft 8 in to 3 ft 8 in] high) and the varieties come in a wider range of colours, from white to blue, violet, pink to carmine and deep red. The varieties exhibit variability in height as well as arrangement of the flowers. An unpleasant feature is that the taller plants tend to flop and need staking. Requirements include a rather damp location and moist, cool air. They make a very attractive effect in the garden and if healthy (they are quite susceptible to mildew) are also suitable for cutting, though they are quite short-lived in a vase.

Aster dumosus

Aster amellus 'Hermann Löns' (top right), *Aster novae-angliae* 'Harrington Pink' (top left), *Aster novi-belgii* 'Winston Churchill' (bottom)

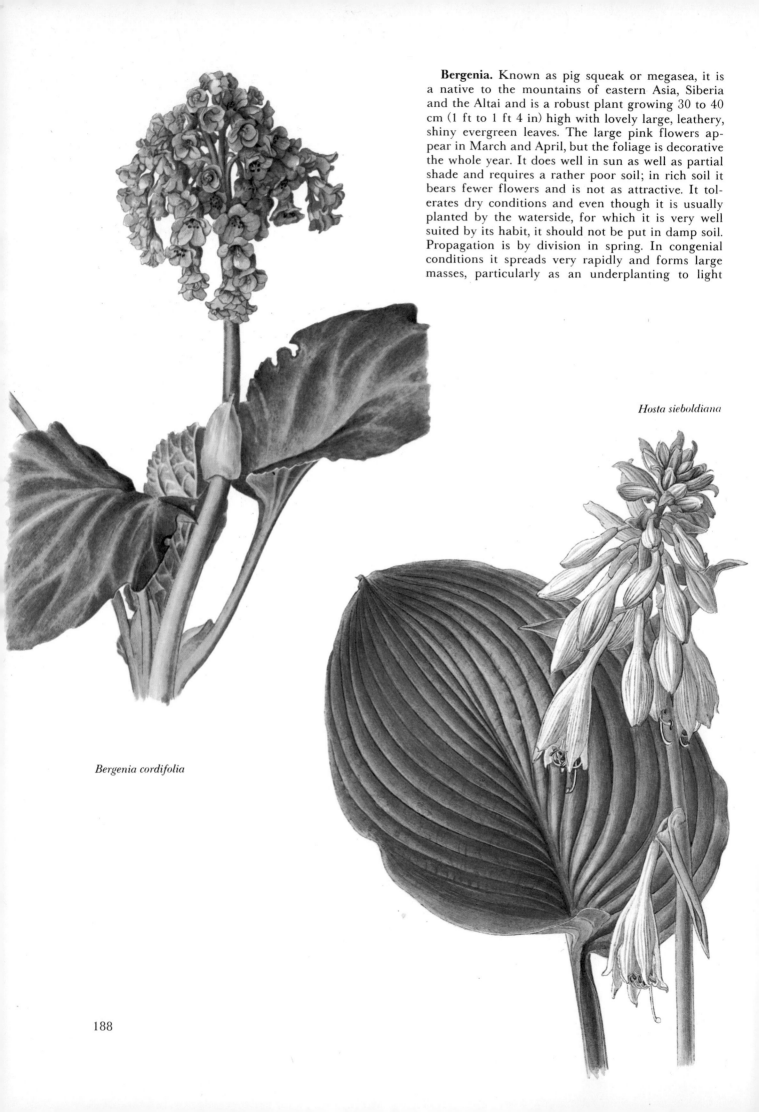

Bergenia. Known as pig squeak or megasea, it is a native to the mountains of eastern Asia, Siberia and the Altai and is a robust plant growing 30 to 40 cm (1 ft to 1 ft 4 in) high with lovely large, leathery, shiny evergreen leaves. The large pink flowers appear in March and April, but the foliage is decorative the whole year. It does well in sun as well as partial shade and requires a rather poor soil; in rich soil it bears fewer flowers and is not as attractive. It tolerates dry conditions and even though it is usually planted by the waterside, for which it is very well suited by its habit, it should not be put in damp soil. Propagation is by division in spring. In congenial conditions it spreads very rapidly and forms large masses, particularly as an underplanting to light

Hosta sieboldiana

Bergenia cordifolia

trees. It is magnificent as a solitary subject near the water garden. There are a number of free-flowering hybrids available in a wider colour range—shades of pink, rose-red and white.

Hosta. Plantain lily or funkia is an important perennial native to eastern Asia, chiefly Japan. They are usually grown for their ornamental, large, handsome, green or variegated leaves. Some plants also have lovely flowers but these are rather inconspicuous. The most widely grown species is *Hosta sieboldiana,* 40 to 50 cm (1 ft 4 in to 1 ft 8 in) high, with pale lilac to pure white flowers in June and July. The leaves are up to 30 cm (1 ft) long. The choice of varieties is quite large but the most popular are those with variegated foliage.

Hosta does best in partial shade but it is adaptable and stands up well to both shade and full sun. It requires ample nourishment and applications of feed. The foliage is loveliest in situations with partial shade and well-drained loamy soil that is rather moist. Propagation is by division, common species and varieties can also be grown from seed. It has many uses in the garden, as a lovely edging for beds, as an underplanting to trees, in unstructured group plantings, near water and in damp sections of the garden.

Dicentra. Bleeding heart, dicentra, is a very popular garden perennial with lovely arching sprays of dangling, pink, heart-shaped flowers. Most widely cultivated is *Dicentra spectabilis* which is an airy shrub 60 to 80 cm (2 ft to 2 ft 8 in) high and flowers in May. In early summer the plants die back. The smaller species *D. eximia* and *D. formosa,* which flower from June until September, are grown in the rock garden.

Dicentra spectabilis does best in partial shade and well-drained soil that is sufficiently moist. It is recommended to apply feeds rich in potash and limit feeds with a high level of nitrogen, as then the shrub retains its compact habit and bears a profusion of flowers. Propagation is by division in spring or autumn. The flower is short-lived and decorative for only about two months, but the effect is striking. Its beauty is lost in groups of perennials; it is most effective planted as a solitary subject, either as the dominating plant in a mixed bed or in grass. However, it is necessary to keep in mind that other plants will have to be put out in its place in the second half of summer. Open flowers can also be used for cutting; most attractive by themselves or with baby's breath in a roughly glazed ceramic-ware vase. Combinations with doronicum, *Anemone sylvestris,* arabis and iberis are charming, but whatever the companion flowers, bleeding heart should be the principal one.

Dicentra spectabilis

Dictamnus. Burning bush, *Dictamnus albus,* is a little-known perennial distributed throughout the northern hemisphere from central Europe to Korea. It is a 60 to 100 cm (2 ft to 3 ft 4 in) high shrub flowering in June and July. All parts of the plant are very aromatic and exude a volatile gas on sultry days. Persons with sensitive skin may get an unpleasant rash if they touch the plant on such a day. It does best in sunny situations and dry, limy soil that is sufficiently nourishing. Propagation is from seed, which should be sown immediately after it is gathered. Seedlings, however, do not flower until the fourth year. It cannot be multiplied by other means and that is perhaps why it is so little grown. The plants are not moved easily; older specimens should be left in the same spot where they will then flower profusely. In a congenial site they seed themselves. Planted as a solitary subject or in small groups in

Dictamnus albus

Polygonatum multiflorum

Polygonatum. Solomon's seal is a lovely, little-known plant for the wild parts of the garden. Some 30 species are distributed throughout the moderate regions of the northern hemisphere. The most widely grown is *Polygonatum multiflorum* of Europe's woodlands, which is 60 to 80 cm (2 ft to 2 ft 8 in) high and flowers in May and June. The nodding white flowers on the leafy arching stems are replaced in autumn by bluish-black berries. This plant does best in partial to full shade and good, rich, slightly acid soil that is sufficiently moist; however, it will grow in a sunny site unless it is too dry. Propagation is easiest by division, even though it can be multiplied from seed, which is a tedious process. It is used chiefly in the damper parts of the garden with ferns and other shade-loving plants. It is lovely in a vase together with fern fronds.

grass or at the top of the rock garden makes the most of the plant's unusual appearance.

Delphinium. Perennial larkspur is one of the handsomest and most widely grown of perennials. Described in the chapter on annuals is an annual species. Of the perennials, only the garden varieties, which number several hundred (hybrids between species such as *Delphinium formosum, D. elatum* and *D. cheilanthum*) are grown in the garden. They need deep, rich soil, regular watering, and in dry weather occasional thorough drenching. The plants should be cut back to about 15 cm (6 in) from the ground as soon as the flowers have faded and they will flower again if provided with ample nourishment. In windy positions they need staking. Propagation is by cuttings or sowing seed.

Delphiniums are striking flowers that should be put in an important part of the garden. Groups of three to five tall plants or a large mass of the more delicate varieties of the same colour or mixture of colours are very attractive. Delphinium is also excellent as a cut flower in a large vase. The flowers open in succession from the bottom up and should be removed as they fade. It is loveliest as a bouquet by itself.

Kniphofia. Red-hot poker or torch lily, native to South Africa and Madagascar, is a very interesting perennial with flowers of unusual shape. The plant is 80 to 130 cm (2 ft 8 in to 4 ft 4 in) high and flowers from July until October. It does best in sun and in well-drained soil that is sufficiently moist. In winter, however, it needs dry conditions and in severe weather should be protected. Propagation is by seed or division. It is good for cutting, used in arrangements with leaves of various bromeliads.

Delphinium formosum

Kniphofia hybrida

191

Dianthus plumarius

Dianthus. Carnation or pink is a very widespread and important genus which includes annuals, biennials, perennials, rock garden plants, as well as greenhouse plants for cutting. The most widely cultivated species are described in the respective sections. Most are native to the Mediterranean region.

The perennial species most widely grown in Europe is *Dianthus plumarius,* which bears a profusion of white, pink or red blossoms, some with a pretty dark centre, either single or double. In time it makes large cushions of flowering stems 20 to 30 cm (8 in to 1 ft) high. The flowering peak is in June and July. For good growth it requires a rather heavy, limy soil and sun and will not tolerate waterlogged conditions. Varieties are propagated by cuttings, single forms can be multiplied from seed.

It is used in the garden as a low-growing, evergreen, attractively flowering mass in informal sections, in prominent beds and in dry walls. Some double varieties are also suitable for cutting. There are many attractive forms. Recommended are 'Excelsior'—double, pink, 'Mrs Sinkins'—double, white, 'Doris'—double, pink with a red centre, and 'Emperor'—double, red.

Helianthemum. Rock or sun roses are actually low-growing, woody plants, mainly evergreen, which are used as perennials. The genus numbers some 80 species native to the Mediterranean region and central Asia. The plants are 15 to 25 cm (6 to 10 in) high with flowers in many different colours, some single,

others double. They are produced from May until July. Sun roses appreciate sun and dry soil, otherwise they have no special requirements. It is advisable to trim the plants after flowering for then they are more certain to survive the winter and make a thicker growth. Propagation is chiefly by cuttings.

Sun roses are used mainly in a dry wall, rock garden, and level plantings, either by themselves or with plants such as thyme (thymus), stonecrop (sedum), low-growing milfoil (achillea). Attractive varieties are 'Praecox'—yellow, 'Old Gold'—single, yellow, brown-

Helianthemum hybridum

Viola cornuta

ish-orange with yellow centre, 'Coppernob'—singie, copper, and 'Supreme'—single, dark red.

Viola. Viola or pansy is a small, well-known flower. Two species, *Viola odorata*, described in the chapter on rock garden plants, and *V. cornuta*, the horned violet, from the Pyrenees, are usually grown in the garden. The latter is 10 to 25 cm (4 to 10 in) high and bears a continuous profusion of small flowers resembling pansies from May until September. The original violet-coloured species is not generally cultivated; the varieties, which are mostly blue and violet though there are also white and yellow forms, are usually grown. For good flowering they require good, light soil that is sufficiently moist but not soggy. Pansies flower best in a sunny site but not in full sun; growth is good in partial shade but flowering is less profuse. Propagation is by division or cuttings, some varieties may also be raised from seed, but this must be select seed. They are ideal for a larger rock garden, as an edging plant for beds, for low, mixed borders, as well as for a flat bedding scheme. They can also be used for cutting for a small posy.

Alyssum saxatile

Iberis sempervirens

Silene schafta

Alyssum. Madwort or gold dust, alyssum, are undemanding plants with characteristic golden-yellow flowers widely grown in Europe's gardens. The genus includes some 80 species distributed throughout the Mediterranean region and in Asia Minor as far as the Caucasus. The one most commonly grown is *Alyssum saxatile,* native to the Balkans and southern Russia. It is about 30 cm (1 ft) high and flowers in April and May. In its native land alyssum grows chiefly on rocks, and thus prefers a sunny site and well-drained soil in the garden; otherwise it is not at all demanding, and is readily propagated from seed. There are several improved varieties: 'Citrinum', which can be propagated from seed, and 'Compactum', which can be propagated only by cuttings. They are of more compact habit than the type species. *A. saxatile* is suitable for dry walls and rock gardens and can be scattered freely in the wild parts of the garden round small country houses and cottages.

Silene. Catchfly, silene, is a typical small plant of the mountains. The genus numbers more than 300 species distributed throughout the northern hemisphere. Only one, *Silene schafta,* however, is usually grown in the garden. It makes low clumps (10 to 20 cm [4 to 8 in] high) with green leaves and a profusion of purple flowers from July until September. Even though it is an alpine plant it adapts well to lowland conditions. It is valued for its flowering period because there are not many low, flowering plants in the garden in late summer. It thrives in any good, well-drained soil in sun, and is readily propagated from seed as well as by division and cuttings. Catchfly is suitable for the rock garden.

Iberis. Candytuft, iberis, is one of the most widely grown of the low, cushion perennials. The genus includes 40 species that grow wild in southern Europe and Asia Minor. There is also an annual species, described in the chapter on annuals. Of the perennials only two are grown in the garden; the low *Iberis saxatilis,* a very slow grower that flowers in April, and the better known *I. sempervirens,* which is taller than the former and has stiff stems. It grows into large evergreen cushions 20 to 25 cm (8 to 10 in) high smothered with white flowers in May and June. Older plants can develop into cushions more than 1 m (3 ft) across. They do best in a sunny situation in good, well-drained soil. After flowering the plants should be cut back lightly so that thick masses of foliage form. Candytuft requires occasional feeding. Propagation is primarily by cuttings. This species is suitable for the larger rock garden, dry walls and flat masses in unstructured perennial groups. There are several attractive compact varieties available growing up to 30 cm (1 ft) high.

Brunnera. Siberian bugloss is a lesser known perennial from the mountain forests of the western Caucasus with flowers resembling forget-me-nots. The thickly leaved stems are 30 to 50 cm (1 ft to 1 ft 8 in) high and the blue flowers appear in April and May. This plant does best in partial shade in warm, rather damp soil. In congenial conditions it spreads rapidly. The foliage is attractive throughout the summer. Siberian bugloss is generally used as an underplanting, mostly to flowering shrubs such as philadelphus, deutzia. In beds it can be planted together with doronicum, polygonatum and primula.

Brunnera myosotidiflora

195

Limonium Sea lavender or statice, limonium, is a large genus of very important flowers which can be dried. It numbers more than 200 species distributed throughout the world. These include annuals and perennials as well as semi-woody plants. One of the loveliest — *Limonium suworowii* — is described in the chapter on annuals. Of the perennials two are generally grown in the garden. *L. latifolium* from southern Russia and Bulgaria is 40 to 60 cm (1 ft 4 in to 2 ft) high and flowers in July and August. The leaves form a rosette from which rise widely branching, leafless stems with sprays of tiny flowers coloured lavender-blue; only the variety 'Violetta' is a dark lilac-violet. It does best in well-drained, rather dry soil that contains lime in a sunny situation. Propagation is by seed. Sea lavender is used mainly in wild parts of the garden. It is very valuable for cutting; the flowers are dried and used as everlastings in bouquets and wreaths.

The second, and equally important, species is *L. tataricum* from south-eastern Europe to Siberia. It is 30 to 40 cm (1 ft to 1 ft 4 in) high, with pinkish-white flowers in July and August. Requirements are the same as for *L. latifolium,* but it needs a more frequent application of feed. Propagation is by seed. It is used chiefly for drying.

Saponaria. Soapwort is a striking plant from the southern slopes of the Alps and from Italy. Of the many annual and perennial species the one usually grown in the garden is *Saponaria ocymoides,* which forms 15 to 20 cm (6 to 8 in) high cushions of branching, prostrate stems with dark evergreen leaves. The cushions are relatively large and loose but in June and July they are smothered with small rosy-violet flowers. This plant thrives in any well-drained, limy soil, in the sun. It also tolerates drought. Propagation is chiefly by seed. It is excellent for the rock garden, dry wall and flat beds. *S.*

Limonium latifolium

Saponaria ocymoides

officinalis is taller (50 to 60 cm [1 ft 8 in to 2 ft] high) and flowers from June until August. Grown chiefly is the double variety *S. o. plena*. It has no special requirements but does best in soil that is sufficiently moist and in a lightly shaded situation. Propagation is by division It is best used in the wild parts of the garden.

Eryngium. Sea holly, eryngium, is a prickly plant with teasel-like flowers although botanically it is not related to the teasles. The genus includes some 200 species native to the region from the Mediterranean to central Asia. One of the popular garden species is *Eryngium bourgatii* from Spain. It is 30 to 50 cm (1 ft to 1 ft 8 in) high, very stiff, greyish-white, with hard spines and flowers in July and August. The plants appear dry even during the flowering period and remain unchanged when cut and dried. They thrive in a sunny location, in stone rubble and gravel in limestone regions. Propagation is by seed, by offshoots, and by root cuttings.

Eryngium bourgatii

Ajuga reptans

Eryngium giganteum is somewhat taller and has similar requirements. This plant, however, is a biennial, but continues to grow in the same spot by seeding itself.

All species of eryngium are suitable for dry spots in the garden with grasses and other drought-tolerating species such as limonium, gypsophila, heliopsis, echinacea. They are planted either singly or in small groups. *E. giganteum* usually colonises in the wild parts of the garden.

Ajuga. Bugle, *Ajuga reptans,* is a European perennial of lesser importance in the garden. It is 10 to 40 cm (4 in to 1 ft 4 in) high and spreads rapidly by means of readily-rooting surface shoots so that thick carpets are soon formed. The blue flowers appear in May and June. The forms with variegated leaves are the most attractive. It thrives in sun as well as partial shade, but does best in soil that is sufficiently damp. It is used as a ground cover, sometimes as a substitute for turf. It is readily propagated by division and cuttings.

Helleborus. This genus includes the Christmas and Lenten rose. The buds of *Helleborus niger* start growing in autumn and open at Christmas. The plant is about 30 cm (1 ft) high with pure white flowers and has green foliage throughout the winter. It is native to the eastern Alps and the Balkans. Hybrids have coloured flowers, ranging from greenish-white to greyish-pink, purple and red which appear in March and April.

Liatris spicata

Helleborus niger

All hellebores are very rewarding garden perennials. They do well in a rich soil and partial shade; in summer they like deep shade. They tolerate quite dry conditions. Propagation is by seed, which must be sown as soon as it is ripe. Only particularly valuable types are multiplied by division. Growth is slow and the plants do not reach the flowering stage until the fourth year after sowing, but they are long-lived and will flower in the same spot for years. Hellebores are used in front of shrubs or in the rock garden. They are also good in the mixed bed, chiefly because of their early flowering. Hellebores suitable for the rock garden are described in the chapter on rock garden plants.

Liatris. Gay feather, *Liatris spicata*, native to North America, is one of the most valuable of garden perennials. Despite its beauty and interesting appearance, however, it is not widely cultivated. Rising from the centre of a tuft of leaves is an unbranched, small-leaved stem terminating in a dense spike of fluffy purple flowers. An unusual feature is that the flowers open from the top downwards. The plants are 80 to 100 cm (2 ft 8 in to 3 ft 4 in) high, the flowering spikes up to 30 cm (1 ft) long; the flowering period is in July and August. This plant has no special requirements, needing only sun and rather dry conditions in winter. In summer it will grow without watering, but requires an occasional application of feed. Propagation is by seed or division. Also grown is the variety 'Kobold' which is only 40 to 50 cm (1 ft 4 in to 1 ft 8 in) high.

Liatris is most effective planted in small groups amidst low-growing perennials or as a solitary subject where its unusual shape is shown to best advantage. It is also very popular for cutting. In a bouquet it is magnificent by itself or with baby's breath.

Paeonia. Peony is one of the basic and most widely cultivated of garden plants. Described in the chapter on rock garden plants is the low growing species *Paeonia tenuifolia*. The common *P. lactiflora* is the Chinese peony of northern China and Manchuria. It makes 60 to 100 cm (2 ft to 3 ft 4 in) high shrubs that flower in June. It is easy to care for but to flower well it needs deep, fertile soil, a sunny site and occasional feeding. It is comparatively tolerant of drought. Once established a fine display of blooms is produced for ten to fifteen years. Propagation is by division in late summer during the resting stage. Each clump should have two to three eyes and a strong root and when inserted in the ground, the eyes should be no more than 3 cm (1 in) below the surface, for otherwise flowering is impaired. In a damp situation it is susceptible to botrytis (grey mould) — the buds turn brown and dry up and occasionally whole stems break.

Peonies are suitable for both small gardens and large parks. They are more effective, however, associated with trees and shrubs or by themselves than in a bed. They are excellent as cut flowers and should be cut while the buds are still tightly closed and just beginning to show colour. In this state they will survive even lengthy transport and will open fully in a vase. They are best by themselves. There are many varieties coloured white, pink, and red, some flowering early, others later.

Paeonia lactiflora

Oenothera. Evening primrose, *Oenothera missouriensis,* a perennial native to North America, is a spreading species, about 20 cm (8 in) high, which from June to October bears fragrant, funnel-shaped yellow flowers, up to 10 cm (4 in) across, in the axils of the leaves, opening in the evening. It has strong, deep roots that supply it with water, enabling dry conditions to be tolerated. It is an undemanding plant which in good soil sometimes grows too luxuriantly, forming carpets more than 1 m (3 ft) across. It starts growth late in spring but then flowers long and untiringly. Propagation is chiefly from seed. It is used mostly in mixed borders, in informal groups, in large rock gardens and for covering large areas.

Monarda. Bergamot, *Monarda didyma,* native to North America, is an interesting perennial with curiously-shaped, dead-nettle type flowers and aromatic foliage. It grows to a height of 60 to 100 cm (2 ft to 3 ft 4 in) and flowers in a wide range of bright colours — white, pink, violet, red — in July and August. There are a great many attractive varieties. Monarda requires full sun, fertile soil and ample space because some varieties make numerous offshoots. Plants that are put out close together become weak after about three years. Propagation is by division or by cuttings. Bergamot is suitable for mixed groups or as a group by itself. It is also good for cutting but the foliage has a pungent odour. It is lovely by itself as well as in arrangements with other bright flowers.

Physalis. Chinese lantern, Cape gooseberry, *Physalis alkekengi,* native to the foothill region of the Tatra

Oenothera missouriensis

Monarda didyma

200

Physalis alkekengi

Trollius hybridus

Mountains in Czechoslovakia, is a 40 to 60 cm (1 ft 4 in to 2 ft) high perennial grown mainly for its showy ornamental fruits that begin to colour in September. The flowers are white and insignificant, but these are followed by red berries enclosed in vermilion seed bags. If cut as soon as they are fully coloured and then dried, the seed bags will make a bright ornament throughout the winter. This is a very undemanding plant that will grow practically anywhere; it makes numerous offshoots and spreads rapidly, thus needing to be kept in check rather than multiplied. It is used chiefly for floral decoration when dried.

Trollius. Globe flower, trollius, is a popular perennial widespread throughout the moderate regions of the northern hemisphere. Breeding has yielded many garden varieties that are taller than the species (up to 80 cm [2 ft 8 in] high) with much larger flowers (up to 4 cm [1¹⁄₂ in] across) and only these are grown in the garden nowadays. They form clumps which flower a long time in May and June. Requirements include a moist soil and a sunny site. Propagation is by seed; garden varieties are increased by division. They are used for the mixed border where they are put in small groups amidst low perennials. They are good for cutting. Also cultivated are the low-growing species, *Trollius patulus* and *T. pumilus,* which are good for the rock garden.

ROCK GARDEN PLANTS

Rock gardening has become very popular in recent years, leading to wider knowledge and specialized gardening. Establishing a rock garden and keeping it attractive requires much knowledge and skill.

A rock garden is a combination of stone, plants and water. Such gardens used to be called rockeries or alpine gardens, reflecting the prevailing tendency to grow only alpine plants. Those grown today also include cultivated varieties and garden hybrids, that in size, appearance and cultivation are suited to a rock garden.

Nowadays we have rock gardens in lowland regions with the possibility of creating mutually different conditions for plants from various altitudes and different environments by making use of exposures, soil and water. Providing plants with congenial conditions and at the same time arranging them so as to create a pleasing and attractive effect is the essence of successful rock gardening.

SITUATION

Before setting about building a rock garden, many aspects should be considered. Where to place it to fit logically into the garden scheme is no problem if the garden is on sloping ground but if it is on flat ground then more difficulties are encountered. A rock garden is a natural formation that is not suited for a formal garden. Its immediate surroundings should have an informal, natural look. Turf is best in front of the rock garden and at the back various shrubs with neutral green foliage. The rock garden should be in an open spot, free of shade cast by buildings or trees. Plants that like sun and dry conditions are the choice for southern exposures, undemanding species that will grow anywhere are the ones to put on a west-facing slope, and slopes facing east or south-east are the best for most of the prettiest rock garden plants. Northern aspects are not suitable for a rock garden.

The size of the rock garden mainly depends on the amount of time to be devoted to its care. A large rock garden should not be considered unless there is adequate time available for its maintenance. Rock gardens require much care, work and interest. Beautiful ones can be created on just a few square metres. However, they cannot contain a large number of different plants and it is always best to have fewer species that have been selected with care and taste.

CREATING A ROCK GARDEN

The beauty of a rock garden is determined first and foremost by the stones used in its construction. Stones are the framework and plants the fillers. Light-coloured stones or ones with a warm hue are best. They should look natural—both in shape and texture—as if they had been there for ages. The rule, then, is to use stones that are weathered, variously cracked and rounded by the elements, even covered with mosses or lichens. Cracked limestone rocks, travertine and tuffa rocks are the most effective. Tuffa is porous, like foam, and can be used to create delightful effects. Another good rock is sandstone, which acquires a weathered look soon after it is cut so that quarried stones can be used. Random boulders of coarsely-grained rock such as granite, porphyry, diorite and old gneiss rocks are attractive, particularly if they are covered with lichens.

Before starting to build the rock garden it is necessary to eliminate all weeds in the area. Later removal of perennial weeds, particularly ones with long invasive roots, is impossible without taking the whole rock garden apart. Annual weeds do not pose such a problem; they can be eliminated if for two years running they are carefully removed before they seed themselves.

Good drainage is essential for a rock garden. With light, sandy soil this is no problem for water passes through readily. In the case of heavier soils it is necessary to prepare a foundation layer of draining material, such as coarse clinker or construction debris.

The first step in making a rock garden is to position the rocks. These should be arranged to give a natural effect, grouped in such a way that the whole looks like one large rock with numerous cracks and crevices. At the bottom of the rock garden large rocks can be placed to resemble natural outcrops with large and smaller spaces to receive the various plants. Small stones by themselves will never make a successful rock garden. Large rocks form the backbone and smaller ones may be grouped around them. The rock garden, particularly if it is a small one, should be built of only one kind of rock; never combine two or more kinds in one section.

Because a rock garden must be tended, weeded, the soil forked over now and then, new plants put out, it is well to remember to include several 'stepping' stones, preferably flat ones, for moving about. In a larger rock garden it is a good idea to make a narrow path for easy access to the various parts. Such paths should be made only of natural-looking stone, of the same kind as those used in the construction of the rock garden. They should follow a crooked, winding course and in spots that afford an attractive view of the rock garden or the surroundings, a low flat stone on which to sit and enjoy the view can be placed. Such a stone blends with the rest and thus does not mar the effect of the whole.

Steps are also a means of getting from one part of the rock garden to another, besides which they are an important aesthetic element. They should not be in a straight line but wind up and down through the rock garden. They, too, should be placed in various directions so as to provide diversity in the rock garden.

WATER
IN THE ROCK GARDEN

Water—either a pool, marshy place or stream with small overflow—should not be missing. Pools are the most common. These are made of concrete, clay, tar paper or polythene. Concrete pools with a run-off pipe are best, their rim masked by natural stones. No matter what kind of pool is decided on it should look as natural as possible without any visible sign of the construction material. Also the area around it should be arranged so as to create a natural-looking effect. If waterlilies are desired, the greater depth needed can be achieved by ma-

king a hollow 40 cm (1 ft 4 in) across in the concrete bottom. Other water plants may be grown in containers, such as wooden troughs or boxes, placed on the pool bottom.

A pool adds beauty and life not only to the rock garden but to the garden as a whole. Water in a pool, however, is still, moving water is far more effective. If there is sufficient height above the rock garden (70 to 100 cm [2 ft 4 in to 3 ft 4 in]), then it is possible to make a small cascade by supplying water through an underground pipe. Water falling into the pool and spraying over stones is also pleasing to the ear.

Once the construction is finished attention can be focused on the plants. Of foremost importance is the soil in which they are to be planted for it is one of the factors that determines the success of the outcome. Most plants have no special requirements and will grow quite well in ordinary garden soil, but in the case of rare and difficult plants the importance of proper preparation of the soil must not be underestimated.

The basic soil mixture for the rock garden should consist of rotted turves, coarse river sand and peat which lightens the soil and is water retentive. To this may be added various admixtures depending on the needs of the given plants. One is stone debris—of limestone for lime-loving plants, of granite (the kind used in road construction) for the calcifuges. This material, consisting of 5 to 10 mm particles, improves soil drainage and if sprinkled on the surface helps keep the soil moist and protects the more tender plants from too much wet. Small pebbles, from screened, coarse river sand, may also be used for this purpose.

CHOOSING THE PLANTS

The rock garden should be attractive even before the plants are put in. The plants are the jewels that give it added beauty. Solitary specimens, conifers and certain deciduous shrubs, should be planted first, then cushion and carpet-forming plants and in their midst the small delicate gems which are placed in rock crevices and small spaces. When choosing plants for the rock garden keep in mind that it should be lovely the whole year long and that beauty is provided not only by flowers but also by foliage.

Selecting plants for the rock garden is not a simple matter. We should start with the easier plants and then gradually progress to the more demanding ones.

Sedum. Stonecrop is a very large group of garden plants. Various species of this genus are among the most widely grown rock garden flowers. All are small plants that brighten gardens and rockeries in the summer and autumn months. *Sedum spurium,* native to the Caucasus, is a fleshy-leaved, mat-forming, herbaceous plant with bright, pinkish-red flowers. Its common name in many languages refers to its fleshy leaves. *S. spurium* is not demanding in its requirements, growing just as well in sun as in partial shade. Many varieties have been derived from this species, some with white flowers.

Soldanella. This is one of the loveliest spring flowers of the primrose family. All species (about ten) are native to the mountains of Europe. They are small, perennial, herbaceous plants with rosettes of long-stalked, rounded leaves and upright stems terminated by a loose cluster of bell-shaped flowers in colours ranging from violet or blue to pink. *Soldanella montana* grows freely in the Pyrenees and Alps, its distribution extending to the Šumava Mountains,

Carpathians and Balkans. The flowers are usually blue-violet, very occasionally white. It is very persistent, grows well and bears a profusion of flowers. It is very good in the rock garden, particularly next to small spring bulbs or *Hepatica triloba,* primula and pulmonaria.

Lewisia. The genus lewisia includes some 20 perennial species with a large rhizome and thick red roots. They are native to the prairies of North America. Most can be grown with success if their special needs are fulfilled. In the rock garden they should be put in vertical crevices between large rocks or in full sun in stone rubble where surplus water can run off. Because summers are very dry in their native habitat they must be protected against too much wet. The plant collars are very sensitive to damp, particularly in winter, and therefore the plants should be covered with a transparent sheet of plastic or glass for the winter. The leaves form decorative ground rosettes and the flowers are borne in clusters on tall stems. Some species have persistent rosettes, others die back. *Lewisia cotyledon* has evergreen leaves, broadest near the tip, and tall stems with clusters of white flowers tinged with pink, later coloured deep pink, sometimes striped white or red.

Cypripedium. Lady's slipper orchid is one of the few orchids that can be grown with comparative ease in the garden. The best time for planting is in spring so that the plants have time to take good root. If planted in autumn the results are usually not successful. Propagation is by division of the rootstock as soon as the ground has thawed. Species most often grown in the rock garden are *Cypripedium reginae,* native to the virgin forests of North America, with large, pink-white flowers, and *C. calceolus,* native to

Sedum spurium

Ramonda pyrenaica

Soldanella montana

Lewisia cotyledon

Cypripedium calceolus

Europe, which grows in the wild in stands of broad-leaved trees on marly limestone or limestone foundations. The flowers have brownish-red petals and yellow pouch with red spots. Both species flower in May and June. They are best planted at or near the edge of the rock garden in the partial shade of trees or thin shrubs with various ferns.

Ramonda. The Pyrenean primrose, *Ramonda pyrenaica* (syn. *R. myconi*), is a native of the Pyrenees. Like the other species of the genus ramonda it makes a flat, ground-hugging rosette of persistent, hairy, evergreen leaves. The leafless stems bear one or two flowers, usually coloured blue, though there are also white *(R. p. alba)* as well as pink *(R. p. rosea)* varieties. The form *R. p. grandiflora* has exceptionally large flowers. Propagation is by leaf cuttings or from seed. *Ramonda pyrenaica* demands a rich leafmould, a northern, sunless aspect and a vertical crevice between rocks so that water drains off and does not remain in the rosettes. It does very well planted beside species of the genus haberlea.

Paeonia. Peonies are lovely garden flowers. They have beautiful single, semi-double or double blooms coloured white, pink or red in many shades. The many species and forms are divided into several groups. *Paeonia officinalis,* the old cottage garden peony of southern and central Europe, belongs to the first group. This peony with large ruby-red flowers has yielded many varieties in all sorts of colours ranging from white to purple.

The second group includes the Chinese peonies — *P. lactiflora,* and the third group the *P. arborea* peonies, rightfully considered the most beautiful. *P. tenuifolia,* which grows in southern Europe, Asia Minor and the Caucasus, belongs to the group of botanical peonies which are best suited for the rock garden because they are only 30 to 40 cm (1 ft to 1 ft 4 in) high and very dainty, with delicate foliage and eight to ten glowing red flowers. They are resolutely hardy and do well in a light soil in sun. They may be grown also in beds but their beauty shows to best advantage in a larger rock garden.

Paeonia tenuifolia

Pulsatilla. This is a very popular rock garden plant. One of the loveliest and most widely grown of the many species is *P. vulgaris* (syn. *Anemone pulsatilla*) which grows wild on limestone rocks in Central Europe. The leaves appear after the flowers, which are large and coloured violet-pink to deep violet, occasionally even white. If grown in alkaline soil and a sunny, well-drained site it is guaranteed to do well and flower profusely. Also good for the rock garden are several of its many forms and varieties, such as *P. alpina,* which has white flowers tinged violet on the outside; the subspecies *P. a. sulphurea* is deep yellow. *P. amoena* has dark, many-partite leaves and bears large reddish-violet flowers somewhat later than *P. vulgaris. P. alba* has pretty white flowers and those of *P. rubra* are velvety red. Extremely lovely is *P. vernalis* which has leathery, hairy leaves and flowers that are violet-brown and hairy outside, smooth inside and white, turning pink as they finish. It is found in very few rock gardens because it is difficult to grow (unlike other pulsatillas it requires acid soil). Planting one of the deep violet pulsatillas together with a few *Adonis vernalis* seedlings or a group of yellow crocuses will make a striking effect in the rock garden when they are in bloom.

Helleborus. This is a well-kown poisonous plant that was used in ancient times as a medicine to treat mental diseases. The deep green leaves of some species last the winter. The flowers (snow white or violet-red, sometimes even green and grey) usually appear in early spring, sometimes in autumn. All species require a rich soil and partial shade (they flower poorly in shade). They are extremely striking in the rock garden in very early spring but they take up much space and thus are more suitable for larger rock gardens. They flower profusely but only after remaining undisturbed in the same spot for several years. Of the many species best for the rock garden are: *Helleborus purpurascens,* native to Hungary, noted for its upright habit and profusion of flowers, which appear in March and April. It makes an attractive contrast with the white *H. niger* (Christmas rose) illustrated and described in the section on perennials. *H. foetidus* (stinking hellebore) is decorative

Primula rosea

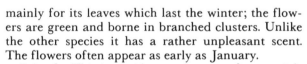

Pulsatilla vulgaris

mainly for its leaves which last the winter; the flowers are green and borne in branched clusters. Unlike the other species it has a rather unpleasant scent. The flowers often appear as early as January.

Primula. This is a widespread genus of perennials described in the section dealing with these plants. The small *Primula rosea* grows in the wild at high-mountain elevations in the northern Himalayas, Kashmir and Afghanistan in damp meadows and often on the very edge of melting snow fields. The leaves generally appear after the flowers, which make a bright splash of colour in the rock garden and are striking even from a distance. The plants require the same conditions as in the wild—a damp situation and rich soil. The variety *P.r.* 'Grandiflora', which is taller and has larger flowers, and *P.r.* 'Gigas' with exceptionally large flowers are best for the rock garden.

Helleborus purpurascens

Erigeron. Fleabane, erigeron, is described in the section on perennials. Only a few small, decorative species may be grown in the rock garden. These include: *Erigeron leiomerus,* native to the Rocky Mountains, which makes pretty masses of decorative flowers with yellow centres and violet ray petals, *E. alpinus,* only 10 to 15 cm (4 to 6 in) high with purplish-red flowers from June until September, and above all *E. aurantiacus,* 20 to 25 cm (8 to 10 in) high and native to Turkestan. It makes a rosette of long, oval leaves and flowers in June and July. This species is exceptionally intolerant of winter wet and often dies at this time. Good drainage is therefore a necessity.

Low-growing species are best put in sunny spots at the top of the rock garden, in dry walls and as edging plants. They are also very attractive in garden beds and borders where, given enough space, they make a large brightly-coloured carpet.

Dodecatheon. Shooting star or American cowslip comprises about 30 species widespread in western North America. They form a ground rosette of leaves like the primrose from which rises a single stalk topped with a cluster of beautiful flowers resembling the blossoms of cyclamen in both shape and colour.

The most widely cultivated species is *Dodecatheon meadia* with broadly oval, longish leaves. The variety *D.m.* 'Splendens' has larger flowers, the variety *D.m.* 'Albiflorum' has white flowers.

Other species that are good for the rock garden include also *D. jeffreyi* which bears a profusion of purple flowers. Dodecatheon requires a heavier, acid soil that is sufficiently moist. It does best in partial shade. After the flowers have faded (the flowering period is from May until June) the plants die back and put out new shoots again in spring.

Achillea. Milfoil or yarrow, achillea, is described in the section on perennials. Most small species are rewarding and easy rock garden plants that thrive in light, limy soil and a sunny situation. They tolerate very dry conditions and full sun. The silvery leaves, which form a thick carpet, are very decorative. Best for the rock garden are: *Achillea aurea,* only 15 cm (6 in) high with golden-yellow flowers from June until September, which is very attractive next to red dianthus species; and *A. tomentosa,* with silvery-green, finely laciniate leaves and golden-yellow, many-flowered clusters, which does well in a sunny spot and light, dry soil.

Erigeron aurantiacus

Dodecatheon meadia

Dryas octopetala

Achillea tomentosa

Lavandula officinalis

Dryas. Mountain avens, dryas, are rock-garden plants from the arctic zone found growing also in the Carpathians. They are small, ground-hugging, evergreen plants with glossy, leathery, scalloped leaves felted on the underside. They are typical rock garden plants of many uses. They may be planted between stones as well as in stone rubble and are also good in dry walls. In May a profusion of flowers resembling anemones are borne. Most widely grown is *Dryas octopetala* which is decorative not only with its leaves and white flowers but also its fruits.

Lavandula. Lavender is a small, evergreen shrublet with grey-green aromatic leaves and usually has blue flowers. The genus, which comprises some 25 species, is distributed from the Canary Islands through the Mediterranean region to India. The true lavender, *Lavandula officinalis,* 25 to 50 cm (10 in to 1 ft 8 in) high, is suitable for edging borders as well as the rock garden. The blue flowers appear in June and July. Noteworthy varieties include: 'Dwarf Blue'—with silvery-grey flowers, 'Hidcote Blue'—violet-blue, 'Munstead'—dark blue, 'Alba'—white, and 'Rosea'—pink. Lavender requires dry, light, well-drained soil containing lime and does not tolerate much damp.

211

Anemone. Snowdrop anemone, *Anemone sylvestris,* has an exceptionally wide distribution. It grows in light deciduous woods from south-western Europe to Kamchatka. Both the pure white, five-petalled flowers and olive-green leaves are decorative. Most widely grown is the large-flowered variety 'Grandiflora', sometimes also the double variety 'Florepleno'. Also belonging to the group of spring-flowerers is the white wood anemone *(A. nemorosa),* which grows in damp deciduous woods and damp meadows. The flowers have six white petals tinged violet or pink on the outside. The rhizome is thin, creeping and coloured deep brown. The cultivated varieties are very good planted in groups between small deciduous shrubs in the rock garden. The yellow wood anemone *(A. ranunculoides)* grows in the same situations as the preceding species. It has deep orange-yellow flowers, sometimes several on a stem, and is best planted with blue, spring-flowering plants.

Euphorbia. Spurge or milkwort has decorative bracts that form terminal clusters on the stems and are coloured during the flowering period, thus resembling large flowers. Described in the section on perennials is the best known plant of this genus *Euphorbia polychroma.* Suitable for the rock garden are the following two; first and foremost *E. myrsinites,* native to the Mediterranean region, which makes broad clumps of grey-green leaves. During the flowering period both the bracts and flowers are coloured yellow. The plant as a whole looks interesting and exotic and is effective on top of a dry wall or in a larger rock garden. The second is *E. capitulata* from Greece, which is a small delicate plant with yellow bracts. It should be planted in rock crevices or stone rubble.

Astilbe. This is described in the section on perennials. Only the small species are suitable for the rock garden such as *Astilbe japonica* and *A. simplicifolia* from Japan, which require partial shade and moist soil. *A. chinensis pumila* makes low clumps (20 to 25 cm [8 to 10 in] high) of decorative leaves with lilac-pink flowers arranged in a slender panicle. It tolerates sun and somewhat dry soil. Breeding accidentally yielded the *A.* × *crispa* varieties which are only 15 to 20 cm (6 to 8 in) high. They have dark, finely divided leaves and low, small panicles of flowers. Low-growing species and varieties of astilbe are effective in the rock garden planted next to omphalodes, waldsteinia, and the like.

Dracocephalum. The genus dracocephalum includes annuals, perennials as well as sub-shrubs. Most are tall plants and thus unsuited for growing in the rock garden. *Dracocephalum austriacum,* native to central and southern Europe, is only 30 to 40 cm (1 ft to 1 ft 4 in) high and is suitable for larger rock gardens. The stems are hairy, the leaves much divided. The large, lipped flowers are usually blue-violet, sometimes also pink or white and appear in July and August. The red variety *D. austriacum rubrum* is very decorative against large limestone boulders or a dry wall. Dracocephalum requires a sunny situation and rather dry soil containing more lime.

Anacyclus. Of the twelve or so species of anacyclus native to the Mediterranean region and Africa only one — *A. depressus* found in the mountains of Morocco — is commonly grown in the rock garden. It is 5 to 10 cm (2 to 4 in) high, with delicate, silvery-grey, ground-hugging leaves. The daisy-like flowers, which appear in May and June, are pink outside and white inside. They open only in sunny weather. This plant does not tolerate unduly moist conditions either in summer or winter. It does best in crevices in tuffa, preferring sandy, rich, well-drained soil and a sunny situation with good drainage. It thrives when planted in a dry wall or rock crevice.

Anacyclus depressus

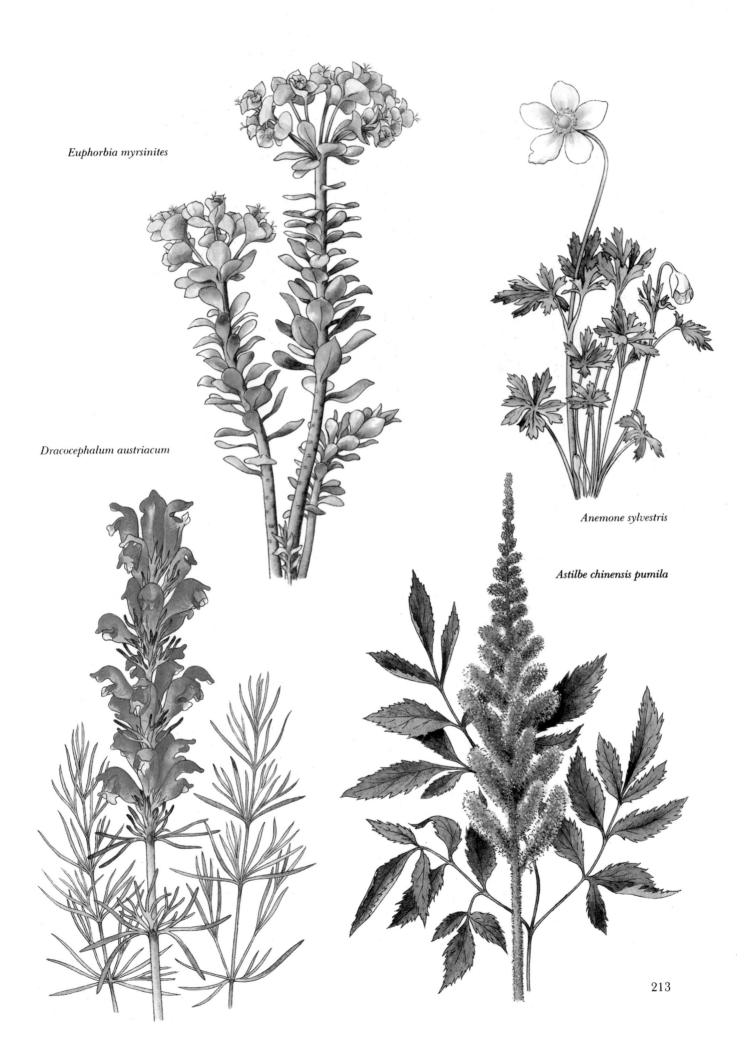

Euphorbia myrsinites

Dracocephalum austriacum

Anemone sylvestris

Astilbe chinensis pumila

213

Papaver alpinum kerneri

Papaver. Poppy, papaver, some 90 species—annual, biennial and perennial in many different forms—grow naturally in the wild. They are described in the section on annuals and perennials. Only a few small species, however, are suitable for the rock garden. First of these is the Alpine Poppy (*Papaver alpinum*) which often grows under very difficult conditions in its native habitat and is therefore very hardy. It makes thick clumps of decorative, laciniate, long-stalked leaves coloured greyish-green. *P. alpinum kerneri* is native to the Alps, Carpathians and Tatras, where it grows mainly in stone rubble or rock crevices. The flowers are yellow with a black mark at the base of the petals, which measure more than 4 cm (1$^1/_2$ in). *P. alpinum burseri* occurs in the same range and is of like habit but the flowers are white and somewhat smaller, 3 to 4 cm (1 to 1$^1/_2$ in). Very similar to this species is *P. pyrenaicum* with leaves less divided and coloured green. The flowers are yellow or white.

Papaver is a decorative subject in the rock garden with its leaves as well as flowers which are borne from May until August; the roots also bind stone rubble and dry walls. It does well in a sunny situation or partial shade in well-drained, unfertilized soil.

Viola. Violet, *Viola odorata*, is our common violet popular for its scent and easy growth. It makes low flowering clumps in spring and again in autumn, spreading freely by means of root-forming shoots as well as by seeding itself. It flowers profusely in any soil that is not too heavy and is tolerant of partial shade as well as sun that is not too strong. Violets are most suitable as an underplanting to trees and shrubs and do fairly well even in naturalised sections of the garden. In the rock garden it is better to plant them at the base of the rockery. The commonest and loveliest are plants with violet flowers but breeding has yielded varieties with much larger flowers coloured white, yellow and even reddish-purple; these are also good for cutting but no longer have the character of true violets.

Phyteuma. Some 30 species of this genus are native to central and southern Europe where they grow at altitudes from 200 to 2,250 m. They are alpines with sparsely leaved stems topped by a dense head of tubular flowers. *Phyteuma scheuchzeri*, native to northern Italy and Switzerland, is decorative in the rock garden in summer when it is in flower (June and July). *P. comosum* is native to the southern limestone Alps, where it grows in crevices in limestone rocks. It makes tufts of dark green leaves and congested heads of bottle-shaped flowers coloured pale blue at the base shading to dark blue at the tips, from which protrude long, curled stigmas.

Phyteuma is a moderately difficult flower which grows well in freely-draining gravelly soil. The best place for it in the rock garden is in rock crevices facing east. It often seeds itself and crops up in various parts of the garden and is generally propagated from seed but sometimes also by division. In the rock garden it is attractive placed next to plants that are its companions in the wild, such as gentiana, *Campanula carpatica*, *Campanula cochlearifolia*, geranium, or next to low-growing ornamental grasses such as *Festuca scoparia*.

Geranium. Crane's bill, geranium, is an annual or perennial plant with branched stems and stalked, divided leaves. The flowers are rarely borne singly, there are usually two to a stem. The only species that are suitable for the rock garden are the low-growing perennials, such as *Geranium argenteum*. Native to the limestone rocks of the southern Alps, it is only 10 to 15 cm (4 to 6 in) high and decorates the rock garden with its large, pink flowers veined dark red. These appear in June and July, when the spring-flowerers are already finishing. Its silvery leaves make it attractive even when not in bloom. It does not tolerate wet, particularly in winter, and thus it is important to make certain the site has good drainage before planting. *G. sanguineum* of central Europe is not suitable for the rock garden because of its height but the varieties 'Nanum' and 'Lancastriense', which are of prostrate habit, are suitable. Native to the Pyrenees is the species *G. cinereum* with silvery leaves and large, pale reddish-violet flowers. It does not tolerate very rich soil. Geraniums do well in sun and light, humus-rich soil and will grow in the same spot for many years.

Phyteuma scheuchzeri

Geranium argenteum

Viola odorata

215

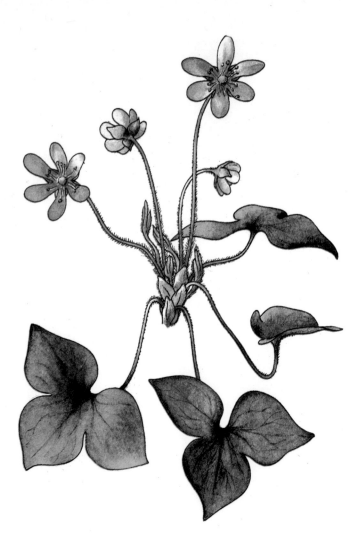

Arabis. Rock cress—most of the 300 species found throughout the world from lowland to high mountain elevations are perennials. They are popular, early-flowering alpines very suitable as edging plants, particularly together with various aubrieta species and varieties, as well as for dry walls and for the rock garden where they are very attractive in larger spaces next to draba, *Dianthus caesius,* androsace. All arabis species have been used for breeding purposes, chiefly *Arabis caucasica* (syn. *A. albida*) from Asia Minor and the Orient. It is 10 to 20 cm (4 to 8 in) high and has stems that are practically leafless and terminated by a thick cluster of flowers. It has yielded a number of garden varieties. Great favourites are the large-flowered forms *A. albida grandiflora, A. a.* 'Variegata', with yellow-white leaves, and the pink *A. a. rosea.* Crossing of *A. aubrietioides* and *A. caucasica* has yielded the *A. × arendsii* forms, of which the most interesting are 'Rosabella'—pale pink, 'Monte Rosa'—dark red, 'Coccinea'—with strikingly large, dark pink flowers, and 'Atrorosea'—bright pink. These require partly shaded or shaded situations, the others like a sunny site and well-drained soil.

Phlox. This genus comprises many perennials and annuals. Only the low, prostrate species are suitable for the rock garden. Of these the most widely grown are: *Phlox amoena* from North America, which makes small shrublets with carmine flowers, about 1.5 cm ($^1/_2$ in) across, carried in thick heads above the leaves, *P. divaricata* from eastern Asia and North America, which makes prostrate shrublets with upright flower stems topped by lilac-blue flowers, about 2 cm ($^3/_4$ in) across, carried in loose heads, *P. douglasii,* which makes compact cushions of narrow leaves and lilac-purple needle-like flowers, and *P. subulata* from

Hepatica triloba

Arabis caucasica

Hepatica. These are undemanding, early spring flowers that require hardly any care and will thrive in the rock garden as well as in the wild, where they grow in open woodland. The typically three- to five-lobed, heart-shaped leaves on long stalks are coloured deep green and appear after the flowers. The flowers are violet-blue, very occasionally pink or white. The plants spread by creeping rhizomes and propagation is by division. They do well in friable soil and partial shade. They like to remain undisturbed and therefore should be transplanted only if absolutely necessary. *Hepatica triloba* grows in shady, mostly deciduous woods in central Europe. Very attractive are the double garden forms 'Alba plena'—white, 'Rosa plena'—pink, and 'Rubra plena'—red. *H. angulosa* flowers somewhat earlier and is also hardier. In the rock garden hepatica is very attractive planted next to *Viola odorata,* anemone and ornamental grasses. In partial shade it can be used as a ground cover instead of turf.

216

North America, the most popular of all phloxes, which makes thick cushions of prostrate stems with needle-like leaves that last the winter. The last has yielded many different varieties of various shapes and colours. They flower from April to May and their compact cushions and brightly coloured flowers make them a must in every rock garden. They do well in sandy or stony soil in a warm, sunny situation.

Dianthus. Only a few of the 270 or so species of pinks are suitable for the rock garden. They are very popular for besides producing lovely, sweetly scented flowers, they fill the gap between the late spring and early summer flowering plants. One that is widely cultivated is the common garden pink—*Dianthus plumarius*—of Europe's mountains. It is a grey-green herbaceous plant with numerous short-leaved stems, each bearing two to five white or pale pink flowers that are usually double. It has many varieties, all of which flower in May. One of the earliest-flowering pinks is *D. alpinus,* native to the eastern limestone Alps, where it grows in stone rubble and meadows at altitudes between 1,000 and 2,250 metres. It makes loose masses of glossy green leaves, 8 to 10 cm (3 to 4 in) high, and bears large, single, fleshy red flowers on stems up to 12 cm (5 in) long. It is grown in crevices between stones with other low-growing rock garden plants as companions.

Saponaria. There are about 30 annual or perennial species of soapwort growing wild in the Mediterranean region and central Europe. In the rock garden they should be put in a dry, sunny spot but they tolerate partial shade. *S. × olivana* is the best species for the rock garden. It makes dense, compact, dark-green cushions smothered with pinkish-red flowers up to 2 cm ($^3/_4$ in) across in June and July. It thrives in a sunny site and light, friable, well-drained soil. It should be planted in a dry wall or in crevices between stones, and is most attractive in the company of arenaria and gypsophila. Other species good for the rock garden are *S. caespitosa* from the Pyrenees, which makes low, round cushions, and *S. pumila* from the Alps and Transylvanian Alps, with bright pinkish-red flowers, which makes dense, low cushions only 3 cm (1 in) high. Unlike the others, this species requires acid soil.

Saponaria × olivana

Dianthus alpinus

Phlox subulata

217

Aster alpinus

Aster. This genus includes about 250 species and varieties, some of which flower in spring, others in summer, and still others in autumn. They are described in the chapter on perennials. Only three, however, are suitable for the rock garden: the autumn-flowering (September, October) *Aster dumosus*—white, pink, blue to violet, the summer-flowering (June, July) *A. yunnanensis*—blue with orange centre, and above all the spring-flowering (May) *A. alpinus*, native to Asia and growing wild in the mountains of Europe, Asia and North America. It makes shrublets or cushions of long, entire leaves with violet-blue, yellow-centred flowers. It is 15 to 20 cm (6 to 8 in) high and thrives in rather dry soil containing lime and in a warm, sunny situation. This species is extremely variable in the wild and thus divided into many natural varieties. The type species has blue flowers but there are also white *(A. a. albus)* as well as pink *(A. a. roseus)* varieties. *A. alpinus* is very attractive planted next to yellow-flowering *Primula auricula* and *Achillea tomentosa*.

Helianthemum. The sun rose, helianthemum, are mostly low subshrubs, 20 cm (8 in) high at the most, with stiff, ovate, entire leaves, which in many varieties are evergreen. The flowers, ranging in colour from white to red, are produced from May until June; double forms flower until the autumn. Single varieties bloom again if cut back when the flowers are finished. *H. apenninum* grows wild in western and southern Europe, its range extending as far as Asia Minor. The varieties *H. apenninum carmineum*—carmine red, and *H. apenninum roseum*—bright red, are very attractive. It is a popular rock garden plant with decorative foliage and short-lived flowers produced daily in great profusion. Generally grown in gardens and rock gardens are the *H. hybridum* garden hybrids described in the chapter on perennials.

Gentiana. This genus includes some 700 species of both annuals and perennials. They are herbaceous plants with leafy stems that are often very short. The flowers generally have a trumpet-shaped calyx and bell-shaped corona. Loveliest are the richly flowering Asiatic gentians, for instance *Gentiana septemfida* from Asia Minor and its hybrids, which flower in late summer; *G. sino-ornata,* from south-western China, makes a central rosette from which emerge numerous stems that put out roots at the nodes. The flowers are long, up to 6 cm ($2^1/_4$ in), blue, greenish-yellow at the base with five reddish-violet, longitudinal stripes. This gentian flowers from September until the frost and grows very well, particularly in heavier, slightly acid soil with good drainage.

218

Gentiana acaulis is a large complex of closely related, slightly varying, stemless gentians which includes the following species: *G. alpina, G. angustifolia, G. clusii, G. dahurica* and *G. dinarica*. Also cultivated are their many hybrids, e.g. *G. × dumonlinii*, which grow best in rock gardens at lowland elevations and are therefore particularly prized. *G. acaulis* grows freely in the wild in the Alps and south-western Carpathians. It flowers in May, often also again in autumn; the flowers are a beautiful gentian blue. Gentians of the acaulis group do best in the rock garden in a sunny or, better, a lightly shaded spot. The soil should be the same as in their natural habitat, that is friable, rather heavy, adequately moist and well drained. Freshly fertilized soil is quite unsuitable.

Helianthemum apenninum

Gentiana acaulis

Gentiana sino-ornata

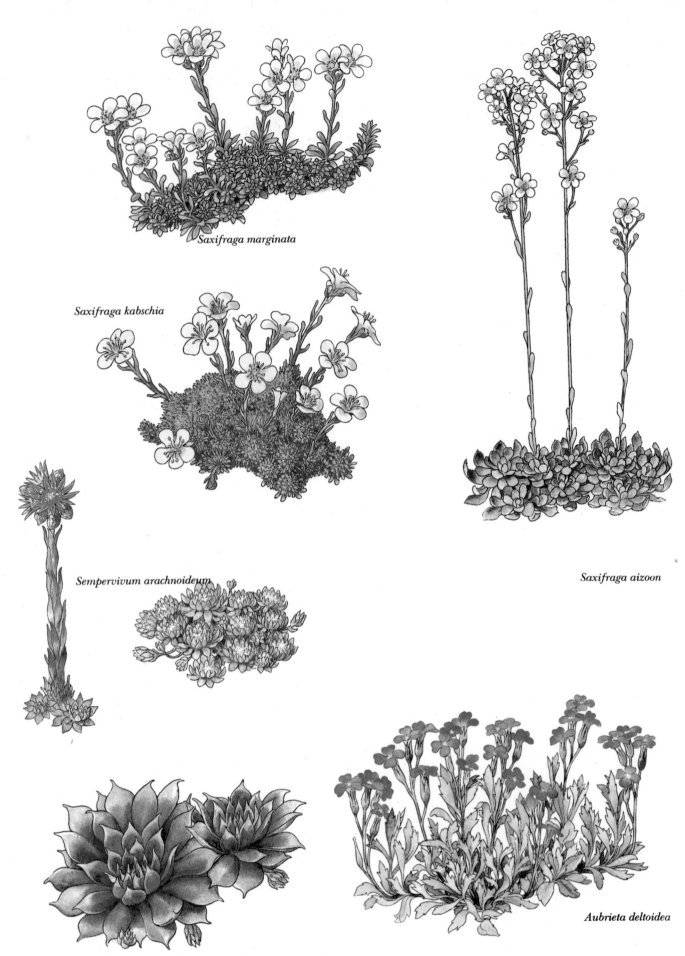

Saxifraga marginata

Saxifraga kabschia

Saxifraga aizoon

Sempervivum arachnoideum

Sempervivum ornatum

Aubrieta deltoidea

220

Sempervivum. Houseleeks are very tenacious plants with fleshy leaves arranged in spherical or flattened, ground-hugging rosettes that stand up well to the severest drought and heat. From the axils of the leaves emerge numerous shoots terminated by tiny, later self-rooting, rosettes. From the centre of the rosette rises an erect, thickly-leaved stem topped by a cluster of white, yellow or pink to carmine flowers. Species with green leaves generally have yellow flowers, red-leaved ones usually have red blossoms. In rock gardens it is recommended to grow several species together. Species are divided into the following four groups according to the colour of the rosettes: 1. species with green leaves, 2. species with leaves coloured brown or brownish-red at the tip, 3. species with brown or brownish-red leaves, 4. species with rosettes spangled with fine hairs, a typical example being the cobweb houseleek, *S. arachnoideum*. *S. ornatum* which makes large rosettes that are red at the centre with green tips is also lovely.

Saxifraga. This genus includes about 300 species some of which are annuals, the remainder perennials. Most are of tufted habit with ascending or upright stems. They require plenty of light but do not tolerate direct sun and should therefore be put in positions facing east or north-east where they will have enough sunlight in the morning but will not be exposed to direct sun at noon. Most should be planted in rock crevices in heavier soil. Saxifrages are divided into 15 separate sections, but not all are good for cultivation. A typical representative of the genus is the species *Saxifraga aizoon*, widespread throughout the northern hemisphere, which bears a profusion of white flowers in late spring and also has decorative grey-green to silvery foliage. Garden varieties derived from this species include: *S. a. rosea* with smaller, pinkish-red flowers, *S. a. splendens* with carmine-red flowers, and *S. a. lutescens* with yellow flowers.

The Kabschia section of saxifrages includes some 45 of the loveliest species, practically all of high alpine origin. In the wild they grow from spring until late summer, but in gardens they flower at the close of winter, the principal flowering period being February until April. Some grow fairly well and make large cushions, such as *S. juniperifolia, S. × haagii, S. × ochroleuca,* others are tender and require much gardening experience such as *S. caesia.* In the rock garden they should be planted in positions facing east or northeast and sheltered from hot sun. They are most effective planted in crevices between rocks or in stone rubble. They require slight permanent moisture but do not tolerate soggy soil. Good drainage is therefore important, as is watering. A very pretty saxifrage belonging to this section is the white-flowered *S. marginata,* native to the Balkans, southern Carpathians, central and southern Italy. It has yielded many hybrids.

Aubrieta. Rock cress, aubrieta, grows freely in the wild in Italy, the Balkans and Asia Minor. It is a very popular and widely cultivated spring-flowering plant. Small tufts or cushions are covered in April and May with a profusion of flowers coloured blue, violet, pink, red or white. Generally grown are hybrids derived from the blue *Aubrieta deltoidea,* which make about 10 cm (4 in) high cushions. In rock gar-

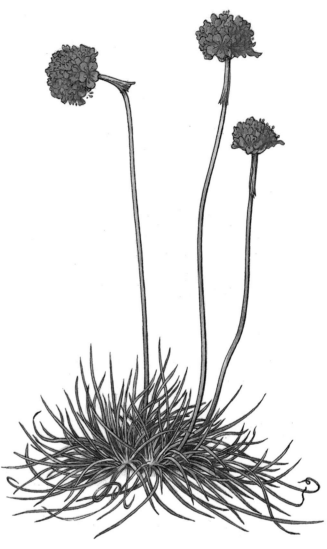

Armeria maritima

dens they are most effective in larger spaces together with *Phlox subulata,* iberis, *Alyssum saxatile.*

Armeria. Thrift, armeria, includes some 50 species growing in the temperate regions of Europe and in the Andes. All make dense tufts of narrow, grass-like leaves and round ball heads of flowers topping leafless stems. They are among the least demanding of rock garden plants and develop into a thick carpet that can serve as a substitute for turf. Thrift are good as edging plants for flower beds, pathways, and at the base of the rockery. They grow in light, sandy soil. Most widely cultivated is the species *Armeria maritima,* which has given rise to several garden forms, such as *A. m. alba*—pure white, 'Crimson Gem'—with smaller, dark red flowers and 'Splendens Perfecta'—a striking bright red.

Artemisia lanata

also found in the Apennines. It is a dwarf, evergreen shrub that makes bright green carpets with a profusion of pink, white or red flowers which appear in March, although sometimes even earlier in winter.

Leontopodium. Edelweiss, leontopodium, are well-known and popular alpine plants native to the mountains of Europe and Asia. They require a sunny situation and poor, stony, dry soil containing lime. In rich soil they do not develop the whitish woolly hairs that make the leaves and flowers so attractive and their growth is too vigorous. The best place in the rock garden is in rock crevices. Best known and most widely cultivated is the species *Leontopodium alpinum*, which grows wild not only in the Alps but also in the Pyrenees, Carpathians, Balkans, Himalayas and Japan. The narrow, felted leaves make a ground-hugging rosette; the lovely star-shaped, flannel-like flowers, which can be pressed and dried, are the plant's chief attraction.

Clematis. *Clematis alpina,* noted for its profusion of flowers, grows in the woodlands of central and southern Europe whence it has spread as far as north-eastern Asia. In gardens, where it grows to a height of 2 m (6 ft), it bears cascades of lovely violet to lilac-pink flowers in May, often flowering once more in summer. It requires a well-drained to gravelly soil, but one that contains humus and is adequately moist. Flowering somewhat earlier is *C. macropetala,* native to China. South-eastern Europe is the home of the upright, 50 to 80 cm (1 ft 8 in to 2 ft 8 in) high *C. integrifolia,* which is used to cover large spaces. Also grown for this purpose are the garden forms, such as *C. montana* 'Grandiflora'.

Erinus. *Erinus alpinus* is a little plant, native to the Alps and Pyrenees, which makes dense mats that fill the spaces between stones in the rock garden. The tiny pink flowers are arranged in dense spikes on short stems and appear in May and June. Erinus seeds itself freely but older plants often disappear. It does well in light, limy soil to which limestone chips have been added, best of all in moderate partial shade. It tolerates sun but then must have sufficient moisture. There is a white form, *Erinus alpinus albus,* and one of the loveliest forms of all is 'Dr. Hanele' with bright carmine flowers.

Artemisia. Wormwood, artemisia, numbers more than 200 species of which only the dwarf, high-mountain species are suitable for the rock garden. The flowers are not particularly attractive and are therefore removed so that the beauty of the silvery leaves shows off to better advantage. Wormwood should be planted in a dry, sunny spot in the rock garden or in a dry wall in light, well-drained soil, ideally in crevices between stones. It soon spreads and makes lovely thick cushions. The most popular species is *Artemisia lanata* (syn. *A. pedemontana*), about 10 cm (4 in) high, with delicate silvery-grey foliage. It grows naturally in the wild in Australia and throughout the world.

Erica. Heathers, erica, flower from early spring until late autumn, the first ones are the *Erica carnea* group. These are followed by the glowing pink flowers of the *E. cinerea* group and in September and October by the *E. vagans* heathers. *E. carnea* grows wild in the Alps, whence it spread westward to Savoy and eastward as far as Moravia and the Balkans. It is

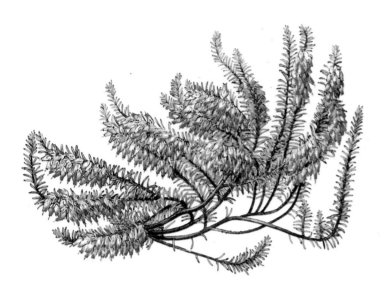

Erica carnea

Erinus alpinus

Leontopodium alpinum

Clematis alpina

Campanula portenschlagiana

Veronica cinerea

Aethionema x warleyense

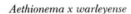

Campanula. Bellflower, *Campanula portenschlagiana,* is native to Dalmatia. It makes low, about 10 cm (4 in) high, thick mats of branching stems covered with small, bright green leaves and bears small flowers in June and July, usually followed by a second flowering in autumn. It grows best in partial shade and humusy, stony soil containing ample lime. 'Birch' is a beautiful gardenworthy form which has a more compact habit and larger, brighter-coloured flowers. It is particularly suitable for dry walls.

Aethionema. Stone cress, Lebanon candytuft, aethionema, has about 40 species native to the Near East and only occasionally are they found in the wild in Europe. Most have grey-green leaves and the flowers are white, pink or purple. Practically all can be grown in the rock garden in full sun and stony soil containing lime. One of the largest is *Aethionema grandiflorum,* up to 20 to 25 cm (8 to 10 in) high, which bears a profusion of pink flowers from May to July. *A. × warleyense,* somewhat similar, includes many differently coloured forms noted for their compact habit. They are very good for planting in dry walls, crevices between boulders, and stone rubble.

Daphne. The dwarf daphnes may be deciduous or evergreen and are generally poisonous. One of the great favourites is garland flower, *Daphne cneorum* — an evergreen shrub 25 to 30 cm (10 in to 1 ft) high smothered in summer with heads of rich pink flowers followed by reddish-brown fruits. It grows wild in the open woodlands of southern and central Europe. In the rock garden it may be grown in partial shade as well as full sun, in stony, humus-rich soil with an admixture of peat.

Daphne cneorum

Hypericum. St John's wort, hypericum, comprises more than 300 species distributed throughout the northern hemisphere from the tropics to the cold regions of the north. They are used in a number of ways in the garden—as bedding plants with low-growing perennials, in dry walls, and in the rock garden. Best suited for this purpose are the low-growing species, such as *Hypericum rhodopeum,* which makes thick, blue-green, cushion-like shrubs with bright yellow flowers borne in profusion in May. It is the earliest to flower. Also good for the rock garden are *H. coris,* about 10 to 15 cm (4 to 6 in) high and *H. olympicum,* 20 to 30 cm (8 to 12 in) high, which bears a profusion of large flowers from July to August and sometimes in September.

Veronica. Speedwell, veronica, of which there are more than 150 species growing in widely different parts of the world. *Veronica cinerea* is from Asia Minor and is 10 to 12 cm (4 to 5 in) high. All green parts of the plant are thickly covered with long grey hairs. It is of prostrate habit and forms thick mats. The pale blue to light pink flowers are arranged in loose spikes. In the rock garden it should be planted in a dry, sunny spot and in poor soil. It has given rise to many garden forms: white—*V. c. alba,* blue—*V. c. pallida,* and pink—*V. c. rosea.*

Hypericum rhodopeum

Globularia elongata

Globularia. Globe daisies, globularia, are low, undemanding, evergreen plants with lovely round heads of violet-blue flowers. *Globularia cordifolia,* native to the Mediterranean Alps, is a prostrate shrublet forming small leaf rosettes from which rise short stems topped by violet-blue powder-puff heads of flowers. It should be planted in rock crevices or stone rubble. It is a hardy rock garden plant and needs no special care. *G. elongata,* native to Asia Minor, is similar but has larger heads of flowers and will thrive in a dry, warm spot with soil containing lime.

AQUATIC PLANTS, FERNS AND ORNAMENTAL GRASSES

Hard and fast rules for laying out and planting a garden would be undesirable, as gardens should differ, no two should be alike. There is such a wide choice of plants and so many ways in which to arrange them that it is almost impossible for two gardens to be identical. Ideas from other gardens can be copied, such as pergolas, pools, the arrangement of pathways, but the overall effect should be unique.

If only the best-known species of plants are grown then gardens may look similar. This may happen when one landscape architect designs the gardens in a community and uses the same or a similar plan for all, including the assortment of plants. Or else the popularity of certain plants may spread. Another reason may be the easy availability of certain plants. Diversity of garden schemes depends on the use of a wide range of plants and on choosing plants that are less widely cultivated, such as water plants, ferns and ornamental grasses.

WATER IN THE GARDEN

Water has a certain magic and soothing effect. Its benefits also include greater atmospheric moisture and the charm of life in and around it. Water plants have a beauty of their own—quite different from that of terrestrial ones. No garden designed for use should be without water.

Garden pools should be shallow, about 30 cm (1 ft) deep is sufficient for most water plants. For water-lilies, which require greater depth, it is necessary to make holes into which they are lowered, and for aquatics requiring a depth of only 5 to 10 cm (2 to 4 in) pockets can be made where the level of the soil below the water's surface can be changed according to need. On the margin of such a pool it is possible to form a bog where many lovely waterside and bog plants will thrive. A fountain can be installed, which besides adding a note of interest also moistens the air, which greatly benefits the plants and keeps the pool supplied with water, an additional asset as water evaporates, particularly on warm days.

AQUATIC PLANTS

Like other plants, aquatics require care, chiefly feeding and the removal of faded top parts. Only organic materials such as well-rotted manure or compost shlould be used. Pebbles should be put on the bottom to keep the soil and fertilizer from rising and clouding the water. Plants that have formed large clumps should be divided now and then as they produce fewer flowers if the clumps are too thick.

Overwintering usually poses a problem. After removing decaying vegetation the pond, if shallow, should be covered with boards and mats on top in severe weather. These should be removed as soon as conditions improve. If the pond is deep covering is unnecessary as most hardy water-lilies will withstand English frosts provided the pool is kept full of water and the crowns well submerged. Ice that forms should be broken to allow the water to be oxygenated. Alternatively plants can be grown in receptacles— boxes, pots, baskets—which are lowered into the water so that the soil surface, which is covered with pebbles, is at the depth required by the given plant. It is then easy to lift the plants for the winter, put them in a frost-proof place and then return them to the cleaned pool in spring.

FERNS

Ferns are unusual plants, attractive with their lacy foliage and graceful fronds. They are not plants for an important spot but for an intimate part of the garden which is quiet and peaceful, the stillness broken only by the whisper of leaves and murmur of water. Ferns are by nature designed for such places, and these are best suited to their needs. They like damp and shady sites where most other plants do poorly for want of light.

Such sites also determine which plants are suitable companions for ferns, these being mainly moisture-loving species such as iris, hemerocallis, large-leaved perennials such as hosta, bergenia, ligularia, rodgersia, and brunnera. Also suitable are forget-me-nots (myosotis) and similar perennials, caltha, trollius, filipendula. Ferns can also be associated with certain ground-carpeting plants such as oenothera, ajuga, armeria, stachys, *Vinca minor,* various saxifrages and ornamental grasses, even though

most are plants of the steppes. Plants which produce bright-coloured blossoms are not attractive with ferns.

Ferns are easy to grow, provided the site is one suited to their needs. Care consists of keeping weeds at bay, occasional feeding and removal of dead dry foliage.

GRASSES

Ornamental grasses are very rewarding plants and cost little. They are a soothing, calming element and soften the visual effect of any planting. The choice of grasses for the garden is wide and varied, ranging from small, 5 to 10 cm (2 to 4 in) high, to huge plants 2 m (6 ft) tall. They can be used to create very attractive arrangements that have the added advantage of being a decorative feature the whole year. That is the great advantage of plants with ornamental foliage, which includes most ferns and grasses. Grasses are generally used as a subsidiary element intended chiefly to help blend and soften the sharp contrasts of flowering plants and the dark effect of certain woody plants. However, they can also be used by themselves to create a 'grass' garden. Such a garden should be combined with water or large, rounded boulders, plus woody plants, suitable perennials, ground-cover plants and bulbs. A grass garden with bulbs has somewhat of an alpine character; if a different type of plant is fitting for the grass garden then it should be included.

Ornamental grasses may be divided into three main groups according to height. The first group includes grasses up to 25 cm (10 in) high, chief representatives being the fescues, festuca; the second includes grasses up to 60 cm (2 ft) high, chief representatives being the oat-grasses, avena; and the third group includes the tall grasses, best known are the various species of miscanthus. The short grasses are used as carpeting plants for ground cover, the ones of medium height for edging or as solitary specimens in the rock garden, and the tall ones only as solitary subjects. To be effective they need a suitable foreground, the best is turf.

Grasses are not particularly difficult to grow or care for. Some should be cut back in early spring so they will form new shoots, and clumps should be thinned and divided so they are not too thick. They should have a light, airy appearance. Further care includes weeding, watering during periods of drought and providing an application of feed in early spring.

229

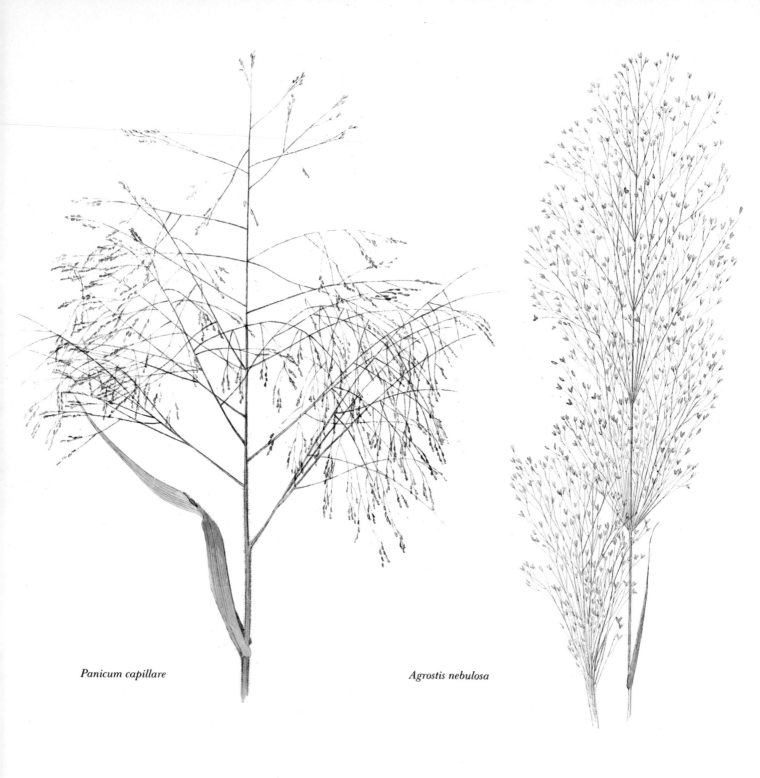

Panicum capillare

Agrostis nebulosa

Ornamental grasses, ferns and water plants are generally last on the list when it comes to selecting plants for the garden. Their importance, however, should not be belittled. They rank, with trees and shrubs, as significant elements in the modern garden scheme and deserve greater appreciation and more widespread use.

Panicum. Of the 400 species the one best suited for decorative purposes in the garden is *Panicum virgatum,* native to eastern North America. It is of upright habit, 60 to 100 cm (2 ft to 3 ft) high, and has pale green leaves tinged with brown. The spikes, which appear in July and August, are also tinted brown. The form 'Strictum' makes a very interesting and attractive solitary subject. It is up to 1.8 m (5 ft) tall, of robust, upright habit, with strong, firm stems and is very effective planted near water. The annual species *P. capillare,* which has delicate spikes 20 cm (8 in) long from July until September, is also very decorative.

Agrostis. This genus numbers 100 species distributed throughout most of the world. Of these several are decorative in the natural and heath garden, and also in mixed beds of brightly coloured flowers where they make restful green patches. The annual species are best sown in early April in a cold frame or directly in the ground. The plants should be spaced 10 to 12 cm (4 to 5 in) apart. *Agrostis nebulosa* is an annual native to Italy, France and Portugal.

Lagurus. The generic name is derived from the Greek words *lagos,* meaning hare, and *oura,* meaning tail, and refers to the resemblance of the inflorescence to a hare's tail, hence the common name—hare's tail. The genus has only the one species, *Lagurus ovatus,* native to the Mediterranean region. It is an annual or biennial, 30 to 40 cm (1 ft to 1 ft 4 in) high, that forms scant tufts. It flowers in May or as late as July, depending on the time of sowing and is attractive associated with gladioli or montbretias, in mixed flower beds as well as in natural layouts. The seeds are sown directly in the ground in April, or, if spring flowering is desired, in late August into boxes which should be put in a light, frost-free room for the winter. The dry spikes are also suitable for floral arrangements.

Arrhenatherum elatius

Lagurus ovatus

Arrhenatherum. This genus includes 40 species distributed throughout Europe, Africa and western Asia. The one usually grown in gardens is the perennial, variegated form *Arrhenatherum elatius bulbosum* 'Variegatum', with decorative leaves longitudinally striped in green and white. It grows to a height of 30 to 40 cm (1 ft to 1 ft 4 in) and the small spikes are borne on stems up to 50 cm (1 ft 8 in) long. It has flat, rounded bulbous roots. The leaves appear early in spring and the plant dies back in June and July. In the garden it is planted in dry, sunny spots, in borders, and in unstructured groups.

231

Festuca gigantea

Festuca glauca

Festuca. This genus includes some 100 species distributed throughout the cooler regions of the world. Many are valuable as crop plants, others as ornamental grasses. Most are tufted, finely-leaved, perennial grasses (commonly called fescues) that grow in dry situations. *Festuca gigantea,* which grows wild in Europe, Asia and Africa, is 30 to 40 cm (1 ft to 1 ft 4 in) high and makes large, loose tufts with wide arching leaves and 60 to 100 cm (2 ft to 3 ft 4 in) long spikes. It thrives in partial shade and is used chiefly in combination with woody plants. *Festuca glauca,* native to the Alps, has stiff, silvery-blue leaves and forms compact tufts 15 to 20 cm (6 to 8 in) high. This evergreen species is one of the most decorative of the fescues. It may be used in the rock garden as well as in all natural layouts, particularly the heath, and naturalised garden, and is also very effective in large groups of perennials. It does best in a sunny situation and rather poor, well-drained soil. Of the many other species, suited to the garden, *F. amethystina* has lovely spreading tufts of fine, blue-green leaves, *F. glacialis* is particularly good for the rock garden, and the undemanding *F. ovina* tolerates even very dry conditions.

Phalaris. This genus includes about 10 species, distributed chiefly in the Mediterranean, of which only the perennial *Phalaris arundinacea* is grown in the garden. In the wild it is found in damp meadows and beside streams throughout Europe and it is, therefore, planted beside pools. The leaves are striped and often 1 m (3 ft) long. It does best in a damp situation, but tolerates dry conditions, though then it is not so tall. It spreads quickly and may become a troublesome weed. It is attractive in flora arrangements with coloured flowers.

Avena. Of this genus the species best suited for decorative purposes in the garden is the perennial *Avena sempervirens*. Growing to a height of 40 to 60 cm (1 ft 4 in to 2 ft), it forms lovely, loose tufts with narrow, bluish-grey-green leaves. In late May and June a great many spikelets on stems up to 1 m (3 ft) long are produced. In summer the stems should be trimmed when they are no longer attractive and in early spring the whole tuft should be cut back hard to the base. This is an ornamental grass that is lovely the entire year round. It may be used in the natural layout and also as a solitary specimen.

Phalaris arundinacea picta

Avena sempervirens

233

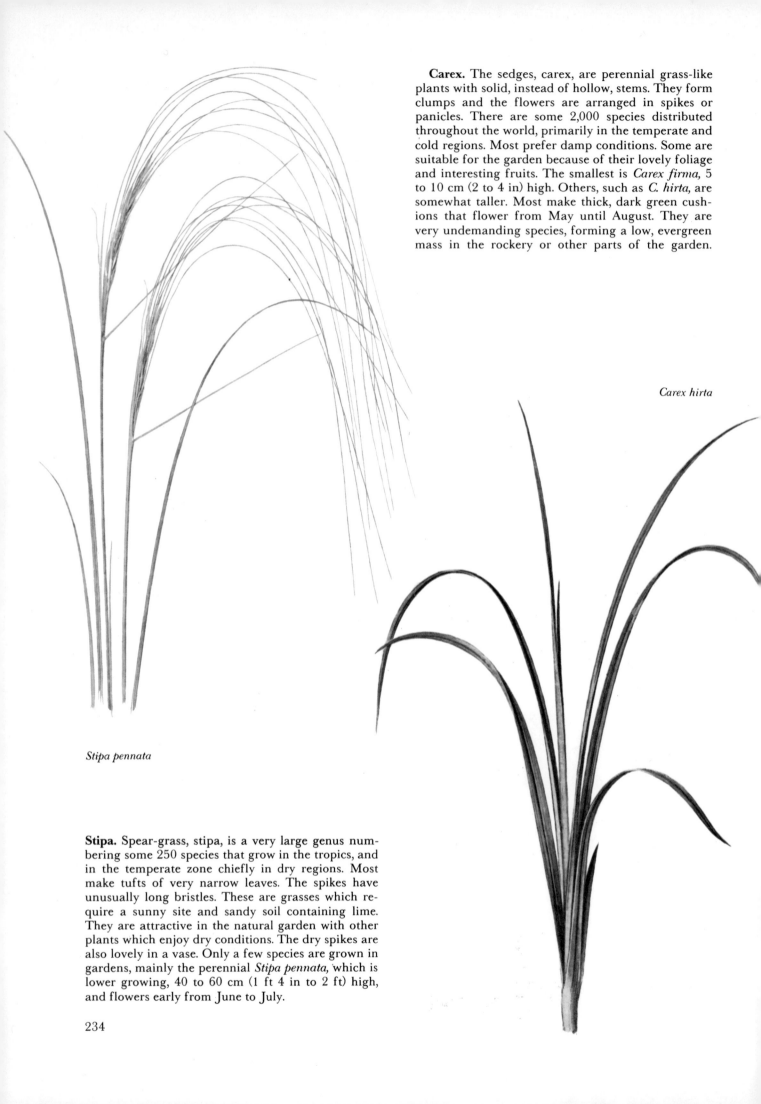

Carex. The sedges, carex, are perennial grass-like plants with solid, instead of hollow, stems. They form clumps and the flowers are arranged in spikes or panicles. There are some 2,000 species distributed throughout the world, primarily in the temperate and cold regions. Most prefer damp conditions. Some are suitable for the garden because of their lovely foliage and interesting fruits. The smallest is *Carex firma*, 5 to 10 cm (2 to 4 in) high. Others, such as *C. hirta*, are somewhat taller. Most make thick, dark green cushions that flower from May until August. They are very undemanding species, forming a low, evergreen mass in the rockery or other parts of the garden.

Carex hirta

Stipa pennata

Stipa. Spear-grass, stipa, is a very large genus numbering some 250 species that grow in the tropics, and in the temperate zone chiefly in dry regions. Most make tufts of very narrow leaves. The spikes have unusually long bristles. These are grasses which require a sunny site and sandy soil containing lime. They are attractive in the natural garden with other plants which enjoy dry conditions. The dry spikes are also lovely in a vase. Only a few species are grown in gardens, mainly the perennial *Stipa pennata*, which is lower growing, 40 to 60 cm (1 ft 4 in to 2 ft) high, and flowers early from June to July.

234

Certain taller species, such as *C. alba, C. baldensis, C. buchananii* and *C. grayi* are a suitable complement to the rock garden sections devoted to grasses.

Cortaderia. The pampas grass, *Cortaderia selloana,* native to the pampas of Argentina and southern Brazil, is one of the loveliest of all grasses grown in the garden. It makes dense tussocks of narrow leaves and is at its best in September when it flowers. The inflorescences are dense, silvery-white spikelets, sometimes more than 50 cm (1 ft 8 in) long, that gleam in the sunlight. This pampas grass is fairly undemanding but needs a warm, sheltered situation and fertile, well-drained soil. Its beauty makes it unrivalled as a solitary specimen. Cut spikes are very long-lived.

Briza. Of the many species of quaking grass only *Briza media* is suitable for the garden. Distributed throughout Europe, it is an undemanding perennial that forms low tufts of narrow green leaves. It flowers from May until June and the airy spikelets are a decorative feature until the autumn. They are also used for dried flower arrangements. Quaking grass thrives in rather dry soil and in a sunny situation. It is suitable for the heath garden.

Cortaderia selloana

Briza media

235

Pennisetum. This is a beautiful grass numbering some 50 annual and perennial species found chiefly in the subtropics and tropics. Most suitable for growing in the garden is *Pennisetum alopecuroides,* a perennial, which has narrow, grey-green leaves and is attractive in late summer, bearing thick, cylindrical flower spikes resembling brushes used for cleaning bottles. It is a delicate grass up to 80 cm (2 ft 8 in) high that gleams in sunshine and does best in a warm, sheltered situation in good, well-drained soil. It is recommended to put some dry leaves over it for the winter and not to cut back the top parts until spring.

Miscanthus. This is a tall, very striking, perennial grass. There are many species and varieties, all of them valuable. The leaves do not appear until late spring and thus they are loveliest from early summer until the winter. The top parts should be cut back in spring. They do best in rich, well-drained soil that is sufficiently moist, particularly in spring and summer. In winter they need dry conditions. It takes two to three years for young plants to attain their full glory. The best species, *Miscanthus sinensis,* is 1.8 to 2 m (5 ft to 6 ft) high; loveliest is the variety 'Gracillimus'. The form 'Zebrinus' has horizontally striped leaves.

Pennisetum alopecuroides

Miscanthus sinensis 'Zebrinus'

Polypodium vulgare

Asplenium septentrionale

Polypodium. A genus which includes some 300 species is found mostly in the tropics. Only one, *Polypodium vulgare,* adder's fern, is hardy and suitable for the garden. It is an evergreen fern of moderate height of 20 to 40 cm (8 in to 1 ft 4 in) with a braching, spreading rhizome. It is a lime-hater and thrives in humus-rich soil in partial shade and will grow as an epiphyte on moss-covered tree trunks and roots. Adder's fern grows rather slowly but is very lovely and can be used as a ground cover in shady areas. The variety 'Serratum' reaches a height of 30 cm (1 ft). If the autumn is dry the leaves die.

Asplenium. The spleenwort, asplenium, is native to Europe, Asia and North America. Most are small ferns growing on rocks and forming clumps. Except for a relatively few species, they thrive in central European conditions and are excellent for the dry wall and rock garden. They do best in soil containing peat and forest litter. The various species are very similar but it is necessary to know which must have lime and which must not. For example, *Asplenium fontanum* and *A. trichomanes,* the maidenhair spleenwort, are lime-lovers whereas *A. septentrionale* does not tolerate lime.

237

Blechnum. This is a large genus numbering some 60 species, many of which grow in the tropics and several in the temperate regions of the southern hemisphere. Only one, *B. spicant,* hard fern, grows in the temperate regions of the northern hemisphere. Its range of distribution includes Europe, Asia Minor, the territory from the Caucasus to Japan, and western North America. It is an evergreen, very decorative fern only about 10 to 20 cm (4 to 8 in) high. Young fronds are arranged in rosettes. It thrives only in acid, pine leafmould with an admixture of peat and loam; further requirements are damp and partial shade.

Phyllitis. This genus occurs in all regions but only one of the six species is hardy in central European conditions. Phyllitis, hart's tongue fern, has typical, tongue-like, entire fronds. It grows wild in mountain forests, attaining a height of 20 to 50 cm (8 in to 1 ft 8 in). Young fronds are pale green, older ones dark green and leathery. It does best in deep shade and moist soil containing lime. There are several varieties with variously frilled and broad fronds.

Blechnum spicant

Phyllitis scolopendrium

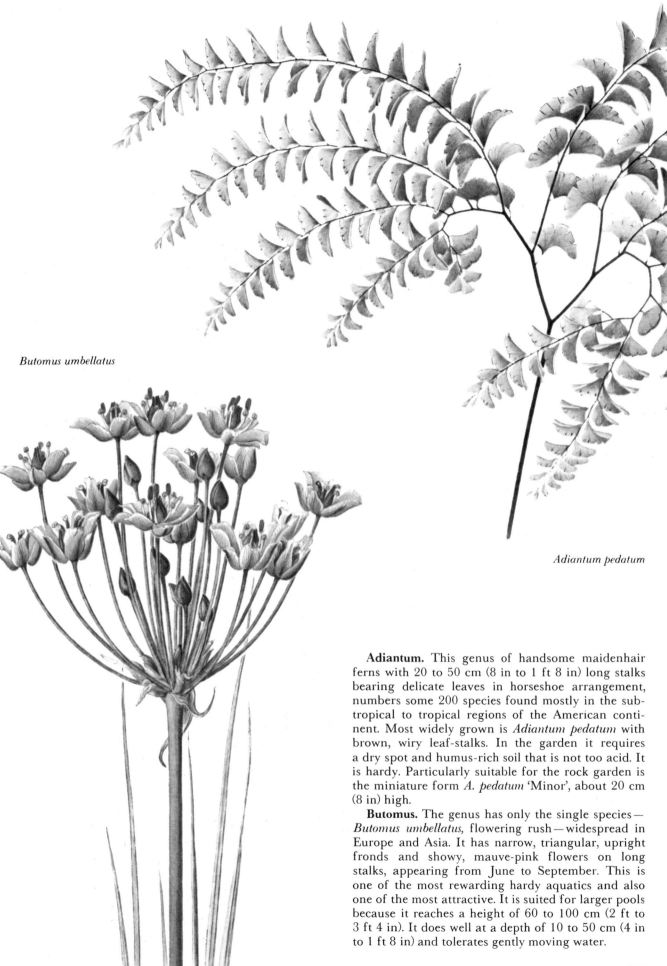

Butomus umbellatus

Adiantum pedatum

Adiantum. This genus of handsome maidenhair ferns with 20 to 50 cm (8 in to 1 ft 8 in) long stalks bearing delicate leaves in horseshoe arrangement, numbers some 200 species found mostly in the subtropical to tropical regions of the American continent. Most widely grown is *Adiantum pedatum* with brown, wiry leaf-stalks. In the garden it requires a dry spot and humus-rich soil that is not too acid. It is hardy. Particularly suitable for the rock garden is the miniature form *A. pedatum* 'Minor', about 20 cm (8 in) high.

Butomus. The genus has only the single species — *Butomus umbellatus,* flowering rush — widespread in Europe and Asia. It has narrow, triangular, upright fronds and showy, mauve-pink flowers on long stalks, appearing from June to September. This is one of the most rewarding hardy aquatics and also one of the most attractive. It is suited for larger pools because it reaches a height of 60 to 100 cm (2 ft to 3 ft 4 in). It does well at a depth of 10 to 50 cm (4 in to 1 ft 8 in) and tolerates gently moving water.

239

Nymphaea hybrida

Nuphar lutea

240

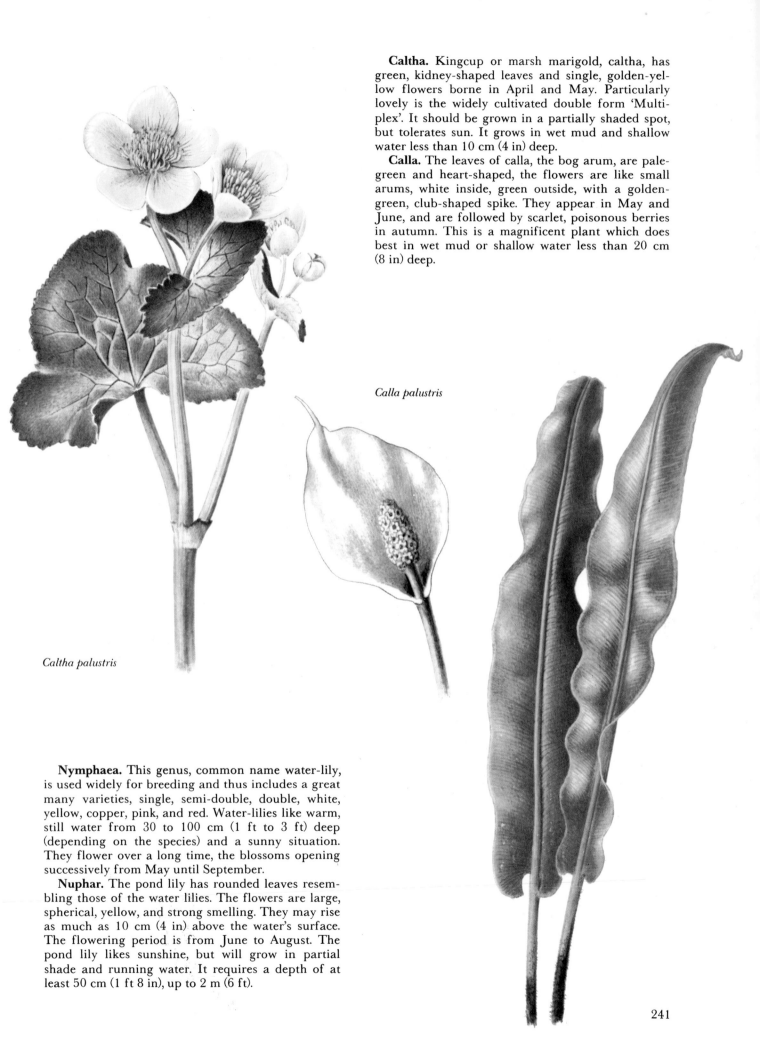

Caltha. Kingcup or marsh marigold, caltha, has green, kidney-shaped leaves and single, golden-yellow flowers borne in April and May. Particularly lovely is the widely cultivated double form 'Multiplex'. It should be grown in a partially shaded spot, but tolerates sun. It grows in wet mud and shallow water less than 10 cm (4 in) deep.

Calla. The leaves of calla, the bog arum, are pale-green and heart-shaped, the flowers are like small arums, white inside, green outside, with a golden-green, club-shaped spike. They appear in May and June, and are followed by scarlet, poisonous berries in autumn. This is a magnificent plant which does best in wet mud or shallow water less than 20 cm (8 in) deep.

Calla palustris

Caltha palustris

Nymphaea. This genus, common name water-lily, is used widely for breeding and thus includes a great many varieties, single, semi-double, double, white, yellow, copper, pink, and red. Water-lilies like warm, still water from 30 to 100 cm (1 ft to 3 ft) deep (depending on the species) and a sunny situation. They flower over a long time, the blossoms opening successively from May until September.

Nuphar. The pond lily has rounded leaves resembling those of the water lilies. The flowers are large, spherical, yellow, and strong smelling. They may rise as much as 10 cm (4 in) above the water's surface. The flowering period is from June to August. The pond lily likes sunshine, but will grow in partial shade and running water. It requires a depth of at least 50 cm (1 ft 8 in), up to 2 m (6 ft).

241

Sagittaria. This genus numbers some 30 species growing in the temperate regions and in the tropics. They are very hardy plants adaptable to the water's depth. Their beauty makes them one of the most suitable plants for pools. *Sagittaria sagittifolia,* arrowhead, native to Europe, has handsome, arrow-shaped leaves up to 70 cm (2 ft 4 in) long and white flowers with a purple blotch at the base borne on stems that are no longer than the leaves. The flowering period is June to July. Shallow water (10 to 20 cm [4 to 8 in] deep) is best as it flowers poorly at depths greater than 50 cm (1 ft 8 in). Sagittaria spreads by shoots, occasionally to an unwelcome extent in congenial conditions. For this reason it is best planted in a pot if in a small pool so it cannot get out of hand.

Acorus. This genus has two species, the only one of importance is *Acorus calamus,* the sweet flag, which grows wild in small lakes and ponds of Europe, Siberia and North America. The narrow leaves resemble those of the aquatic irises. The thick, fleshy rhizomes have a distinctive aromatic taste and smell. The flower heads, produced in June and July, are 10 to 20 cm (4 to 8 in) long, yellowish-green at first, later brown, and inconspicuous. Acorus is a hardy, undemanding plant that can be used in bog gardens and pools up to 20 cm (8 in) deep. It is readily propagated by division of the rhizomes. There is an attractive and decorative, variegated form, 'Variegatus', with leaves longitudinally striped in yellow and white, new leaves edged with red.

Sagittaria sagittifolia

Acorus calamus

Scirpus. The plants of this genus are mostly large and robust. Best known is *Scirpus lacustris,* bulrush, a large plant 1 to 2.5 m (3 ft to 8 ft) high forming clumps of thick round rushes. The brown heads of flowers are interesting and appear in July and August. The bulrush is a very undemanding and hardy plant that spreads quickly, crowding out other aquatics, and therefore it is best put in a large receptacle on the pool bottom. It adapts itself to various depths and will even grow in water 1 m (3 ft) deep. It is interesting to note that the height of the plant above the surface is always the same no matter at what depth it is put. The species *S. tabernaemontani* is somewhat smaller, about 80 cm (2 ft 8 in) high; there is a very attractive variety 'Zebrinus' with the rushes horizontally barred in green and white. It does well at a depth of 30 cm (1 ft).

Typha. Reed mace or cat-tail; this genus numbers some 15 species found in the tropical and temperate regions. The reed mace is a typical plant of the ponds of central Europe. The leaves are long and narrow and the poker-like heads of flowers are very popular as indoor decoration. They are also attractive water plants for a large garden pool. The more robust species such as *Typha angustifolia* and *T. latifolia* are suitable for pools with water about 50 cm (1 ft 8 in) deep. They grow to a height of 2 m (6 ft), have no particular requirements and are hardy. The flowering period is in July and August. Propagation is by division. *T. minima,* which is only 60 cm (2 ft) high, is suitable also for small pools with water less than 20 cm (8 in) deep. The leaves are very narrow (only about 2 mm across) and the small flower heads ovate to spherical.

Typha minima

Scirpus lacustris

243

ANNUALS

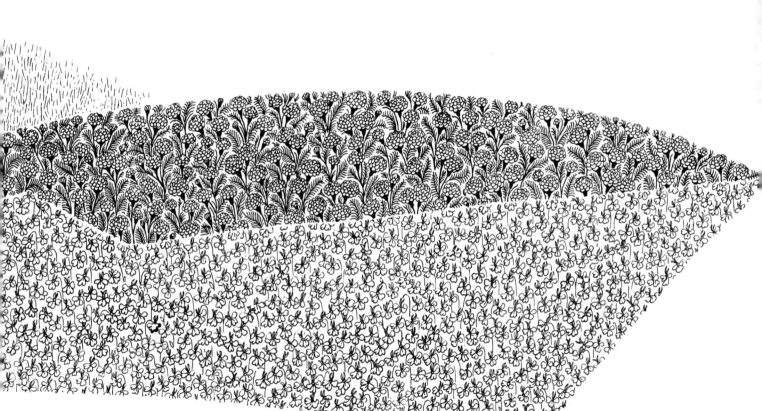

Annuals add a bright spot of colour to the garden for the second half of the growing season. They are not permanent plants and thus can be experimented with. Those that do not fit into the general scheme may simply be left out the following year.

A mixed annual bed should contain a number of species planted in groups to form a pattern in which the colours create a harmonious effect. When planning the layout species with similar uses should be put beside each other. To have a fine display of colour as long as possible the bed should contain both early-flowering species as well as ones that flower until the autumn.

Annuals for cutting are very important. A bed of such plants serves a twofold purpose — it brightens both the garden and home. Many species put out new side shoots after the main stem is cut off, such as China asters (callistephus), snapdragons (Antirrhinum), pot marigolds (calendula), chrysanthemum, sweet peas (lathyrus). The choice of pretty annuals for cutting is wide, including, for example, the Chabaud carnations *(Dianthus caryophyllus)*, stock (matthiola), zinnia, African marigolds (tagetes), sea lavender (limonium), cosmea (cosmos), larkspur (delphinium), sunflowers (helianthus), phlox, scabious (scabiosa), tickseed (coreopsis), baby's breath (gypsophila), and venidium.

Climbing annuals are widely grown, planted beside fences, porches, to climb up various poles and lattice-work, which may be of thin wire or twine because the plants are usually not heavy. Best known and most rewarding are the sweet peas (lathyrus), and nasturtiums — *Tropaeolum*

majus. Both are well-loved climbing plants.

Annuals are also planted in perennial beds to provide a display of colour before the perennials come into their places or to fill empty spaces. Best for this purpose are those with similar habits to the perennials, such as blanket flowers (gaillardia), coneflowers (rudbeckia), vervain (verbena), cornflowers (centaurea), sunflowers (helianthus), and chrysanthemum.

Annuals used to make a bright splash of colour in the rock garden and to provide a display of flowers there in late summer and autumn include rose moss (portulaca), dorotheanthus, treasure flower (gazania), Californian poppy (eschscholzia), sweet alyssum (alyssum), and floss flower (ageratum).

A number of pretty, low growing species are good as edging plants for beds, such as sweet alyssum (alyssum), Californian poppy (eschscholzia), treasure flower (gazania), lobelia, floss flower (ageratum), short-growing Chinese asters (callistephus), rose moss (portulaca), salvia, vervain (verbena), bedding petunias (petunia), *Begonia semperflorens* and low French marigolds *(Tagetes patula, T. tenuifolia)*. For this purpose, they should be planted close together.

In beds where bulbs have finished flowering annuals provide a further display of colour. These include the sun-loving species which are planted in the second half of May, such as Chinese asters (callistephus), African marigolds (tagetes), coneflower (rudbeckia), treasure flower (gazania), balsam (impatiens), zinnia, scabious (scabiosa), bedding petunias and *Begonia semperflorens.*

The best for drying and winter decoration as an everlasting is statice (limonium), but a great favourite is the true everlasting flower (helichrysum).

For growing in ceramic bowls and urns in the garden the more striking annuals such as salvia, godetia, lobelia, catchfly (silene), rose moss (portulaca), candytuft (iberis) and many others are best. Two or even three different species may be put out one after the other during the growing season.

Many annuals are lovely potted as house plants. Commonly used for this purpose are the wallflower (cheiranthus) — a biennial — *Begonia semperflorens*, balsam (impatiens), and others that form clumps.

Annuals are also suitable for planting in boxes and on balconies. Best are petunias, but the choice is wide, including lobelia, candytuft (iberis), French marigolds (tagetes), balsam (impatiens), low-growing Chinese asters (callistephus), and even sweet peas (lathyrus).

Annuals with striking leaves or of unusual habit are interesting. These are primarily summer cypress or burning bush (kochia), love-lies-bleeding (amaranthus), particularly lovely next to architectural elements in the garden, as well as castor oil plant (ricinus), a robust annual that can be used in place of ornamental shrubs.

Many annuals are used for forcing, for example stock (matthiola), sweet peas (lathyrus), pot marigolds (calendula), snapdragons (antirrhinum).

Theoretically all annuals may be sown directly outdoors. Some, however, have a long growth period and would not flower until late autumn and furthermore would not be as attractive. These must be grown-on so that they will flower when their beauty can be fully appreciated. Growing-on speeds up the growth cycle. On the basis of these requirements annuals may be divided into the following five groups:

1. Species that must be grown-on in the greenhouse; this is usually done at a nursery from which the gardener purchases the seedlings which he then plants in his garden (for example, petunias).
2. Species that must be grown-on in a semiwarm frame; here, too, the gardener usually purchases seedlings from the nursery (for example, snapdragons—antirrhinum).
3. Annuals that can be grown under a polythene sheet or in a cold frame; seedlings can be purchased but often these are grown by the gardener (for example, Chinese asters—callistephus).
4. Annuals that are sown in a nursery bed and then pricked out into the permanent bed, or else sown directly in the ground where they are to grow (for example, pot marigolds—calendula).
5. Annuals that must be sown in their permanent site because they do not tolerate transplanting; when they have sprouted they are thinned to the required spacing (for example, Californian poppy—eschscholzia).

Some species may be grown in several of the above ways and the requirements need not be strictly observed; however, if we wish to have a good and lengthy flowering period it is best to observe the guidelines.

Annuals are not difficult to grow. All should be put in a sunny position; in partial shade they do poorly and in full shade they won't grow at all. They should not be exposed to wind, particularly the taller species and varieties, for they all have fragile stems that can be bent or broken by wind. Some require staking, others need to be tied with soft twine or raffia to keep the clump from spreading out too much. The richer the soil, which should be neither too dry nor too wet, neither too light nor heavy, the better the flowers. During the growth period it is recommended to feed those species that have a lot of foliage (climbing annuals and annuals for cutting). Regular watering and regular weeding are also necessary. Furthermore the soil must not be allowed to become caked; light hoeing when weeding will prevent the formation of a crust and will also promote good growth by providing the plant roots with air. After the flowers have faded they should be removed, for the formation of seed weakens the plants. Diseased plants should also be removed and burnt.

Many annuals have only a brief growing period and so for a lengthier display either the seedlings are put out into the bed at successive intervals or else, if grown from seed, they are sown in succession. The sweet pea (lathyrus) is a typical example. The seeds are sown every two weeks from the end of March until mid-June. Plants sown in March flower in June and July, those sown in July flower until the frost. The same can be done with others such as pot marigolds (calendula), cornflowers (centaurea), larkspur (delphinium), convolvulus, Californian poppy (eschscholzia), poppy (papaver), candytuft (iberis).

Antirrhinum. The snapdragon, antirrhinum, is an annual of many uses. It is native to the warmer regions of Europe, Asia and America, where it grows as a perennial, which would also be the case in central Europe if it could survive the winters there. The generic name is derived from the Greek words *anti,* meaning resembling, and *rhinos,* meaning nose. Its common name in many languages refers to its resemblance to a lion's, hare's, or dragon's mouth.

Snapdragons are of two basic kinds according to height; tall ones up to 90 cm (3 ft) high and low ones less than 25 cm (10 in) in height. There are also intermediate varieties 40 to 50 cm (1 ft 4 in to 1 ft 8 in) high, but these are not grown as frequently. Snapdragons also come in a wide range of colours, mostly pure ones, but there are also several attractive bi-coloured forms. Flowering begins in late June and continues until the first frost. Removal of the terminal shoots promotes branching.

The seeds germinate after 7 to 12 days and remain viable up to 6 years. They should be sown in a cool frame in late February or March or in a nursery bed in April. When the seedlings are about 10 cm (4 in) high they are moved to their permanent site; this may be as early as late April because they are not unduly sensitive to cold. They should be put in a sunny position, in fertilized soil, and should be watered adequately throughout the growing period.

Snapdragons are suitable for mixed annual or carpeting beds. Both the tall and low-growing species may be combined with plants of similar habit. Snapdragons have rich colours and thus the choice of companion plants requires careful consideration; recommended are ones of more delicate hues for contrast. Snapdragons may also be put in a bed by themselves in a bright mixture of colours. For edging, however, it is best to use a single colour.

Tall and intermediate forms are mostly used for cutting. Good associates in the vase are white daisies *(Chrysanthemum maximum),* and blanket flowers (gaillardia) are lovely with yellow, orange or white snapdragons. A simple and attractive arrangement is a combination of snapdragons and pot marigolds (calendula). Another good companion is cosmea (cosmos), and African marigolds (tagetes) with snapdragons produce a striking effect. A bouquet of snapdragons alone, either of the same or different varieties, is also beautiful. When planning arrangements one should keep in mind that white and yellow snapdragons create a delicate effect whereas dark red ones make a bold contrast.

Callistephus. Chinese aster—*Callistephus chinensis*—is one of the most rewarding and most widely grown annuals. It is native to China and was introduced into Europe in 1732, first of all to France, whence it spread rapidly elsewhere. The generic name is derived from the Greek words *kallos,* meaning beautiful, and *stephos,* meaning crown.

Asters come in a wide range of colours with variously shaped flowers on stems 15 to 70 cm (6 in to 2 ft 4 in) high. The genus is a very large one and includes a great many species and varieties. Most countries have their own assortment. They can be divided according to height—tall species more than 50 cm (1 ft 8 in) high, intermediate species 35 to 50 cm (1 ft 2 in to 1 ft 8 in) high, and low ones less

Antirrhinum majus

than 35 cm (1 ft 2 in) high. Tall and intermediate asters are used primarily for cutting and decoration in the vase, low-growing species as edging plants for beds, and the lowest, which form compact clumps, also for potting.

They are also divided according to the shape of the flower. The first group includes the single varieties. These are not the most modern of flowers and are more often found in country gardens in a variegated mixture with other annuals. Ray-petalled asters, on the other hand, are very popular because of the elegant shape of the flower composed of narrow petals. Many varieties resemble chrysanthemums, others may have petals that are thread-like or recurved at the tip. The group of asters with quilled petals is the hardiest, stands up well to transport and is long-lived in the vase. The 'Ostrich Plume' group has globose flower heads.

All groups are marked by a wide range of pure and glowing colours. Multicoloured asters are not cultivated. Plants put out in the bed in mid-May flower in succession from the second half of July until September. Removal of the first terminal flower will promote branching and further flowering. Plants that are put out later (after the bulbs have finished in June) produce flowers until the frost.

Seeds germinate after 7 to 14 days and remain viable for 3 to 4 years. They are sown in March or April in a cool frame or nursery bed, seedlings are pricked out and when the first two true leaves appear they are moved to their permanent site. Tall varieties should be spaced about 40 cm (1 ft 4 in) apart, moderately tall ones 30 cm (1 ft 2 in) and low varieties 20 cm (8 in) apart. They should be put in a sunny position in weathered soil that does not cake after watering. They should not be put in beds fertilized with fresh manure or where tomatoes have previously been grown because in such soil they are susceptible to fusarium wilt, which survives in the ground a number of years.

Asters are the most important annuals for cutting. In the vase they should be used by themselves, without any supplementary feature, best of all in a mix-

ture of colours. The water should be changed frequently. In modern, mainly spiked dish arrangements, they may be combined with other flowers of similar character. Asters and snapdragons (antirrhinum), make a very striking arrangement, the same being true of asters and zinnias. Yellow pot marigolds (calendula) make a pretty contrast with asters of different colours. An attractive, delicate effect is achieved by combining pink cosmeas (cosmos) with white asters. African marigolds (tagetes) make an interesting arrangement with blue or pink asters.

Clarkia. This is a native of North America. Two species are grown in the garden: *Clarkia elegans,* up to 60 cm (2 ft) high, and *C. pulchella,* about 40 cm (1 ft 4 in) high, as well as the variety *C. p. nana,* less than 30 cm (1 ft) high. The flowers, in shades of red, pink and white, are borne in the axils of the leaves in slender spikes in July and August.

This is an undemanding annual. The seed is sown in April in the bed in full sun and the seedlings are then thinned to a spacing of 30 cm (1 ft). They make fragile bushy plants that require adequate watering. After flowering the plants should be cut back to about half their height and then they will flower once again. The seed remains viable for 3 to 4 years.

Clarkia is not suitable for cutting, but is excellent for mixed beds. It is best to grow clarkias of various colours than to combine them with other annuals in the bed.

Tagetes. African and French marigolds, tagetes, are indispensable annuals for bedding schemes and for cutting. They are native to Mexico and North America and are named after the Etruscan god Tages, who was the son of Jupiter. The following three species are grown in the garden: *Tagetes erecta,* up to 80 cm (2 ft 8 in) high, *T. patula,* only 15 to 40 cm (6 in to 1 ft 4 in) high, and *T. tenuifolia,* less than 20 cm (8 in) high, with narrow, linear leaves. The flowers are single or double, yellow, orange or with brownish-red shading, and with a characteristic pungent smell.

These are undemanding plants. They are either sown in a frame in March or directly in open ground in April. Tall marigolds are used mainly for cutting and should be thinned out to a spacing of 25 cm (10 in). They should be put in full sun and may be transplanted at any time, even during the flowering period. The seed germinates after about 7 days and remains viable for 3 to 4 years.

For decoration in the vase tagetes is very attractive by itself; combinations with blue flowers—delphinium, liatris, *Iris kaempferi, Verbena hybrida*—make colourful arrangements, with zinnia or the white blossoms of *Chrysanthemum maximum* they are also lovely.

Zinnia. This is a widely grown annual. It is native to Central America, whence it was introduced into Europe in 1759, and is named in honour of the German botanist J. G. Zinn. There are a number of spe-

Clarkia elegans

cies but only two are grown in the garden. One is *Zinnia elegans*—up to 90 cm (3 ft) high with single as well as double blooms, 7 to 10 cm ($2^3/_4$ to 4 in) across, in various colours. The second is *Z. haageana,* which is shorter, only about 40 cm (1 ft 4 in) high, with smaller blooms that are orange or a mixture of colours.

Both are fairly difficult to grow. The seed is sown in a frame and the seedlings pricked out in mid-May—lower plants 10 cm (4 in) apart, taller plants up to 20 cm (8 in) apart. They require good soil and a sunny situation. The seed germinates in 4 to 7 days and remains viable for 4 to 6 years.

Tagetes erecta

Zinnia elegans

The shorter-growing zinnias are suitable chiefly as edging for beds or for mixed beds. Taller ones are excellent for cutting, lasting up to 2 weeks in the vase. In floral arrangements they are used by themselves, particularly if they come in a mixture of colours. Delicate gypsophila is sometimes added to highlight the effect. A striking arrangement may be obtained by combining red zinnias and yellow rudbeckia, the combination of zinnia and antirrhinum offers a wide choice of possibilities, red zinnias are good with pale yellow tagetes, and white zinnias with orange tagetes.

251

Papaver somniferum

Papaver. The poppy, papaver, is an age-old medicinal plant grown also for its oily seeds. In ancient Egypt the infusion from this plant was used as a remedy to relieve pain. Several of the 100 species, mostly native to Europe and Asia, have been grown for garden decoration for several centuries. One is *Papaver somniferum,* the opium poppy, which has striking flowers in all shades excepting yellow and blue. The many varieties are divided into two groups according to the shape of the flower: peony-flowered—single or double, with wavy, entire or only slightly notched margins; and carnation-flowered—double, with delicately cut, feathery petals. The exotic blooms are magnificent but are produced only for a brief period in July and thus other plants must be put out in their stead after they have finished. They are most effective as solitary subjects or in larger groups by themselves. They are also used for cutting, even though they are not long-lived in the vase and the petals soon fall. The flowers should be cut while still in bud, when they are beginning to open.

Calendula. Pot or garden marigold, calendula, flowers continuously throughout the year and hence its generic name (the Latin word *calendula* means the first day of the month, figuratively the whole year long). *Calendula officinalis* is native to southern Europe and was originally grown only as a medicinal plant. Nowadays it is one of the best known of our garden flowers, its yellow and orange hues brightening the scene the whole summer long. It is one of the easiest plants to grow in almost any soil, though it does best in soil containing lime and in sun. The seed is sown where the plants are to flower from April onward; successive sowing will give full and continuous flowering throughout the summer. Seeds may also be sown in autumn. The flowers should be removed promptly as they fade because if seed is allowed to ripen the blooms that appear later are single and smaller and the plant ceases to bear flowers. With its glowing colours the pot marigold is striking not only in mixed annual beds but also in separate groups by itself, particularly in front of dark conifers or tall blue larkspur (delphinium). It may also be used for cutting, even though the branching stems are short.

Matthiola. The stock is named in honour of the famous 16th-century botanist Matthioli. *Matthiola incana annua* is native to the Mediterranean region and has been grown in gardens since the 16th century. It is a magnificent annual with flowers arranged in loose or dense spikes coloured white, pink and many shades of violet. They are either single or double and have a penetrating scent. Only the double varieties are grown in the garden—either single

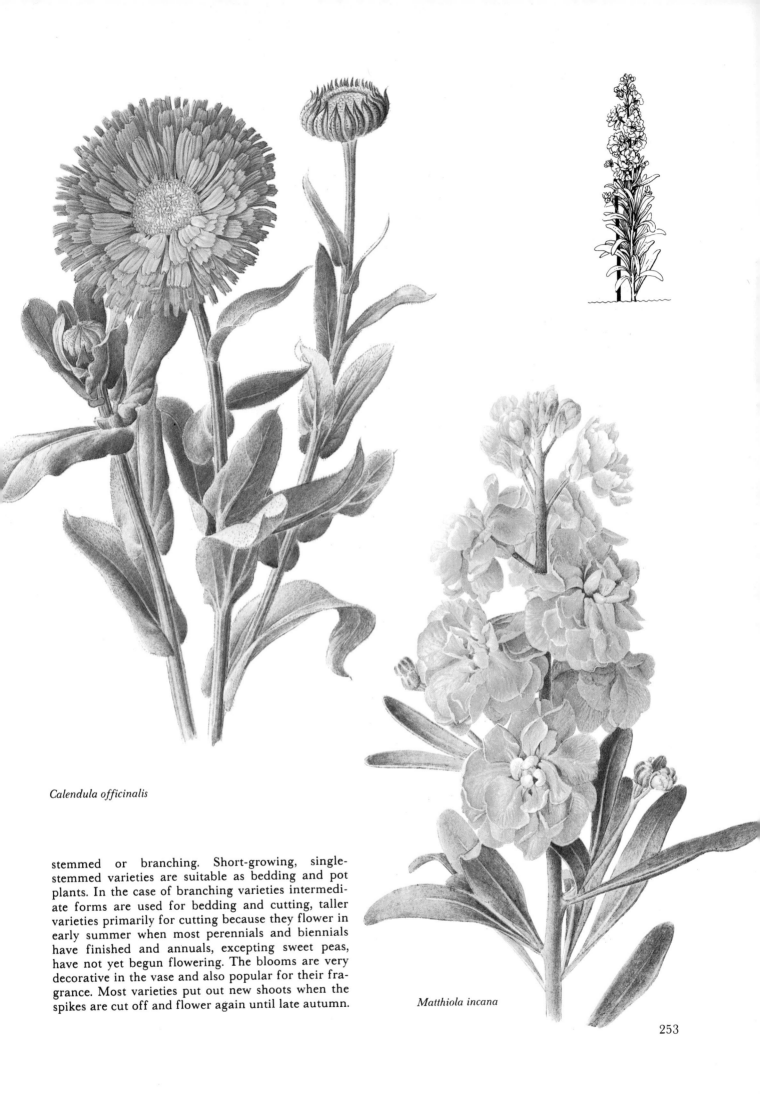

Calendula officinalis

stemmed or branching. Short-growing, single-stemmed varieties are suitable as bedding and pot plants. In the case of branching varieties intermediate forms are used for bedding and cutting, taller varieties primarily for cutting because they flower in early summer when most perennials and biennials have finished and annuals, excepting sweet peas, have not yet begun flowering. The blooms are very decorative in the vase and also popular for their fragrance. Most varieties put out new shoots when the spikes are cut off and flower again until late autumn.

Matthiola incana

253

Rudbeckia. Coneflower, rudbeckia, named in honour of the Swedish botanist K. Rudbeck, is native to North America and Mexico. Most species are perennial but two are grown as annuals. One is *Rudbeckia bicolor,* 30 to 50 cm (1 ft to 1 ft 8 in) high, with pale yellow, black-centred flowers. New varieties are taller, up to 1 m (3 ft) high, with yellow flowers that have a reddish-brown zone round the dark centre. Better known is *R. hirta,* which forms shrubby, branching plants bearing as many as 60 flowers up to 10 cm (4 in) across. These are yellow with black raised centres; some varieties have a reddish-brown zone round the centre.

Their long flowering period, from July until the frost, makes them very rewarding annuals. They are planted 30 cm (1 ft) apart in large groups by themselves or in mixed beds. This is also one of the best annuals for cutting, producing flowers that will last up to 14 days in water over a period of two to three months. They should be cut when fully open and immersed in water right away, for partly open buds soon wilt. Rudbeckia is not put with other flowers in the vase, being loveliest by itself.

Delphinium. This is better known as a striking perennial. *Delphinium ajacis,* larkspur, from the Mediterranean region, is one of the annuals grown in the garden. The plants are tall and slender with flowers in shades of pink, violet, blue and yellow. They should be staked so that they are not broken by winds. They flower in summer for only a fairly brief period.

They are raised from seed, best sown in autumn or early spring, and the seedlings should be thinned to a spacing of 15 cm (6 in), leaving two seedlings at each spot. They are good in mixed annual beds, both in single colours and in a mixture of colours; they are also suitable for cutting—the plants are pulled up whole for decoration in tall vases.

Rudbeckia bicolor (left),
Rudbeckia hirta (right)

Helianthus. The sunflower, helianthus, is derived from the Greek words *helios,* meaning sun, and *anthos,* meaning flower, and it is known as the sunflower in all languages because its golden-yellow heads resemble the sun. It is native to North and South America and includes both perennial and annual species. The most widely grown of the annuals is *Helianthus annuus,* a double form of tree-like habit growing to a height of 1.2 m (4 ft) with rough leaves and bright yellow flowers up to 15 cm (6 in) across.

The seed is sown directly in the ground about 40 cm (1 ft 4 in) apart. The seedlings should be thinned to one plant at each spacing. Sunflowers are suitable for demarcating areas and beds, to mask walls, fences. If grown for cutting they should be spaced closer together, about 25 cm (10 in) apart.

Delphinium consolida

Helianthus annuus

255

Godetia grandiflora

Godetia. This native to North and South America was named in honour of the 19th-century Swiss botanist C. H. Godet. The species generally grown in the garden is *Godetia grandiflora*. It is 30 to 40 cm (1 ft to 1 ft 4 in) high and makes compact shrubby plants with flowers up to 8 cm (3 in) across. Best known forms are the ones with single, symmetrical, four-petalled flowers and the double azalea-flowered sorts, *G. azaleiflora plena*, so called because they resemble azaleas.

This is a gay flower, but only in sun. It requires light soil and tolerates drought; many plants die if watered in full sun. Godetia flowers for only a brief period, in late June and early July in the case of grown-on seedlings, and a month later if sown in the open. It is used by itself as an edging or bedding plant; it is not as striking in a mixture with other flowers. Because of the brief flowering season the gardener should keep in mind that other flowers will have to be put out in its stead when it has finished. Godetia is also used for cutting. Open flowers soon fade but all the buds will open in the vase.

Chrysanthemum. This is a large and popular group of plants. The generic name is derived from the Greek words *chrysos,* meaning gold, and *anthemos,* meaning flower. Most are perennials; of the annuals the following are the ones generally grown in the garden: *Chrysanthemum carinatum* (painted lady), native to North America. The flowers, 6 to 8 cm (2¹/₄ to

3 in) across, come in various colours; many forms have rings or zones of colour round the central boss. *C. coronarium* (crown daisy), native to southern Europe. The flowers, about 4 cm (1¹/₂ in) across, are double and coloured white or yellow. *C. segetum* (corn marigold), is native to North Africa. The flowers, about 8 cm (3¹/₂ in) across, are generally pale yellow with brown centre. There are as many as 80 flowers on a plant. *C. parthenium* (feverfew) is native to Asia Minor. The flowers, about 1.5 cm (³/₄ in) across, are small, clustered, and coloured white or yellow.

Since the annual forms usually have firm stems they are used for bedding or for cutting. Flowering is long and continuous; the flowers open in succession and should be removed as they fade. Cut flowers are very long-lived in the vase.

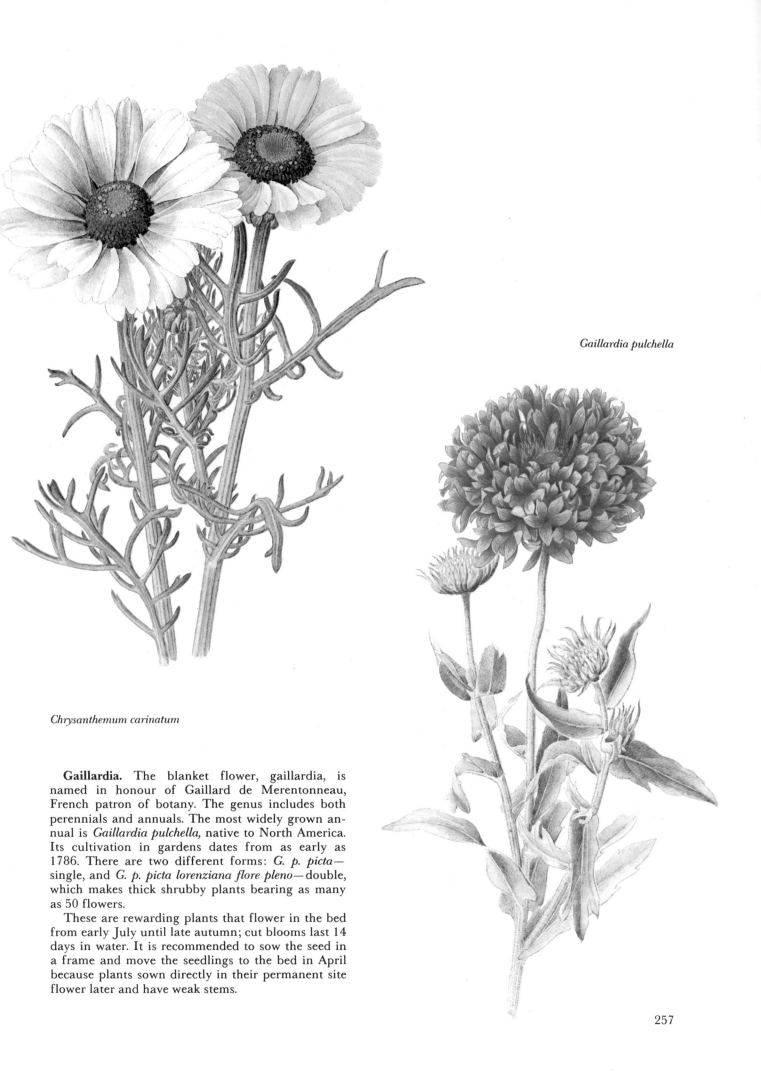

Gaillardia pulchella

Chrysanthemum carinatum

Gaillardia. The blanket flower, gaillardia, is named in honour of Gaillard de Merentonneau, French patron of botany. The genus includes both perennials and annuals. The most widely grown annual is *Gaillardia pulchella,* native to North America. Its cultivation in gardens dates from as early as 1786. There are two different forms: *G. p. picta*— single, and *G. p. picta lorenziana flore pleno*—double, which makes thick shrubby plants bearing as many as 50 flowers.

These are rewarding plants that flower in the bed from early July until late autumn; cut blooms last 14 days in water. It is recommended to sow the seed in a frame and move the seedlings to the bed in April because plants sown directly in their permanent site flower later and have weak stems.

257

Centaurea. Cornflower or sweet sultan, centaurea, is named after the Centaur Chiron of Greek mythology who healed wounds with its leaves. It grows wild throughout the world and numbers more than 500 species of annuals and perennials. Best known of the annuals is *Centaurea cyanus,* the cornflower or blue bottle, grown in gardens for years. It is an erect, richly branched, bushy plant, 60 to 90 cm (2 to 3 ft) high. The flowers are generally blue but some cultivated forms are white, pink or red. Breeding has also yielded double forms *C. c. flore pleno* with enlarged central florets. This character, however, is not firmly established; plants from further sowings are not reliable and include increasingly greater numbers with single and semi-double instead of double flowers. Another cultivated species is *C. moschata,* the sweet

sultan. The plants are 80 to 90 cm (2 ft 8 in to 3 ft) high with delicately coloured, fragrant flowers, 5 to 7 cm (2 to 2³/₄ in) across from early July until autumn. *C. moschata* is grown chiefly for cutting, as the plants are too broadly-branched for bedding. The one used for mixed beds is *C. cyanus,* particularly the blue forms. Cut flowers last 4 to 8 days in the vase, but they gradually lose colour. Plants should be sown where they are to flower because they do not transplant well.

Dianthus. Chinese pink, *Dianthus chinensis* is the only species, besides the Chabaud carnations, grown as an annual. It is native to China, whence it was introduced into Europe in its garden forms. There are a great many varieties, all of which, however, have the typical characteristics of the species—deli-

Centaurea moschata

Dianthus chinensis

cate, branching habit, rich foliage, flowers single and double, multicoloured, often streaked, and unscented, borne singly or 2 to 3 on a long stem. They are usually grown in mixture. *D. chinensis* varieties include: *D. c. imperialis*—about 25 cm (10 in) high with large flowers, *D. c. imperialis nanus*— 15 cm (6 in) high, of compact habit, and the interesting, new form *D. c. heddewigii laciniatus* with deeply incised petals. *Dianthus* Wee Willie is a single form, only 13 cm (5 in) high, smothered with flowers 1 cm ($^1/_2$ in) across. Blossoms are produced by plants when they are still small, barely 5 cm (2 in) high. The Japanese form 'Bravo' is an unusual scarlet hue. The Chinese pink and its varieties is grown only as an annual in the border, generally in groups. The short stem limits its suitability for cutting but the flowers are very striking in the vase.

Scabiosa atropurpurea

Scabiosa Sweet scabious or pincushion flower; the generic name scabiosa is derived from the Latin word *scabies,* meaning rough, referring to the rough surface of the leaves. There are some 80 annual and perennial species distributed in southern Europe, Africa and Asia. Grown in gardens as an annual is *Scabiosa atropurpurea* from southern Europe. This species has yielded many varieties of varying height and colour. Most widely grown are members of the *S. atropurpurea grandiflora flore pleno* group which come in shades of white, yellow, pink, pale blue, and dark red. All are 70 to 90 cm (2 ft 4 in to 3 ft) high, branch from the base, and flower profusely. The flowers have a long, firm stem and thus are very good for cutting; they last 5 to 10 days in the vase. In floral arrangements they are most attractive by themselves in a mixture of colours, and if combined with other flowers, white daisies—*Chrysanthemum leucanthemum*—or tickseed—*Coreopsis grandiflora* —are lovely as companion plants. Scabiosa is very easy to grow but requires a sheltered spot, for the plants are easily uprooted or laid flat by strong winds. When cutting flowers for the vase the best time to do so is when they are half-open. Scabiosa is also planted amongst moderately tall annuals in mixed beds or amongst perennials that have finished flowering. Faded flowers should be removed promptly because they are not attractive and also because the plants stop flowering if seed is allowed to develop.

Venidium fastuosum

Salpiglossis sinuata

Venidium. Namaqualand daisy, Monarch of the Veldt, *Venidium fastuosum*, native to South Africa, is interesting in that the flowers close at night and in rainy weather and also that they follow the sun. There are as many as 50 on a single plant coloured white, yellow, orange and red with a coloured zone round the centre. They are borne in profusion for several weeks in a dry, sunny situation but in rainy weather the plants die. They are suitable for mixed flower beds as well as for cutting, lasting a long time in the vase, particularly if the flowerheads are occasionally immersed in water.

Salpiglossis. Trumpet flower, *Salpiglossis sinuata*, is native to South America. The two Greek words from which the generic name is derived — *salpinx*, meaning trumpet and *glossa*, meaning tongue — refer to the shape of both the flower and the leaf. This is an elegant but fragile flower, easily broken by the wind. Its blooms measure 7 to 8 cm ($2^3/_4$ to 3 in) across. It requires a sunny and rather dry situation. It is used in mixed annual beds, in ornamental containers, and for cutting, lasting 7 days in water.

Coreopsis. Tickseed, coreopsis, the generic name of which is derived from the Greek words *koris*, meaning tick, and *opsis*, meaning resembling, referring to the resemblance of the seeds to a bug. It grows wild in North and South America as well as in Africa. Of the many species, which also include perennials, the most widely grown annual is *Coreopsis drummondii*, 30 to 60 cm (1 to 2 ft) high, with flowers up to 8 cm (3 in) across. This is a fragile plant easily damaged by wind and rain. It is used for mass plantings and also for cutting; the flowers last up to 10 days in the vase.

Coreopsis drummondii

Arctotis hybrida

Arctotis. African daisy, *Arctotis grandis*, from South America, derives its name from the two Greek words *arctos*, meaning bear, and *otos*, meaning ear, probably in reference to the felted stems and leaves. The flowers come in various colours and open fully only in sun; otherwise they open in the morning and close in the afternoon. The flowering period is from June until autumn. The situation should be a sunny and rather dry one. African daisies are used in mixed beds and for cutting.

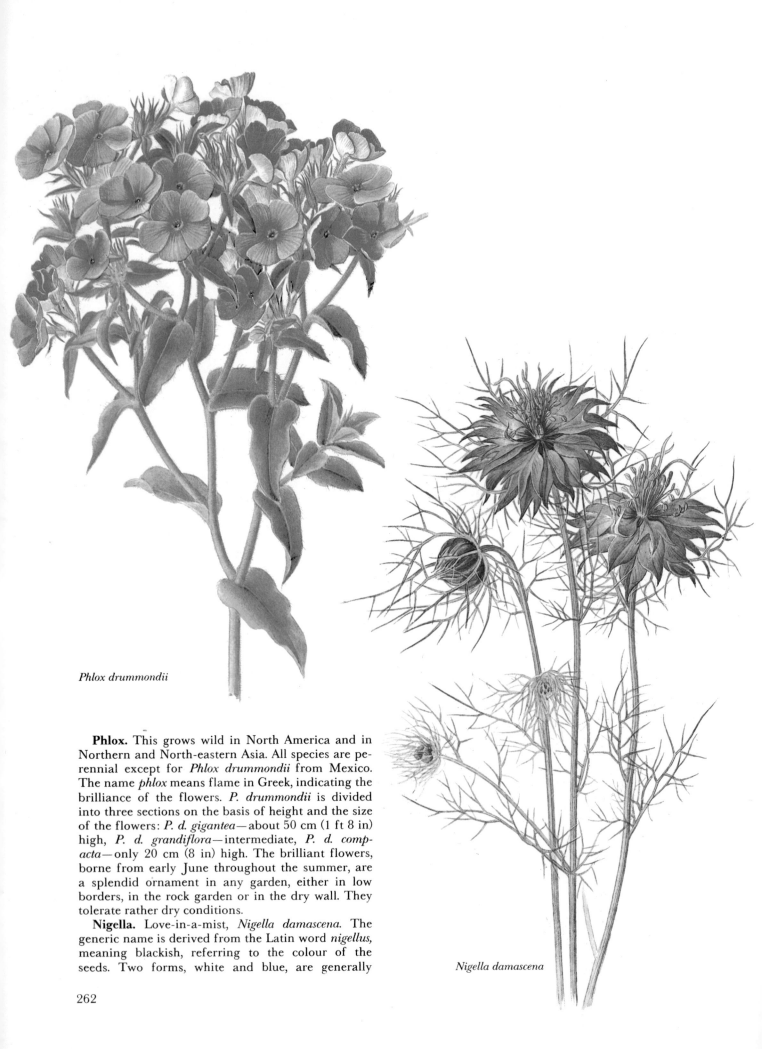

Phlox drummondii

Phlox. This grows wild in North America and in Northern and North-eastern Asia. All species are perennial except for *Phlox drummondii* from Mexico. The name *phlox* means flame in Greek, indicating the brilliance of the flowers. *P. drummondii* is divided into three sections on the basis of height and the size of the flowers: *P. d. gigantea*—about 50 cm (1 ft 8 in) high, *P. d. grandiflora*—intermediate, *P. d. compacta*—only 20 cm (8 in) high. The brilliant flowers, borne from early June throughout the summer, are a splendid ornament in any garden, either in low borders, in the rock garden or in the dry wall. They tolerate rather dry conditions.

Nigella. Love-in-a-mist, *Nigella damascena*. The generic name is derived from the Latin word *nigellus*, meaning blackish, referring to the colour of the seeds. Two forms, white and blue, are generally

Nigella damascena

grown in the garden. Flowering is fairly brief but the foliage is also decorative, as are the seed pods, which are dried and used in modern floral arrangements. Nigella is used in mixed bedding schemes and for edging.

Reseda. Mignonette, *Reseda odorata*, has insignificant, but pleasantly scented flowers. It grows wild in North Africa. The small, fragrant flowers, arranged in dense spikes, are coloured green or yellow-green with striking red or yellow anthers. The flowering period is from July until late autumn. Reseda is often grown in country gardens for its sweet fragrance and as food for bees. Its deep green foliage also looks good amidst the bright colours of other annuals.

Gypsophila. Baby's breath, chalk plant — *Gypsophila elegans*. The generic name is derived from the Greek words *gypsos* and *phile* meaning 'lime or chalk loving'. The more than 80 species are native to Asia Minor and Central Asia and are mostly perennials; only a few are annuals. The short-growing varieties are suitable for the rock garden and dry places, such as dry walls, but the plant is mostly used for cutting, primarily as a supplement to other flowers in bouquets.

Reseda odorata

Gypsophila elegans

263

Salvia. This was cultivated already in ancient times for its medicinal qualities and used to treat a great many diseases, hence its generic name (the Latin word *salvare* means 'to heal'). Of the several hundred species only a few are of ornamental value. *Salvia coccinea,* from southern North America, is a broadly-branching, grey-felted plant, 30 to 60 cm (1 ft to 2 ft) high, with scarlet flowers opening from June until autumn.

Salvia horminum, from southern Europe, is the same height and also flowers from June until autumn. The flowers, coloured white, carmine or purple, are attractive, as are the coloured bracts surrounding them.

Verbena hybrida

Salvia coccinea (left), *Salvia horminum* (centre), *Salvia farinacea* (right)

Salvia farinacea grows as a perennial in Texas, but in Europe it is treated as an annual. The plants are 60 to 80 cm (2 ft to 2 ft 8 in) high, richly branched, and grow throughout the summer until late autumn. The flowers are dark violet and arranged in long spikes.

Verbena. Vervain, verbena, was a sacred flower in ancient times upon which oaths were sworn, hence its name, derived from the Latin word *verbum*, meaning word. Multiple crossing of the original perennial species, mostly native to America, yielded many forms and varieties grown as annuals and great favourites in the garden.

Verbena bonariensis is native to America, where it grows as a perennial. In Europe this upright, 50 to 100 cm (1 ft 8 in to 3 ft 4 in) high, richly branching plant is grown as an annual. The flowers are pale to dark violet and borne in dense heads from July until the frost. The plants are decorative even after flowering has finished. They are used in bedding schemes together with other tall annuals and for cutting.

Verbena rigida is a widespread perennial in America but in the garden it is treated as an annual. The plants are 30 to 40 cm (1 ft to 1 ft 4 in) high and of loose, broadly-spreading habit. The flowers are pale purplish-violet.

Verbena is suitable for long, narrow beds in the lawn or beside paths, for ornamental walls, patios, balconies as well as window-boxes and earthenware containers. It is also used for cutting. It is attractive in arrangements by itself as well as with other flowers in a suitable blend of colours. It is one of the several annuals that are put out in beds after bulbs have finished.

Verbena bonariensis (left), *Verbena rigida* (right)

265

Dimorphotheca aurantiaca   *Linum grandiflorum*

Dimorphotheca. The generic name of the Star of the Veldt is derived from the Greek words *dimorphos,* meaning two-shaped, and *theca,* meaning box, indicating that two forms of seed vessels are produced. The plant is native to South Africa. The stems and leaves are covered with small glandular hairs that give off a strong scent when touched. The flowers are white with violet centre (*Dimorphotheca pluvialis*) or pale to dark orange (*D. aurantiaca*), and are produced from June until autumn; they open fully only in sun. The seeds are sown where the plants are to flower. They are used for edging, in the rock garden, and on a dry wall.

Linum. The only flax plant of ornamental value is

the scarlet flax, *Linum grandiflorum,* of Algeria. It is up to 50 cm (1 ft 8 in) high, of loose, branching habit, with wide-open flowers, 3 to 4 cm (1 to $1^{1}/_{2}$ in) across, coloured bright carmine with dark centres. It is used in mixed annual beds and the seeds are sown where the plants are to flower.

Brachycome. The Swan River daisy has hairy seeds, hence its generic name, which is derived from the Greek words *brachys,* meaning short, and *kome,* meaning hair. Grown in gardens is the blue form of *Brachycome iberidifolia* from Australia. The plants are 26 cm ($10^{1}/_{2}$ in) high and the flowers are pleasantly scented. There are also white and red varieties. Brachycome flowers from mid-June throughout the

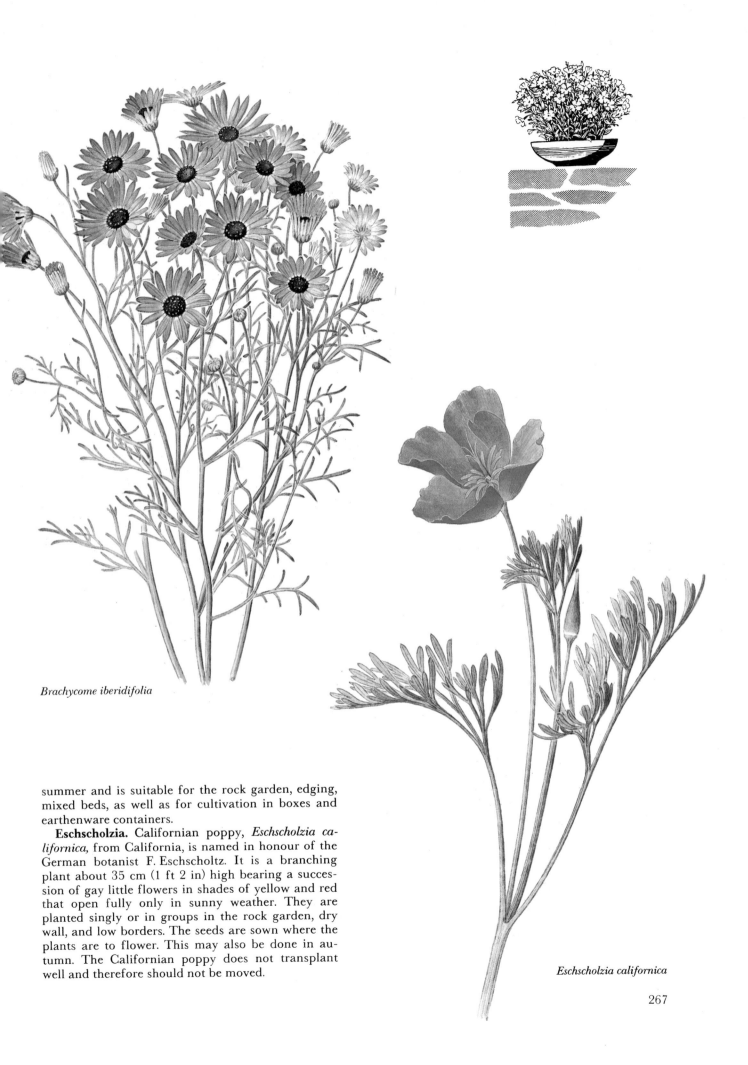

Brachycome iberidifolia

summer and is suitable for the rock garden, edging, mixed beds, as well as for cultivation in boxes and earthenware containers.

Eschscholzia. Californian poppy, *Eschscholzia californica,* from California, is named in honour of the German botanist F. Eschscholtz. It is a branching plant about 35 cm (1 ft 2 in) high bearing a succession of gay little flowers in shades of yellow and red that open fully only in sunny weather. They are planted singly or in groups in the rock garden, dry wall, and low borders. The seeds are sown where the plants are to flower. This may also be done in autumn. The Californian poppy does not transplant well and therefore should not be moved.

Eschscholzia californica

267

Iberis. Candytuft is native to the Iberian Peninsula, hence the botanical title iberis. There are some 20 species, mostly perennials, growing wild in southern Europe and Asia Minor. Two annual species are cultivated in the garden: *Iberis amara* (rocket candytuft) with small, symmetrical flowers in dense clusters, and *I. umbellata* (globe candytuft), more branching, with many more flower clusters (18 to 25) in white as well as several other colours. Both flower briefly in June and early July after which other annuals are planted out in their stead. The plants are about 30 cm (1 ft) high and resemble hyacinths. The seeds are sown where the plants are to flower. They are used in the rock garden, mixed beds, boxes, and as pot plants, and are also good for cutting, lasting 7 to 10 days in the vase.

Nemesia. *Nemesia strumosa,* native to South Africa, makes a spherical small bush, about 25 cm (10 in) high, which flowers from May until August. If cut back when the flowers have faded they will put out new shoots and flower again. The flowers have an interesting shape and come in a wide range of bright, glowing colours, which makes them excellent for mixed beds or by themselves, either in one colour or a mixture of colours. They may also be grown in pots or earthenware containers. Cut flowers are very long-lived in water.

Impatiens. Balsam, touch-me-not, *Impatiens balsamina.* The Latin name *impatiens* refers to the fact that when ripe seed pods are touched they immediately burst. It is native to East India. The plants are about 50 cm (1 ft 8 in) high with thick, fleshy stems,

Iberis umbellata

268

Impatiens balsamina

Nemesia strumosa

usually reddish, with distinct swollen nodes and sessile leaves. The large flowers, coloured red, are borne on short stalks in the axils of the leaves from June until late September. They are used in mixed beds. The low, double varieties are grown in boxes and flower bowls and also make attractive pot plants. They may be moved even during the flowering period, but, being fragile, they break easily and should therefore be handled with care. The flowers may be used for decoration in shallow dishes the same as camellias.

Petunia hybrida

Begonia semperflorens

Petunia. This is one of the most rewarding annuals but also one of the most demanding. The name is taken from the Brazilian name for this plant, 'pet-un', as it is native to southern Brazil and Argentina. Countless hybrids have been raised by breeders throughout the world, chiefly in the United States, Japan and Czechoslovakia. Since World War II the ones generally grown are the varieties which are more resistant to unfavourable weather and bear a greater profusion of flowers. The seeds of these varieties are obtained by the crossing of two pure breeding strains every year, otherwise the variety rapidly loses the desirable characters which are present only in the first generation, designated as F_1 hybrids. Petunias are divided into two basic groups on the basis of use. Large-flowered varieties, *P. hybrida grandiflora nana,* are used chiefly for window-boxes; they may be grown as bedding plants only in warm and dry regions. They are also good for cutting. Small-flowered varieties, *P. hybrida multiflora nana,* are used chiefly for bedding but they are also suitable for window-boxes and balcony boxes. Besides these, there are many other different varieties, such as with frilled flowers, with double blooms, and trailing forms.

Petunias are planted out in the second half of May, usually as grown-on seedlings already starting to flower. They should be put in sun in well-fertilized soil and given occasional applications of feed and water as they produce many blooms during the summer. Faded flowers should be removed. Petunias flower continuously until they are destroyed by frost.

Begonia. *Begonia semperflorens* is the only species of this large genus which is treated as an annual. The genus is named in honour of Michael Begon, Governor of San Domingo in the late 17th century, and ranks second to petunias in importance and demanding requirements. They are divided according to height into two groups—intermediate and dwarf—and within these groups according to the colour of the foliage—green-leaved and red-leaved. The best intermediate varieties for cultivation in European conditions are the 'Variation' F_1 hybrids with both red and green foliage and flowers in shades of white, pink and red. They are about 25 to 30 cm (10 in to 1 ft) high. Most widely grown are the low varieties up to 15 cm (6 in) high. The flowers come in a wider range of hues, from white to pink to dark red, and the foliage is likewise red or green. Best, again, are the F_1 hybrids.

Begonia semperflorens varieties should not be planted out until the second half of May, after which they will flower continuously until the frost. They are used in parks and gardens as bedding and edging plants. They do quite well even in partial shade but require adequately rich soil and watering in periods of drought.

Ageratum. The generic name of floss flower is derived from the Greek word *ageratos*, meaning ageless, in reference to the long-lasting nature of the flowers which are produced the whole summer long, with new ones covering the old faded blooms. Of the many species only *Ageratum houstonianum pumilum*, 15 to 25 cm (8 to 10 in) high, is grown in the garden. Varieties are coloured blue, such as 'Blue Star', 'Blue Mink', and white, the best known being 'Little Dorrit'.

Ageratum does well in any garden soil, best of all in a warm, sunny situation. The seedlings should not be planted out until the second half of May. The first autumn frost completely destroys the plants. They transplant well and thus may be moved to pots and taken indoors where they will continue to flower. Ageratum is generally used as an edging plant, in borders, and in parks. It is also suitable for window-boxes.

Ageratum houstonianum

271

Lobelia. This genus is named in honour of the Flemish botanist de l'Obel. The many species are widespread in the moderate regions of the world, some also in the tropics. In the wild they occur as annuals, perennials and sub-shrubs, but in the gardens of Europe they are treated as annuals. The one of greatest merit is *Lobelia erinus*, which has yielded a great many varieties, mostly blue, but also white, pink and carmine. The plants are 15 to 20 cm (6 to 8 in) high and begin flowering while still in the frame or shortly after being moved outdoors, continuing to do so throughout the summer. They do not tolerate frost and are therefore not put out until the end of May. They transplant well, even in full bloom. Prompt cutting back after flowering will force the plants to flower again. They are killed by the first autumn frost. Lobelia is used chiefly for edging, in separate borders, and in groups of several plants in low, mixed beds. It is very good with other flowers for decoration in urns. The trailing varieties are useful for window-boxes and hanging baskets on the balcony or patio.

Silene. The catchfly, silene, is named after Silenus, constant companion of the god Bacchus. More than 300 species are distributed throughout the world. Usually the following two are grown in gardens: *Silene coeli-rosa oculata* (syn. *Lychnis coeli-rosa, Viscaria oculata*), up to 35 cm (1 ft 2 in) high with thickly clustered flowers, often a pale colour with darker centre, and *S. pendula,* from the Mediterranean coast, only 10 to 15 cm (4 to 6 in) high, often of trailing habit, with flowers in shades of white, pink, glowing red and lilac. Most widely-grown is the glowing pink variety *S. pendula compacta florepleno* 'Triumph', which is a compact, broadly spreading to prostrate plant 17 cm (7 in) high and with a spread up to 40 cm (1 ft 4 in). Uses are in mixed beds, dry walls and on dry slopes where the glowing colours make a striking effect from early July to August. If the seeds are sown in August and the seedlings overwintered in a frame then they may be put outdoors early in spring and will flower from May until June when most perennials are finishing and most annuals have not yet begun flowering.

Tagetes. The tall African marigold — *Tagetes erecta* — is shown on p. 251; depicted on the opposite page is the most widespread group of the genus, namely the French marigolds — *T. patula nana* — which is divided into the following sections:

Intermediate, double, 30 to 40 cm (1 ft to 1 ft 4 in) high, well branched with a profusion of flowers. The flowers are small, yellow, orange to reddish-brown, either chrysanthemum like or carnation like, and borne fairly early.

Dwarf, double, 20 to 30 cm (8 in to 1 ft) high, well branched, of compact habit, producing from 60 to 100 flowers. These are in the usual colours or bicoloured, and either chrysanthemum like or carnation like.

Dwarf, single, 20 to 30 cm (8 in to 1 ft) high, resembling the double forms in habit. There are as many as 200 flowers to a single plant, which when in full bloom form whole sheets of colour.

Tagetes is one of the most widely grown annuals because it tolerates both dry and rainy weather, thrives in any garden soil and has many uses. The taller double varieties are planted as separate groups or in combination and may also be used for cutting. Cut flowers will last a week to 14 days in the vase. Dwarf varieties are sown or planted out as edging plants or in larger spaces by themselves in pure colours. They are also attractive in window-boxes and as a decoration in urns. They have a characteristic pungent smell.

Lobelia erinus

Tagetes patula

Silene pendula

273

Gazania splendens

Dorotheanthus bellidiformis

274

Gazania. Treasure flower 'gazania' is named in honour of the Italian scientist Theodore Gaza, who lived in Rome in the late 15th century. It is native to Africa where some 20 species, sub-shrubs, perennials as well as annuals, grow wild. *Gazania splendens* is the outcome of the cross-breeding of several species. The plants are about 1 cm (½ in) high with a branching rosette of leaves and large flowers on firm, smooth stems, in a wide range of colours, mostly yellow. One drawback of this lovely flower is that the blooms open only in full sun at about 10 a. m. and close at 4 p. m. The same is true of cut flowers in the vase. The flowering period is from the end of June until late autumn; the first light frosts do not harm the plants. Gazania may be used for edging, on sunny slopes, in the rock garden, as well as in mixed beds. The beauty of the flowers shows off to better advantage in larger groups than if it is planted by itself.

Dorotheanthus. The botanical name of the Livingstone daisy is made up of the name Dorothy plus the Greek word *anthos,* meaning flower. The plant was so named by the German botanist Schwantes in honour of his mother. Native to South Africa, it is better known under its previous name mesembryanthemum. *Dorotheanthus bellidiformis* is of spreading to prostrate habit with flat, elongate, fleshy leaves and reddish stems. The single, wide-open flowers are large and come in lovely glowing shades of whitish-pink, salmon and deep carmine. It does best in drier, sandy soil and a sunny situation. It does not tolerate wet and is killed by lengthy spells of rainy weather. The seeds are sown where the plants are to flower or else they may be grown-on in pots. They are best in separate groups by themselves, after bulbs when those have finished flowering, also for dry walls, the rock garden, dry sunny slopes, and between stone slabs in the patio. The multicoloured flowers make a beautiful carpet in bedding schemes. One drawback, however, is that they open only in bright sun.

Salvia. Scarlet sage, *Salvia splendens,* native to Brazil, is the most important and most widely grown species. The plants are 30 to 40 cm (1 ft to 1 ft 4 in) high and the flowers are red, white or violet; most popular are the low varieties with brilliant scarlet flowers commonly seen in parks. The original Brazilian form, a sub-shrub which is no longer cultivated, has yielded many pretty, low and richly flowering varieties of firm, compact, upright habit. They should be planted out in the second half of May in a sunny spot where they will flower profusely until the first frosts. The long flowering period and brilliant colour make this a favourite annual for the mixed border, particularly with flowers of contrasting hues. The lowest forms may be grown in pots, boxes and earthenware containers. It transplants well and seedlings may be put out when already in bloom.

Salvia splendens

Mimulus. The generic name of the monkey flower is derived from the Latin word *mimus,* meaning mime or mimic, referring to the supposed resemblance of the flower to a mask or monkey face. There are some 150 species distributed throughout the temperate regions of the world. They generally overwinter well. However, the plants are usually treated as annuals because they flower best the first year. Of the many species the following are the most widely grown:

Mimulus guttatus, native to North America. It is up to 40 cm (1 ft 4 in) high with 2.5 cm (1 in) long flowers coloured yellow with throat blotched purple or brown. They are arranged in multiflowered racemes.

Mimulus luteus

Mimulus luteus native to Chile. It is a perennial but in gardens it is treated as an annual. The plants are 20 to 60 cm (8 in to 3 ft) high with loose racemes of yellow flowers blotched with red.

Mimulus cupreus. This resembles the preceding species but is shorter (15 to 25 cm [6 to 10 in]).

Mimulus tigrinus grandiflorus. This is a mixture of hybrids of the preceding species. The plants are of loose, bushy habit, 25 cm (10 in) high, with broadly funnel-shaped flowers coloured yellow with dark red markings. In congenial conditions a single plant will produce 100 to 150 flowers. They are easy to grow and thrive even in partial shade. Pinching of young plants promotes branching and thereby more profuse flowering. Mimulus is suitable for low borders as well as mixed beds, particularly in rather damp, slightly shaded locations. It may also be planted in boxes on the patio or balcony but in a spot that is shaded at least part of the day; unduly dry conditions must be guarded against in containers.

Portulaca. Sun plant or rose moss, portulaca, are low, creeping plants for poor, dry, sandy soil. Some 100 species grow in the tropical and subtropical regions of the world. *Portulaca grandiflora* is native to Argentina and Brazil. The fleshy, creeping stems are coloured green in the white forms and reddish in the coloured forms. The leaves are linear and fleshy. The lovely flowers are single and double, 4 cm (1¹/₂ in) across, in shades of white, yellow, pink to carmine. They open only in full sun. Long spells of cold and rainy weather often completely destroy the plants. Portulaca do poorly in shade and do not tolerate heavy, clay and wet soil. In full bloom they are most decorative with their glowing colours, whether planted singly or in larger groups. They are suitable for rock gardens, dry walls and dry sunny slopes. They do very well in earthenware urns in full sun and are excellent for brightening places where, because of excessively dry conditions and insufficient soil, most other plants would grow very poorly.

Phacelia. The generic name of the California bluebell is derived from the Greek word *phakelos,* meaning cluster or bundle, an indication of the way the flowers are arranged. Some 100 species are distributed in North America and Chile. It is grown more as food for bees than as an ornamental plant. Of the previously cultivated species the one of greatest merit as an ornamental is *Phacelia campanularia* of North America. The plants are 15 to 25 cm (6 to 10

276

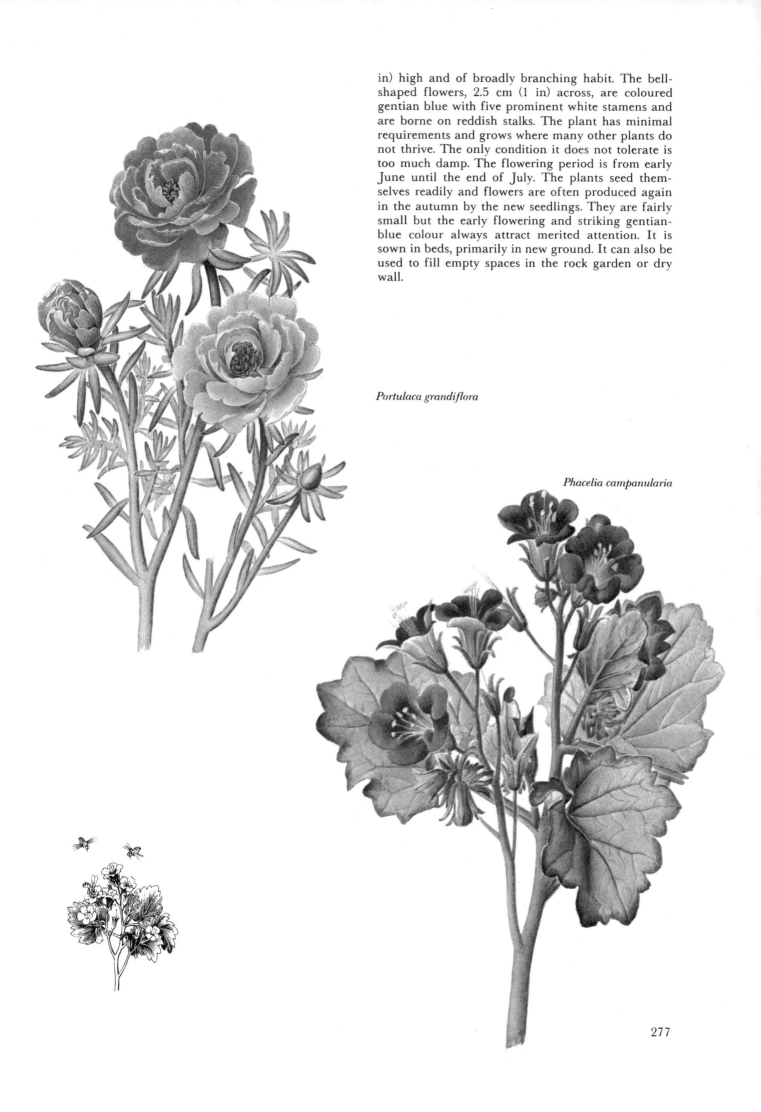

in) high and of broadly branching habit. The bell-shaped flowers, 2.5 cm (1 in) across, are coloured gentian blue with five prominent white stamens and are borne on reddish stalks. The plant has minimal requirements and grows where many other plants do not thrive. The only condition it does not tolerate is too much damp. The flowering period is from early June until the end of July. The plants seed themselves readily and flowers are often produced again in the autumn by the new seedlings. They are fairly small but the early flowering and striking gentian-blue colour always attract merited attention. It is sown in beds, primarily in new ground. It can also be used to fill empty spaces in the rock garden or dry wall.

Portulaca grandiflora

Phacelia campanularia

277

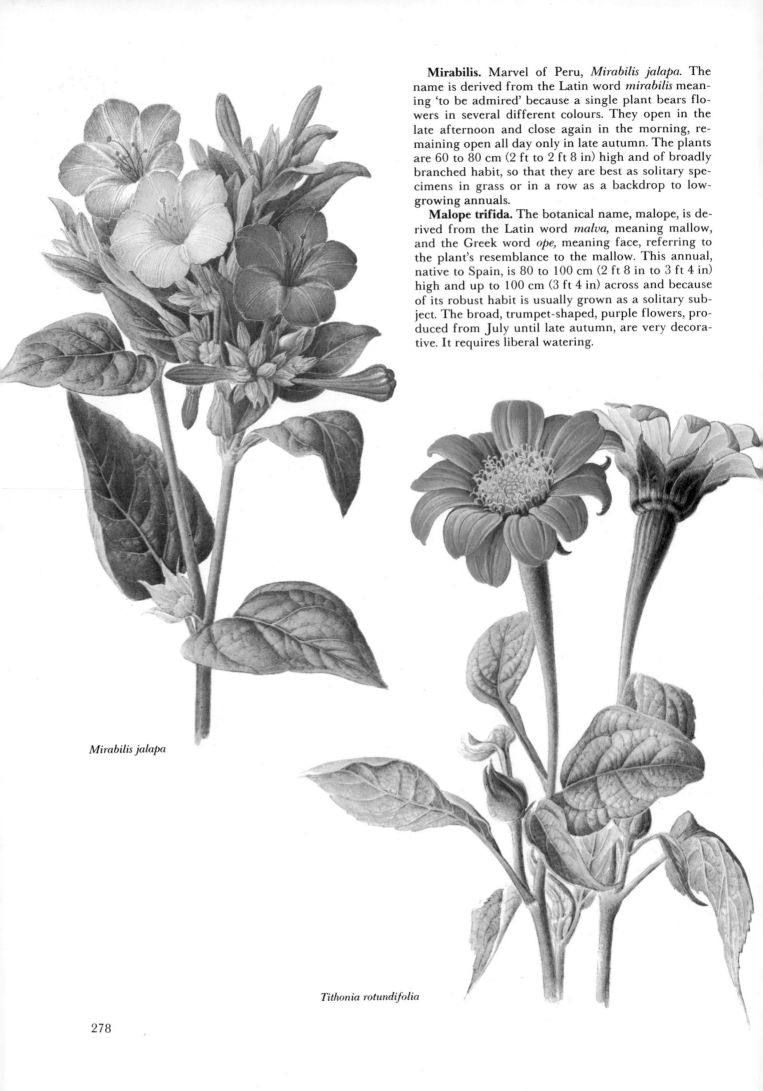

Mirabilis. Marvel of Peru, *Mirabilis jalapa.* The name is derived from the Latin word *mirabilis* meaning 'to be admired' because a single plant bears flowers in several different colours. They open in the late afternoon and close again in the morning, remaining open all day only in late autumn. The plants are 60 to 80 cm (2 ft to 2 ft 8 in) high and of broadly branched habit, so that they are best as solitary specimens in grass or in a row as a backdrop to low-growing annuals.

Malope trifida. The botanical name, malope, is derived from the Latin word *malva,* meaning mallow, and the Greek word *ope,* meaning face, referring to the plant's resemblance to the mallow. This annual, native to Spain, is 80 to 100 cm (2 ft 8 in to 3 ft 4 in) high and up to 100 cm (3 ft 4 in) across and because of its robust habit is usually grown as a solitary subject. The broad, trumpet-shaped, purple flowers, produced from July until late autumn, are very decorative. It requires liberal watering.

Mirabilis jalapa

Tithonia rotundifolia

278

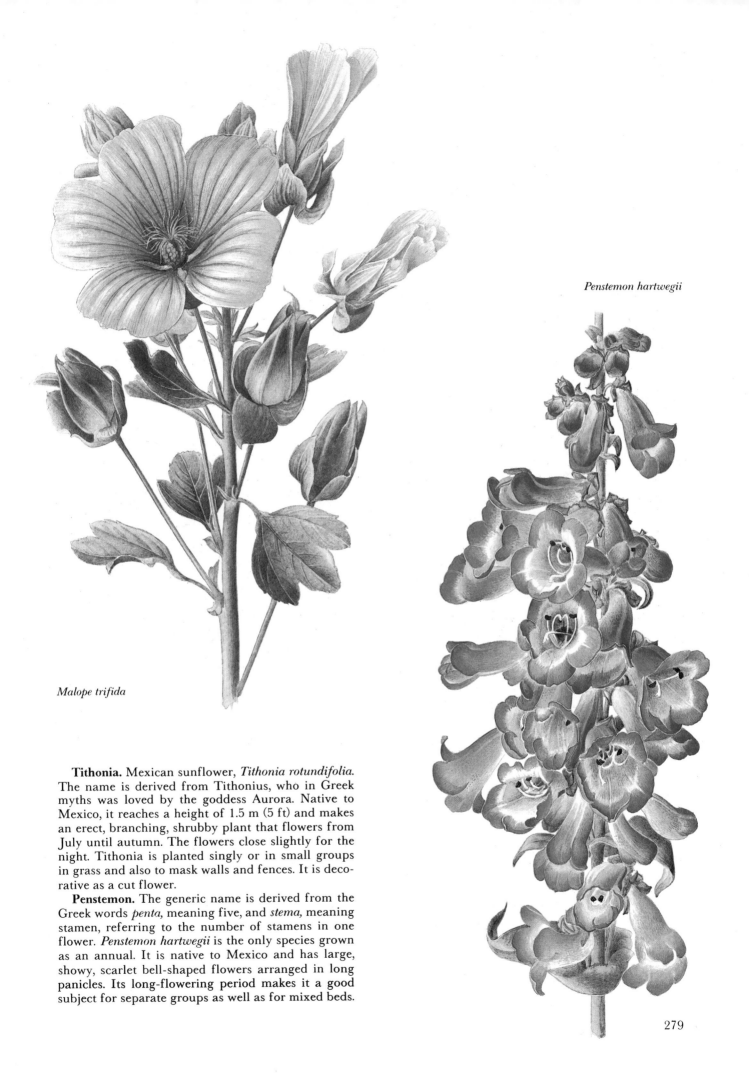

Penstemon hartwegii

Malope trifida

Tithonia. Mexican sunflower, *Tithonia rotundifolia.*
The name is derived from Tithonius, who in Greek
myths was loved by the goddess Aurora. Native to
Mexico, it reaches a height of 1.5 m (5 ft) and makes
an erect, branching, shrubby plant that flowers from
July until autumn. The flowers close slightly for the
night. Tithonia is planted singly or in small groups
in grass and also to mask walls and fences. It is decorative as a cut flower.

Penstemon. The generic name is derived from the
Greek words *penta,* meaning five, and *stema,* meaning
stamen, referring to the number of stamens in one
flower. *Penstemon hartwegii* is the only species grown
as an annual. It is native to Mexico and has large,
showy, scarlet bell-shaped flowers arranged in long
panicles. Its long-flowering period makes it a good
subject for separate groups as well as for mixed beds.

279

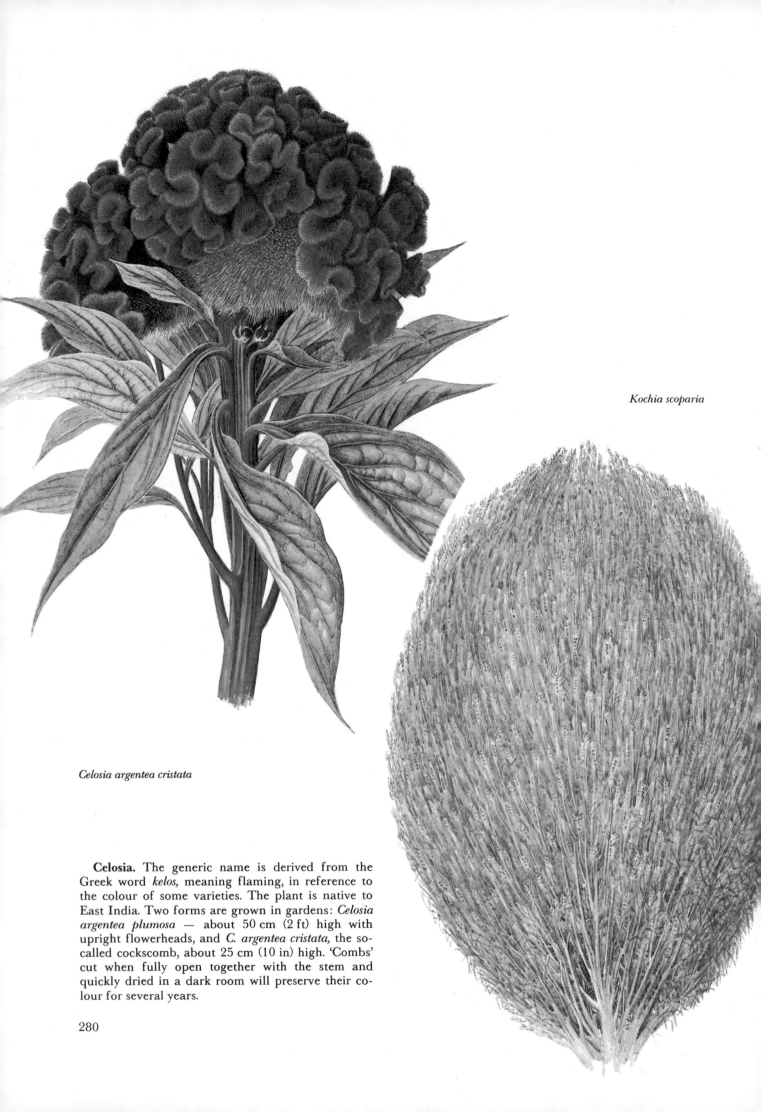

Kochia scoparia

Celosia argentea cristata

Celosia. The generic name is derived from the Greek word *kelos,* meaning flaming, in reference to the colour of some varieties. The plant is native to East India. Two forms are grown in gardens: *Celosia argentea plumosa* — about 50 cm (2 ft) high with upright flowerheads, and *C. argentea cristata,* the so-called cockscomb, about 25 cm (10 in) high. 'Combs' cut when fully open together with the stem and quickly dried in a dark room will preserve their colour for several years.

Kochia. Summer cypress, burning bush, kochia, is named in honour of the German botanist W. D. J. Koch. It grows wild in Australia, Asia, Africa, North America and southern Europe. *Kochia scoparia* is the species grown for garden decoration. It is an erect, compact bush of finely-cut, tender-looking foliage. The flowers are insignificant. It is an unusual annual.

Amaranthus. The generic name of love-lies-bleeding is derived from the Greek word *maranein,* to wilt, because its blooms look always as if they are fading. *Amaranthus caudatus,* native to southern Asia, is a robust plant up to 1.2 m (5 ft) high with long, drooping racemes of dark red flowers. It is used in mixed annual beds.

Ricinus. Castor oil plant, *Ricinus communis,* the generic name of which is derived from the Latin word *ricinus,* meaning tick, which the seed is said to resemble. It has been cultivated since ancient times for its oily seeds. The fully grown, brownish green plants have an exotic appearance and are used to mask walls and fences or as a backdrop for other, contrasting flowers. It is poisonous.

Amaranthus caudatus

Ricinus communis

Xeranthemum. The name, derived from the Greek words *xeros* and *anthemon* meaning dry flower, refers to the dry papery character of the blooms. *Xeranthemum annuum,* which is native to southern Europe, makes an upright, bushy plant, 50 to 65 cm (1 ft 8 in to 2 ft 2 in) high, with flowers, either single or double, up to 4 cm (1 $^1/_2$ in) across. It is suitable for planting on dry slopes exposed to direct sunlight. The flowers are dried for winter decoration.

Helipterum. The generic name is derived from the Greek word *helios,* meaning sun, and *pteron,* meaning wing, in reference to the flower which has a golden-yellow central disc surrounded by dry, papery bracts. *Helipterum roseum* is native to Australia. Some varieties are double with a greater number of incurved bracts. The plants do best in acid soil. They flower from June until the autumn and are grown chiefly for cutting and for winter decoration as everlastings. Flowers to be dried should be cut, partly-opened, at mid-day, tied in small bunches, and hung upside down in a dark, well-ventilated room.

Helichrysum. The generic name of the strawflower is derived from the Greek words *helios,* meaning sun, and *chrysos,* meaning gold, referring to the predominant colour of the flower. *Helichrysum bracteatum* is native to Australia where it grows as a perennial. In Europe, however, it is grown as an annual. There are many varieties, tall as well as dwarf. A recent development are forms notable for their large flowers. Helichrysum is used in mixed beds; some plants are left in the bed as garden decoration (from July until late autumn), others are cut before the

Xeranthemum annuum

Helipterum roseum

flowers are fully open and dried for winter decoration. Freshly cut flowers are decorative in the vase.

Limonium. The sea lavender, limonium, formerly named statice, is a well known flower for drying as an everlasting. It grows wild in steppes, deserts, and on the shores of salt lakes throughout the world. *Limonium suworowii*, from western Turkestan, has small pink flowers arranged in dense cylindrical spikes up to 35 cm (1 ft 2 in) long. These are pretty and interesting plants which, when used in bedding schemes, merit the attention they attract. The flowers may also be cut and dried. The better-known *L. sinuatum* has flowers coloured white, pink and blue borne in dense clusters on branching stems resembling brushes. They, too, are dried as everlastings and used for decoration in wreaths.

Helichrysum bracteatum

Limonium suworowii

283

Lathyrus. The botanical name for the sweet pea is derived from the Greek name for this plant. *Lathyrus odoratus* grows wild in Sicily and southern Italy. It is a splendid climbing plant growing to a height of 1.8 to 2 m (6 ft to 6 ft 8 in). Varieties come in many pastel hues. Each plant produces a great profusion of marvellously scented flowers. If seeds are sown in succession (from April to July) there will be continuous flowers throughout the summer until the frost. Faded blooms should be removed because if seed is allowed to develop the plants will stop flowering. Plants should be provided with a support; seeds may be sown beside fences, arbors, railings, as well as on balconies and in window-boxes. They climb best up wire netting. Very effective are 1.5 to 1.8 m (5 ft to 6 ft) high pillars of wire netting covered with sweet peas sown round the base. Sweet peas are often used for cutting; they make a delicate and very fragrant bouquet.

Convolvulus. The name is derived from the Latin word *convolvere,* meaning to entwine, as many species are climbing plants. *Convolvulus tricolor,* native to southern Europe and North Africa, is a bushy plant with branching, prostrate stems growing vertically at the tip. The large, funnel-shaped flowers are coloured blue with a white ring round a yellow throat; some varieties are pink or red instead of blue. Flowering is continuous from June until the end of summer. The flowers close in the afternoon, which is a drawback. Convolvulus is a rapid grower and thus may be used to cover empty spaces quickly; it is also good as a border and edging plant.

Ipomoea. The generic name of the morning glory is derived from the Greek words *ipos,* meaning worm, and *omoios,* meaning like, which refers to the twining nature of the plants. Of the many species native to the Mediterranean region and South America the following are grown as annuals in Europe: *Ipomoea hederacea,* growing to a height of 3 m (10 ft), with azure-blue flowers. It is very tender and must also be handled with care. *I. nil,* which resembles the former, but is more robust and has larger leaves as well as flowers. *I. purpurea,* growing to a height of 3 m (10 ft), with large, funnel-shaped flowers in many colours.

Ipomoea tricolor is the most widely cultivated species. It grows to a height of 3 to 5 m (10 to 16 ft) and has large, trumpet-shaped flowers up to 8 cm (3 in) across. They are mostly dark blue, changing colour during the day, from dark blue in the early morning to pale red (almost pink) before they close. They open at dawn and close at noon, which is a disadvantage. In rainy weather they do not open at all and in autumn they close at a later hour. A great advantage is the long flowering period (from June until the frost) and the plants' rapid growth which enables them to cover a large area in a very short time. They must be provided with a support such as wire, wire netting, twine. Morning glory is used for covering walls, arbours and balconies.

Lathyrus odoratus

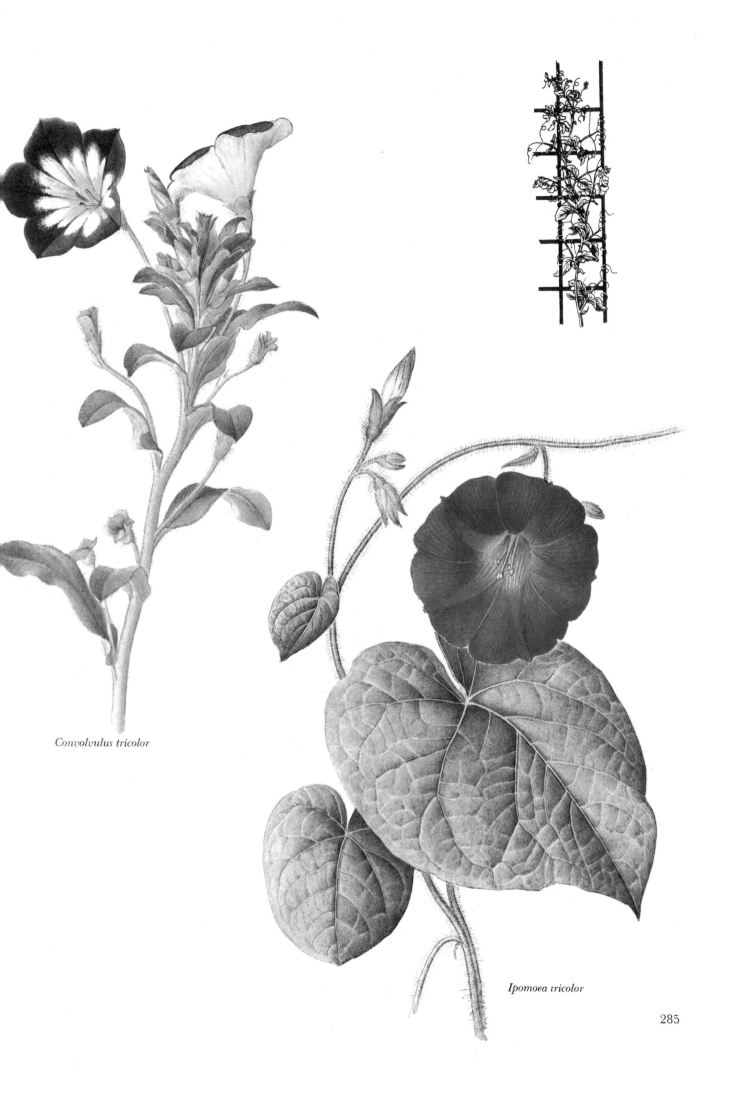

Convolvulus tricolor

Ipomoea tricolor

285

Phaseolus coccineus

Tropaeolum majus

286

Phaseolus. The bean grows wild in tropical America as well as in southern Asia, where there are more than 150 species. The only bean grown as an ornamental, however, is *Phaseolus multiflorus* (syn. *P. coccineus*) from South America, where it is usually a biennial, although in gardens it is treated as an annual. The firm stem, which always twines spirally upward from right to left and normally does not branch, grows to a height of 4 m (13 ft). The small flowers, borne in loose clusters, are white, fiery red or bicoloured. Most widely grown is the bicoloured form *P. m. bicolor* (the keel red, the wings white). The plants should be provided with a support such as a pole, wire, or netting. They flower from June to September but must be watered in periods of drought, otherwise the leaves turn yellow from the bottom up. This is a very attractive, rapid growing, climbing plant used in balcony boxes, to cover pergolas and fences. With the aid of a framework one can easily have a thick shaded screen as a divider for the garden or a cover for masking unsightly objects. The young tender beans are eaten.

Tropaeolum. Nasturtium or tropaeolum; the generic name is derived from the Latin word *tropaeolum,* meaning trophy, because the leaves are of shield-like appearance while the flowers resemble a helmet (both battle trophies in ancient times). There are some 50 species of these fleshy, branching plants growing in the mountains of Mexico and South America. These no longer occur in their original forms; mutual interbreeding has given rise to many varieties only a few of which are cultivated in the garden nowadays. These are divided into two groups: *Tropaeolum majus* and *T. minus.* The first are climbing plants up to 2 m (6 ft) long; this group also includes the double, fragrant forms *T. m. odoratus flore pleno,* mostly with semidouble flowers 6 to 7 cm ($2^1/_4$ to $2^3/_4$ in) across in shades of orange, pale yellow, red and salmon pink. The *T. minus* group includes dwarf, bushy plants only about 40 cm (1 ft 4 in) high, coloured yellow, orange or bright red. Flowering is profuse from spring until the first frost, which kills the plants. The fresh foliage and large glowing flowers are very decorative. Dwarf forms are used in narrow beds, as edging plants, and in irregular patches in large expanses of turf where they make beautiful carpets. They are also good for planting in boxes on the patio or balcony; the climbing forms may be used for this purpose as trailing plants. Flowering stems or only the flowers themselves are attractive as decoration in small hanging vases or in flat dishes.

Cosmos. The generic name of cosmea is derived from the Greek word *kosmos,* meaning ornament, a tribute to the beauty of the flower. It grows wild in Bolivia and Arizona. *Cosmos bipinnatus,* native to Mexico, is a tall, branching annual, 80 to 90 cm (2 ft 8 in to 3 ft) high, with fern-like foliage and large flowers, up to 10 cm (4 in) across, coloured white, pink or red. They are produced from July until late autumn. The plants will grow in any soil but require a sunny and sheltered location because they may be broken by strong winds when in full bloom. The finely cut foliage is also decorative. They are not suitable for very small gardens because of their size. They may be planted singly or in smaller groups in grass but are primarily grown for cutting, cut flowers lasting more than a week in the vase. However, they must be cut before they are fully open. Partly-open buds will also flower in the vase.

Cosmos bipinnatus

Dianthus. This genus includes pinks and carnations. The botanical name is derived from the Greek words *dios,* meaning divine, and *anthos,* meaning flower. *Dianthus barbatus,* the Sweet William, is a favourite biennial for cutting. The year it is sown it makes a clump of dark green leaves from which emerge the following spring 25 to 50 cm (10 in to 1 ft 8 in) long stems bearing terminal clusters of flowers in a wide range of colours. The plants should be provided with a light cover of evergreen boughs in winter and with some form of fencing to protect them from hares and rabbits if these are likely to be a problem. Taller forms are used mostly for cutting, lower forms as edging plants.

Myosotis alpestris

Dianthus barbatus

Viola. Pansy, violet or viola is referred to by its Latin name in the verses of ancient poets. Today there are more than 400 known species, with characteristic, symmetrical, five-petalled flowers. Various individual species have been grown in gardens for years. The present garden form, *Viola wittrockiana,* combines the best features of the botanical species. Varieties are divided into two groups according to the flowering period. Early-flowering forms bear their first blooms in autumn, later and late-flowering forms produce blooms in spring. They are used mainly as edging plants and for the mixed bed, often with tulips. When the seed pods are ripe the seeds are ejected some distance and this makes gathering difficult.

Bellis. The generic name is derived from the Latin word *bellus,* meaning beautiful. *Bellis perennis* 'meadow daisy' grows wild in grass. It is a small plant that seeds itself and is a troublesome weed in a lawn. Cultivated forms are more robust and some have flowers up to 5 cm (2 in) across. They come in several colours, white and carmine are prettiest and flower from late April until the beginning of July. They are used usually for borders and window-boxes but also as pot plants and for cutting. They should always be put in full sun and never in grass. Large-flowered forms have smaller and scantier blossoms if left in the same spot for more than one year and should therefore be planted out anew every year, either as grown-on seedlings raised from seed or ones obtained by the division of clumps.

Viola wittrockiana

Bellis perennis

Myosotis. The generic name of the forget-me-not comes from the Greek word *myos,* meaning mouse, and *otus,* meaning ear, referring to the shape of the leaves. Its name in all European languages, however, refers to the blue colour of the flowers as a symbol of faithfulness. *Myosotis alpestris* grows wild throughout the northern and temperate regions in damp meadows as well as high in the mountains. This is a popular flower grown as a biennial. The flowering period is from the end of April until the end of May and the flowers are mostly various shades of blue. Taller forms are suitable for cutting, smaller ones for edging or bedding. They are generally planted with tulips. They are also good for planting in pots, boxes and bowls.

289

Digitalis. The generic name of foxglove is derived from the Latin word *digitus*, meaning finger because the flower resembles a thimble. The common name in all European languages also refers to the shape of the flower. Eighteen species found their way to Europe from western and central Asia. Of these the ones grown for ornamental purposes are *Digitalis ferruginea*, up to 1.5 m (5 ft) high with yellowish-grey to yellowish-red flowers, and *D. lanata*, about 1 m (3 ft) high with whitish or whitish-yellow flowers and calyx covered with long, white, glandular hairs. Both do well on dry slopes.

Digitalis purpurea

The best for garden decoration, however, are the cultivated varieties of *D. purpurea* listed under the name *D. p. gloxiniaeflora*, These are taller and have larger, wide-open flowers in a colour range which includes white, yellow, pink and purple. They are biennials that make a rosette of rough leaves the first year, followed in the summer of the next year by slender racemes of lovely flowers. The garden forms of digitalis are planted in smaller groups either by themselves or in mixed beds. The plants flower in June and July and are most decorative. They will grow in the same spot for 2 to 3 years unless killed by frost. They are also interesting flowers for home decoration in a vase. The leaves yield an important drug used by the pharmaceutical industry.

Campanula. The generic name and the common name bellflower are derived from the shape of the flower which resembles a bell (campanula in Latin). The genus numbers some 200 species, most of which are perennials and many rock garden plants. The only one of importance as a biennial is *Campanula medium* 'Canterbury bell', a robust plant about 70 cm (2 ft 4 in) high, which makes a rosette of felted leaves the year the seed is sown, followed in the spring of the next year by a branching stem bearing pyramidal panicles of large, bell-like flowers from the end of June until August. The original forms were coloured dark blue but breeding has also yielded pale blue, white, pink and violet forms. For successful flowering it is important that the leaf rosettes survive the winter in good condition. To overwinter well the plants must be well rooted and the leaf rosettes well developed. *C. medium* is very striking and decorative. It is planted as a solitary subject or in groups, also in mixed beds, being most effective by itself in grass or in front of shrubs. Cut flowers are attractive in a tall vase.

Althaea. The generic name of hollyhock is derived from the Greek word *altheis*, meaning healing, referring to the medicinal qualities of some species. The genus includes both annuals and biennials which make a characteristic ground rosette of felted leaves and a tall, thick stem bearing a spike of large, showy flowers. *Althaea rosea*, the most widely distributed, was introduced into Europe from the Orient. The numerous present forms are the result of many years

Althaea rosea

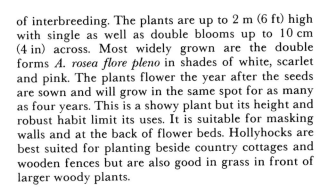

of interbreeding. The plants are up to 2 m (6 ft) high with single as well as double blooms up to 10 cm (4 in) across. Most widely grown are the double forms *A. rosea flore pleno* in shades of white, scarlet and pink. The plants flower the year after the seeds are sown and will grow in the same spot for as many as four years. This is a showy plant but its height and robust habit limit its uses. It is suitable for masking walls and at the back of flower beds. Hollyhocks are best suited for planting beside country cottages and wooden fences but are also good in grass in front of larger woody plants.

Campanula medium

TABLE SHOWING THE MOST IMPORTANT CHARACTERISTICS OF GARDEN PLANTS

Species, Variety	Height of stem		Flowering period	Colour of flower	Life in the vase (days)	Note
	cm	in				
BULBS						
Narcissus	30—50	12—20	April—May	yellow, white, orange	6—12	there are many varieties and species
Tulipa	30—60	12—14	April—May	varied	5—10	only tall forms
Lilium	30—70	12—28	June—August	varied	8—14	only large-flowered forms
Muscari	8—15	3—6	April	blue, white	3—6	
Allium	15—60	6—24	April—May	violet, red	10—14	mainly large-flowered forms
CORMS-TUBERS						
Gladiolus	40—100	16—39	July—September	varied	8—14	flowers in succession
Anemone coronaria	25—35	10—14	June—August	red, blue, white	5—8	single and double
Freesia	15—30	6—12	June—July	varied	6—10	flowers in succession
Convallaria	15—25	6—10	May	white	8—12	very fragrant
Crocosmia	25—45	10—18	June—July	orange	8—14	flowers in succession
Dahlia	50—100	20—39	August—October	varied	4—7	mainly pompon dahlias
PERENNIALS						
Paeonia	30—60	12—24	May—June	white, pink, red	10—14	cut closed buds
Chrysanthemum	40—80	16—32	May—August	white, red, yellow	12—18	only tall forms
Rudbeckia	40—80	16—32	July—September	yellow	12—20	
Doronicum	40—60	16—24	April—May	yellow	6—10	
Liatris	30—40	12—16	June—July	violet	8—12	flowers in succession
Astilbe	50—90	20—36	June—July	varied	8—12	
Iris barbata	50—80	20—32	May—June	varied	5—8	only tall forms
Gaillardia	35—60	14—24	June—August	reddish-brown	6—10	tends to flop
Eryngium	40—80	16—32	July—August	silvery- blue	all winter	dried for decoration
Limonium	30—40	12—16	July—August	blue, white	all winter	dried
Gypsophila	60—100	24—39	July—August	white, pink	20—30	dried
Physalis	40—70	16—28	September— October	decorative fruits, orange lanterns		
Sedum spectabile	30—50	12—20	August—September	pink	15—20	fleshy stem
Pennisetum	60—80	24—32	June—August	pale yellow	20—30	grass
Heuchera	40—60	16—24	June	pink, red	6—8	
Aquilegia	50—80	20—32	May—July	varied	6—8	
Erigeron	50—80	20—32	June	pink, violet	15—18	
Campanula glomerata	30—60	12—24	June—July	violet	10—15	
ANNUALS						
Lathyrus	15—30	6—12	June—September	varied	8—10	very fragrant
Callistephus	30—60	12—24	July—October	varied	10—12	only tall forms
Dianthus var. Chabaud	30—50	12—20	July—September	varied	8—10	
Matthiola	30—60	12—24	May—June	varied	5—6	very fragrant
Rudbeckia	40—100	16—39	August—October	yellow with eye	10—20	
Limonium	30—50	12—20	July—August	blue, white		dried
Zinnia	40—100	16—39	June—October	varied	5—8	
Cosmos	80—150	32—60	July—October	white, red	6—8	
Antirrhinum	60—80	24—32	July—October	varied	8—10	
Calendula	30—60	12—24	June—July	yellow, orange	6—10	
Helichrysum	80—100	32—39	July—October	varied		dried
Helianthus	100—250	39—96	July—October	yellow, orange	5—8	
Chrysanthemum	40—80	16—32	July—October	varied	4—7	
Delphinium	100—120	30—44	June—July	blue, white	6—9	
Tagetes	50—70	20—28	August—September	yellow, orange	8—10	only the tall *T. erecta*
Scabiosa	80—90	32—36	July—October	varied	5—8	
Verbena	50—100	20—39	July—October	violet	5—8	only a few species
BIENNIALS						
Dianthus barbatus	25—60	10—24	May—June	varied	8—10	
Campanula medium	40—50	16—20	May—June	blue, white, pink	10—12	
SHRUBS/ WOODY PLANTS						
Rosa	30—80	12—32	June—October	varied	5—8	only large-flowered forms

Species	Height		Spread		Shape of crown	Rate of growth	Soil
	metres	feet	metres	feet			
Chamaecyparis lawsoniana	4—6	13—20	2—3	6—10	narrow, conical	slow	light, moist
Chamaecyparis obtusa	2	6	1.5	5	broadly conical	slow	moist
Chamaecyparis pisifera	3—5	10—16	2—3	6—10	broader, looser	slow	light, moist
Juniperus communis		according to variety			varied	moderate	light, may be acid
Juniperus horizontalis	0.5	1$^1/_2$	2—3	6—10	prostrate, creeping	slow	light, may be dry
Juniperus chinensis	2—4	6—13	2—3	6—10	broadly conical	moderate	light, may be acid
Juniperus squamata	3	10	1.5	5	spreading	moderate	light, may be dry
Juniperus virginiana	3—5	10—16	0.5—1	1$^1/_2$—3	narrow, conical	slow	better moist
Picea abies	up to 30	up to 100	up to 5	up to 16	conical	rapid	moist
Picea glauca	2	6	0.5	1$^1/_2$	conical	slow	moist, may be acid
Picea pungens	3	10	1.5	5	conical	moderate	moist
Pinus mugo	1.5	5	3—4	10—13	prostrate	slow	light, may be acid
Pinus sylvestris	up to 20	up to 65	up to 4	up to 13	pyramidal	moderate	light, may be acid
Pinus strobus	up to 25	up to 80	up to 5	up to 16	irregularly shaped layered	rapid	moist
Taxus baccata	3—5	10—16	3—5	10—16	broadly conical	slow	limy
Taxus cuspidata	0.5—1	1$^1/_2$—3	2—3	6—10	broadly spreading	slow	deep, moist
Taxus media	3—4	10—13	0.5	1$^1/_2$	upright	slow	deep, moist
Thuja occidentalis	3—4	10—13	1—1.5	3—5	conical	slow	deep, may be acid
Berberis julianae	1.5	5	0.5	1$^1/_2$	sturdy, upright	slow	dry, well-drained
Buxus	1	3	1	3	symmetrical	moderate	light, may be dry
Hedera helix	up to 16—20	up to 53—65			climbing	rapid	moist
Ilex	3—5	10—16	2	6	pyramidal	slow	heavier, moist
Prunus laurocerasus	1.5	5	2	6	spreading	rapid	moist, limy
Rhododendron hybr.	1—3	3—10	2—3	6—10	spreading	slow	moist, acid
Rhododendron japonicum	1	3	0.5	1$^1/_2$	upright	slow	moist, acid
Viburnum rhytidophyllum	2—3	6—10	1.5	5	upright	rapid	rich, may be dry
Acer palmatum	2—3	6—10	2—3	6—10	spherical	slow	rich
Buddleia	1.5—2	5—6	1.5—2	5—6	arching	slow	rich, well-drained
Campsis	up to 8	up to 26			climbing	moderate	rich, well-drained
Carpinus	up to 20	up to 65			bushy	moderate	light, moist
Clematis hybr.	2—3	6—10	1	3	climbing	moderate	rich, moist
Cornus mas	5	16	3	10	spreading	moderate	dry, limy
Corylus	4	13	3	10	spreading	rapid	rich, moist
Cotoneaster	1—2	3—6	1—3	3—10	upright, prostrate	moderate	well-drained, dry
Deutzia	1.5	5	1	3	upright	moderate	light, well-drained
Euonymus	2—4	6—13	1—2	3—6	upright	moderate	moist
Forsythia	2—3	6—10	1—2	3—6	drooping	moderate	rich, well-drained
Hibiscus	2—3	6—10	1	3	upright	slow	rich, well-drained
Chaenomeles	1—2	3—6	1	3	upright	moderate	light, may be dry

Light	Colour of leaves	Autumn coloration	Flowering period	Ornamental fruits	Good for hedges	Note
light partial shade	blue-green, yellow	—	—	—	freely growing	damaged by frost
light partial shade	green	—	—	—	no	protect against frost, attacked by rodents
partial shade	according to the variety	—	—	—	no	protect against icy winds
sun	grey-green	—	—	black	no	has sharp, prickle-pointed needles
sun	blue-green	—	—	—	no	
partial shade	slightly greyish	—	—	—	freely growing	
sun	silvery	—	—	—	no	
sun	according to the variety	—	—	—	no	attacked by rodents
partial shade	dark green	—	—	—	clipped	
sun	pale green	—	—	—	no	
sun	blue-grey	—	—	—	no	good as solitary subject
sun	dark green	—	—	—	no	
sun	blue-green	—	—	—	no	
sun	green/grey	—	—	—	no	good as solitary subject
shade	dark green	—	—	—	clipped	
shade	green	—	—	—	clipped	
shade	dark green	—	—	—	clipped	
sun	green, yellow	brownish	—	—	clipped	thins out in dry conditions
partial shade	green	red	May—June	blue	freely growing	thorny
partial shade	dark green	—	May—June	—	clipped	very easy to grow
partial shade, shade	dark green	—	August—September	—	no	does not need to be tied to a support
partial shade	glossy green	—	May—June	red	no	provide roots with protective cover in winter
partial shade	dark green	—	May	black	no	provide roots with protective cover in winter
partial shade	dark green	—	May—June	—	no	provide roots with protective cover in winter
sun	pale green	red	May	—	no	
sun	green/grey	—	May—June	red, then black	no	provide roots with protective cover in winter
partial shade	red, yellow	red	April—May	—	no	good as solitary subject
sun	green/grey	—	July—August	—	no	top parts damaged by frost
sun	green	—	July—September	—	no	must be tied to a support
sun	green	brown	April	winged nutlet	clipped	good only for hedges
sun	green	—	June—August	—	no	soil at the base of the plants should be shaded
sun and partial shade	green	—	March—April	red	no	
sun and partial shade	green	yellow	March	brown	freely growing	
sun	green	red	May—June	red or black	freely growing	there are many species
sun	dark green	—	May—June	—	freely growing	top parts destroyed by frost
partial shade	green	—	May	red	freely growing	
sun	green	—	April	—	no	
sun	green	—	August—October	—	no	less hardy
sun	green	—	April—May	greyish-red	freely growing	

295

Species	Height		Spread		Shape of crown	Rate of growth	Soil
	metres	feet	metres	feet			
Laburnum	4—5	13—16	2	6	drooping	moderate	well-drained, limy
Ligustrum	3	10	2	6	spreading	rapid	light, may be dry
Lonicera	3	10	1	3	upright	rapid	may be sandy, dry
Magnolia	3	10	3	10	spreading	slow	light, acid
Paeonia suffruticosa	1.5	5	1	3	upright	slow	moist, well-drained
Parthenocissus	up to 10	up to 33			climbing	rapid	light
Philadelphus	1—2.5	3—8	1—2	3—6	spreading	moderate	moist, rich
Rhamnus	4—6	13—20	2	6	upright	moderate	moist
Sorbus	8—12	26—40	3—4	10—13	upright	moderate	moist, may be poor
Spiraea	1.5—2	5—6	2	6	arching	moderate	rich, well-drained
Symphoricarpos	1—1.5	3—5	1—2	3—6	spreading	moderate	light, may be poor
Syringa	2—3	6—10	1—1.5	3—5	upright	moderate	rich
Tamarix	3—5	10—16	2—3	6—10	airy, broad	slow	rich, well-drained
Viburnum	3	10	2	6	upright	moderate	deep, moist
Weigela	2	6	1.5	5	upright	moderate	light, well-drained
Wisteria	up to 10	up to 33			climbing	moderate	dry, limy

Light	Colour of leaves	Autumn coloration	Flowering period	Ornamental fruits	Good for hedges	Note
sun	green	—	May	—	no	attacked by rodents
sun and partial shade	green	bronze	June—July	black	clipped	
sun and partial shade	blue-green	—	May	red	freely growing	there are a great number of species
sun	pale green	yellow	March—April	black, brown	no	must be protected against frost when young
light partial shade	grey-green	—	May—June	—	no	provide roots with protective cover in winter
sun and partial shade	dark green	red	May—June	black	no	must be tied to a support when young
sun	green	—	June	—	freely growing	very fragrant
partial shade	pale green	yellow	May—July	red, then black	freely growing	
sun	green	—	May—June, June—August	red	no	there are a great number of species
sun	green	orange	June—August	—	freely growing	there are a great number of species
sun and partial shade	green	—	May	white	freely growing and clipped	spreads by suckers
sun	green	—	May	—	freely growing	spreads by suckers
sun	violet	yellow	May, June—September	—	in seaside areas	tender
sun and partial shade	green	yellow, red	May—June	red	no	
sun	green	—	May—June	—	no	
sun	green	—	May—June	—	no	should be tied-in horizontally to a support

Note: Most trees and shrubs are very adaptable to the given conditions; most species have several cultivated varieties differing in size.
The above data refers to the ideal conditions for the most widely grown species or cultivated varieties.

BIBLIOGRAPHY

Alpine Garden Society: A Handbook of Rock Gardens. Alpine Garden Society

Bean, W. J.: Trees and Shrubs Hardy in the British Isles, 4 Vols. John Murray

Bloom, A.: Conifers for your Garden. Floraprint

Bloom, A.: Perennials for your Garden. Floraprint

Clayton, J.: Herbaceous Plants. R.H.S.

Collingridge: Standard Guide. Roses. Hamlyn

Gault, S. M. and Synge, P. M.: The Dictionary of Roses in Colour. Michael Joseph

Gault, S. M.: Roses. R.H.S.

Green, R.: Asiatic Primulas. Alpine Garden Society

Griffiths, A.: Collins Guide to Alpines. Collins

Hanson, R.: Dahlias. R.H.S.

Harkness, J.: Roses. Dent

Harrison, G.: Ornamental Conifers. David and Charles

Hellyer, A.: The Collingridge Encyclopedia of Gardening. Hamlyn

Heritage, W.: Lotus Book of Water Gardening. Hamlyn

Hillier: Manual of Trees and Shrubs. Hillier

Hubbard, C. E.: Grasses. Penguin

Ingwersen, W.: Alpines without a Rock Garden. R.H.S.

Jeffreys, J.: Perennials for Cutting. Faber and Faber

Johnson, H.: International Book of Trees. Mitchell Beazley

Kay, R.: Ferns. R.H.S.

Kay, R.: Modern Water Gardening. Faber and Faber

Lancaster, R.: Trees for your Garden. Floraprint

Leathart, S.: Trees of the World. Hamlyn

Le Grice, E. B.: Rose Growing Complete. Faber

Mathew, B.: Dwarf Bulbs. Batsford

Mathew, B.: The Larger Bulbs. Batsford

Phillips, R.: Trees in Britain, Europe and North America. Pan

Proudley, D. and V.: Heathers in Colour. Blandford

Reader's Digest: Encyclopedia of Garden Plants and Flowers. Hodder and Stoughton

Sanders': Encyclopedia of Gardening. Hamlyn

Seabrook, P.: Shrubs for your Garden. Floraprint

Smith, J. F.: Chrysanthemums. Batsford

Smith, J. F.: Chrysanthemums. R.H.S.

Synge, P.: Collins Guide to Bulbs. Collins

Synge, P. and Hay, R.: The Dictionary of Garden Plants and Flowers. Michael Joseph

Thomas, G. S.: Climbing Roses Old and New. Dent

Thomas, G. S.: Perennial Garden Plants. Dent

Thomas, G. S.: Plants for Ground Cover. Dent

Thomas, G. S.: Shrub Roses of Today. Dent

Thomas, G. S.: The Old Shrub Roses. Dent

Thrower, P.: Encyclopedia of Gardening. Hamlyn

Underhill, T.: Heaths and Heathers. David and Charles

INDEX OF COMMON AND BOTANICAL NAMES

INDEX OF LATIN NAMES